IMAGES
of America

SUISUN CITY AND VALLEY

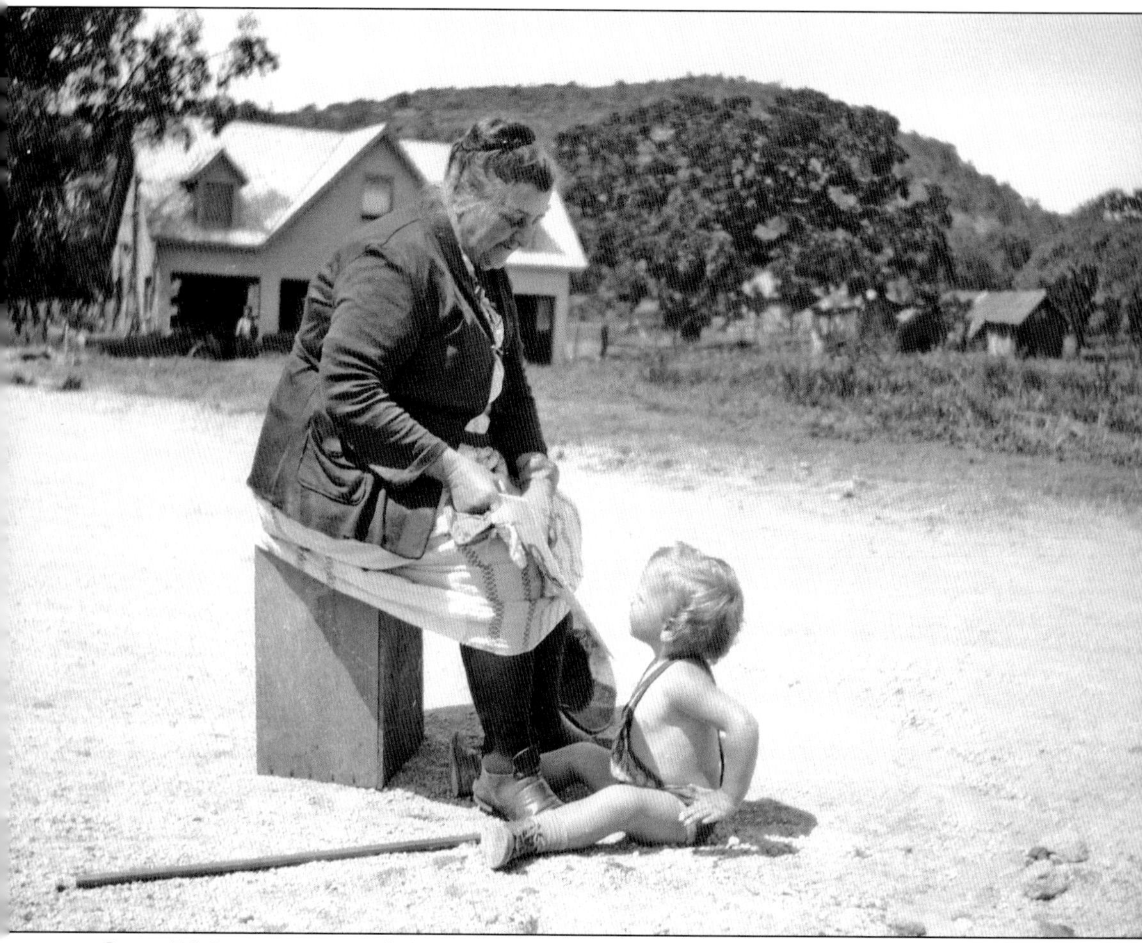

Carrie E.J. Pittman Martin (left) and grandson "Nic" William Henry Martin Smith are enjoying afternoon storybook time on the grounds of the Samuel Martin estate Stonedene with the carriage house designed by architect Julia Morgan visible in the background around 1930. Nic was the last Martin family member to live at the storied estate in Suisun Valley when he sold it in the 1970s. (Courtesy of Vacaville Heritage Council.)

ON THE COVER: The Mayfield Hotel was one of the first lodging establishments in Suisun. It provided comfort to weary travelers from all points of the country. (Courtesy of Vacaville Heritage Council.)

IMAGES
of America

SUISUN CITY AND VALLEY

Elissa A. DeCaro and L.M. Ewing

ARCADIA
PUBLISHING

ISBN 978-0-7385-9517-7

Published by Arcadia Publishing
Charleston, South Carolina

Printed in the United States of America

Library of Congress Control Number: 2012933255

For all general information, please contact Arcadia Publishing:
Telephone 843-853-2070
Fax 843-853-0044
E-mail sales@arcadiapublishing.com
For customer service and orders:
Toll-Free 1-888-313-2665

Visit us on the Internet at www.arcadiapublishing.com

For Ian and Zoë

Contents

ACKNOWLEDGMENTS

We are especially thankful for all of the people who assisted and generously shared their knowledge, photographs, stories, and expertise. In particular, we would like to thank the following individuals: Connie Adams, Leslie Batson, the Darville family (truly, we cannot thank them enough), Dick Day, James Delehanty, Marlene Dessel, Nancy Dingler, the Donaldson family, Jan Greene, Patty Huyssoon, Robert Lockefeer, Lois Monez, Joe Neitzel, Marline Newall, Helena Oberlander, Jim Perry, the Pienovi family, Paul Puente, Doug Rodgers, Warren and Carolyn Sheldon, David Griffiths Sox, Ian Thompson, Barbara Van Putten, Duane Alexander Vick, and Larry Welch.

We are indebted to the following organizations: Ancestry.com, Native Sons of the Golden West, Solano County Archives, Solano County Historical Society, Solano History Exploration Center, Solano County Genealogical Society, Solano Land Trust, Vacaville Heritage Council, and the Vacaville Museum.

A very special thank you must go to Brian Irwin at the Vacaville Heritage Council for his assistance with the preliminary scans and for the invaluable database he created at www.solanohistory.org. We also thank the historical research of Bob Allen, Jerry Bowen, Kristin Delaplane, Nancy Dingler, Gil Richardson, and Sabine Goerke-Shrode.

Our sincerest gratitude goes to Jared Nelson, our editor. He was patient, kind, and encouraging. This book would not have been possible were it not for his assistance. Nor would it have been possible to complete the book without the support of our families and friends. Thank you, Mom, Dad, Daniel, Ian, Zoë, Clyde, Eileen, Casey, and Cricket! There might actually be sleep and real food in our future.

Lastly, we thank the "ghosts" of Hank and Mary Higham, Clyde Low, Rod Rulofson, Ernie Wichels, and Wood Young; late at night in the quiet hush of the old town hall, they all seemed to lend a hand when our attention was inexplicably drawn to lost treasures tucked in nooks and crannies or sequestered in old dusty files. It was their past dedication to preserving history that helped us document it for the future.

(DF) Courtesy of the Darville family
(DGS) Courtesy of David Griffiths Sox
(ED) Courtesy of the author's collection
(MD) Courtesy of Marlene Dessel
(SCHS) Courtesy of Solano County Historical Society
(SHEC) Courtesy of Solano History Exploration Center
(VHC) Courtesy of Vacaville Heritage Council

INTRODUCTION

Valleys awash with golden wild oats; hills carpeted with dewy grass under the shade of ancient, plentiful oaks; the glimmering surface of the marsh teaming with life—these are the timeless vistas of the wondrous Suisun region.

It is awe-inspiring to consider the immense biodiversity of the area. There were birds and fish by the thousands, grizzlies and tule elk roaming free, and an unending supply of acorns, soap root, and native plants. It is no wonder the Suisunes thrived for thousands of years prior to Spanish occupation, sustained by the seemingly limitless supply of natural resources. It is also no wonder Suisun City would become the central trade link between San Francisco and Sacramento. Today the resources, though only a fraction of what they were, still inspire amazement and continue to sustain those who have settled in the region.

It is easy when documenting history to get caught up in the minutiae of dates, facts, and figures. One gets so busy squeezing in every tidbit of information that the essence of the story gets lost in translation (or worse—boredom). Yet Suisun is anything but boring. We learned so much in writing this book!

The history of Suisun and its environs has been fairly well documented from its humble beginnings as the "island" nestled in the tules to its heyday as a thriving metropolis. What has not been conveyed as fully is the vibrancy, generosity, and resilience of the people of Suisun City and Valley. Suisun was a contradictory mix of rough and tumble with intellectual enlightenment. If the town burned down, was knocked over, or flooded, the people simply picked themselves up, dusted themselves off, and started over. Fortunes were made. Fortunes were lost. Regardless, the community always seemed to work together—lessons we would be well suited to learn today.

The Suisun region is in transition. Suisun City is once again becoming a destination spot. The waterfront has been cleaned up. There are community events such as outdoor movies and music festivals. The historic Lawler House has been restored and is now host to an art gallery and the Solano History Exploration Center. The Suisun Wildlife Center down the street gives children opportunities to learn about the animals who call the largest contiguous estuarine marsh on the West Coast home. The Rush Ranch, a part of the Solano Land Trust, blends history, science, and nature in programs that inspire and enlighten. The Western Railway Museum highlights the transportation that connected communities to the world.

Suisun Valley is flourishing and has been featured in national publications such as *Sunset* magazine for its wine and art. It is a welcome local retreat from the congestion and homogenized shopping chains of the surrounding areas. Wineries, such as Mangels Vineyards, its fellow Suisun Valley Co-Op member Winterhawk, Wooden Valley Winery, and Ledgewood Creek Winery (just to name a very few), are continuing the viticulture tradition established over 150 years ago by producing world-class wines that rival our more famous neighbor, Napa Valley.

Farming has evolved as well. The vast orchards that once supplied a nation have been replaced by more intimate endeavors that capitalize on the current movement for people to get healthy, organic food fresh from local growers, such as Shooting Star CSA, Erickson Ranch Produce Stand and Dahlia Garden, Larry's Produce, Castaneda Bros. Produce, and Cal Yee Farms. Artisan specialty foods are also thriving with companies like the Il Fiorello Olive Oil Company and Sepay Groves Olive Oil.

The valley serves as inspiration for artists Phillip and Chad Glashoff with their whimsical sculptures and their latest project—one-of-a-kind mailboxes made for fellow valley residents to highlight the beauty and uniqueness of the area. (They also make one of the best potluck dishes we have ever seen, but not actually eaten—trout Jello!) Other artistic endeavors may also be found at the Mankas Potters at the Clay Station.

Despite the renaissance that has been occurring with art, wine, and history, the region still hangs in the balance. Developers have a way of trying to capitalize on the ephemeral, and as a result, many a special place has been torn down, paved over, and needlessly lost forever. Subdivisions and strip malls loom at the valley's edge. Thus, we are grateful to the families and community groups who continue to keep the rural and historic setting of Suisun Valley.

Due to the sheer magnitude of the project, we intentionally only covered the history of the area up until the early 1950s. Hopefully, inspiration will lead someone to write a book covering where we left off. It was also our intention not to duplicate any images already published in other Arcadia Publishing books. After pouring over 10,000 images, scanning 900 images, and then whittling those down to the images within, inevitably, we have forgotten the names of some people and events, and for that, we offer our humble apologies. Quite simply, there is far more information than can be contained in the confines of this book. We hope this will serve as inspiration to learn more about this special place.

One

People of the West Wind

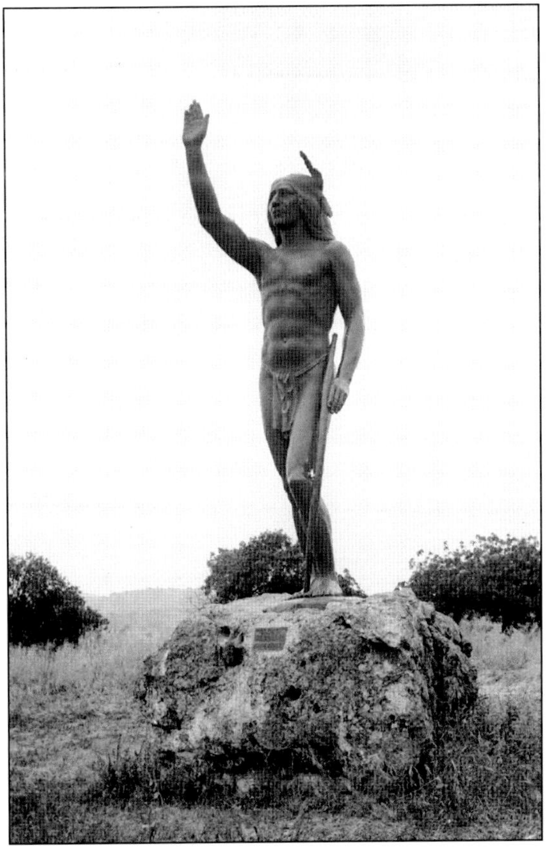

Artist William Gordon Huff's sculpture of the county's namesake, Chief Solano, or more accurately Sem Yeto or Francisco Solano, once greeted highway passersby from a knoll in Solano's ancestral home at Suisun Valley. The sculpture was dedicated in a special ceremony on June 3, 1934. Although this image resonates most with locals when they think of Solano, in actuality, he looked quite different. The sculpture itself was moved into town to protect it from vandals and unruly teenagers. (VHC.)

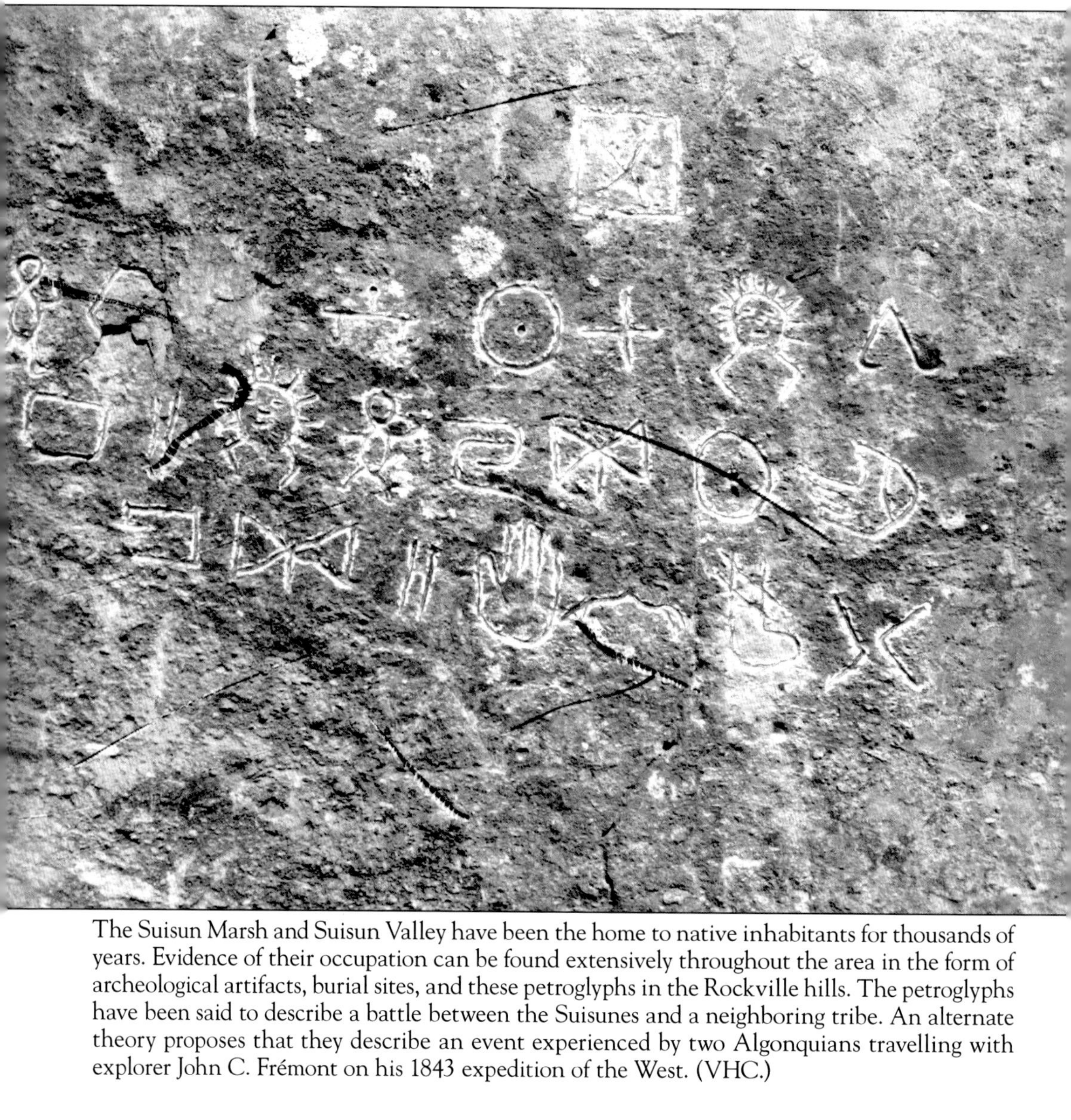

The Suisun Marsh and Suisun Valley have been the home to native inhabitants for thousands of years. Evidence of their occupation can be found extensively throughout the area in the form of archeological artifacts, burial sites, and these petroglyphs in the Rockville hills. The petroglyphs have been said to describe a battle between the Suisunes and a neighboring tribe. An alternate theory proposes that they describe an event experienced by two Algonquians travelling with explorer John C. Frémont on his 1843 expedition of the West. (VHC.)

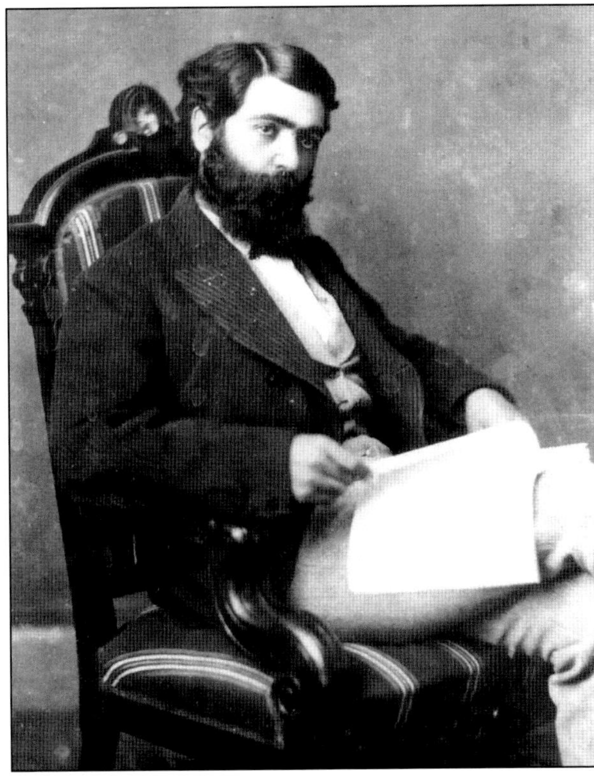

The seventh son of Gen. Mariano G. Vallejo, Dr. Platon Vallejo was a scholar and physician. He personally knew Chief Solano and considered him a friend. As a young child, Platon learned to speak the Suysun (Soo-eee-sun) dialect of the Suisunes, who were of Patwin ancestry, and set about translating the intricate language to preserve it for future generations. This is a copy in Platon's own hand of his translation of the Lord's Prayer to Suysun. (Both, VHC.)

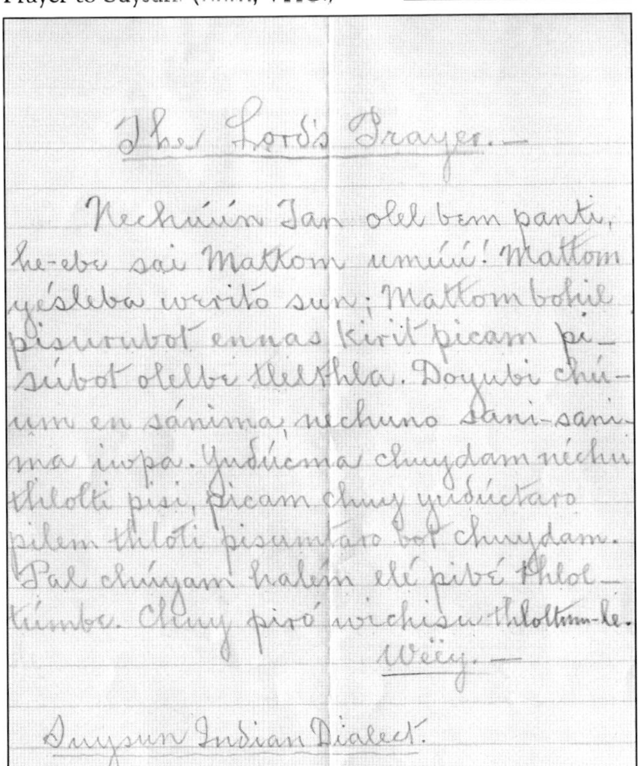

The Lord's Prayer.—

Nechúún Jan olel bem panti, he-ebe sai Mattom umúú! Mattom yésleba weritó sun; Mattom bohil pisurubot ennas kirit picam pi-súbot olelbe thelthla. Doyubi chú-um en sánima, nechuno sani-sani-ma iwpa. Yudúcma chuydam néchu thilolti pisi, picam chuy yudúctaro pilem thlóti pisumtaro bot chuydam. Pal chúyam halém elé pibé thlol-tiimbe. Chuy piró wichisu thloltum-le.

Wéiy.—

Suysun Indian Dialect.

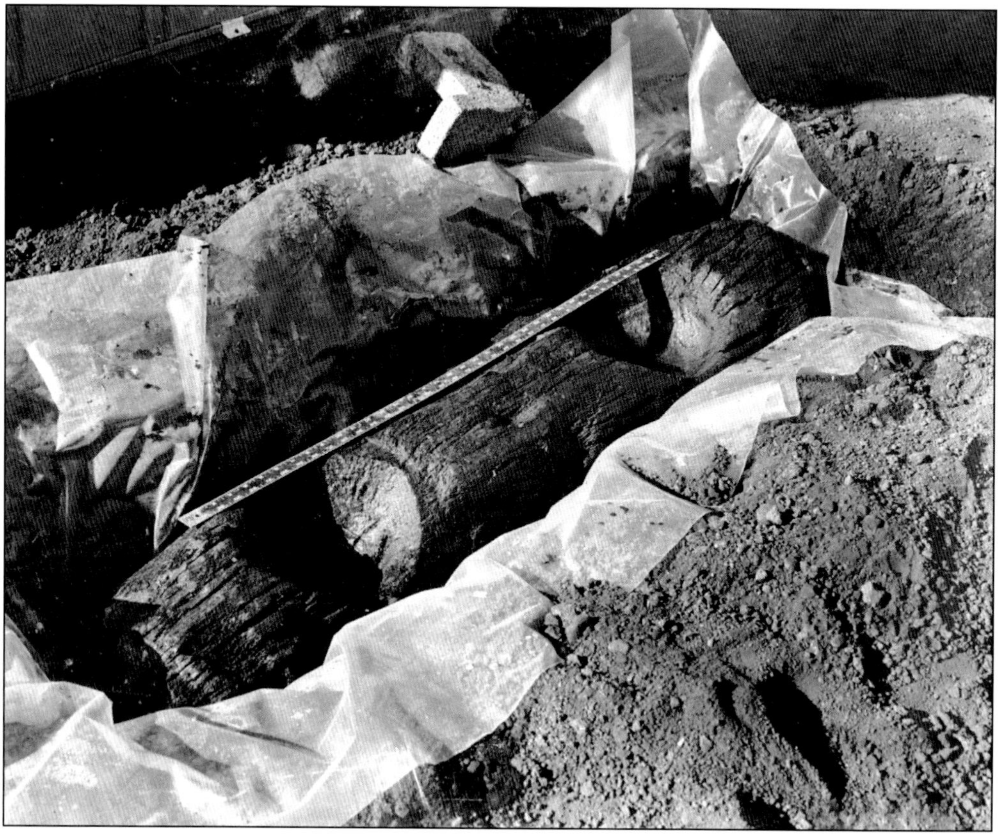

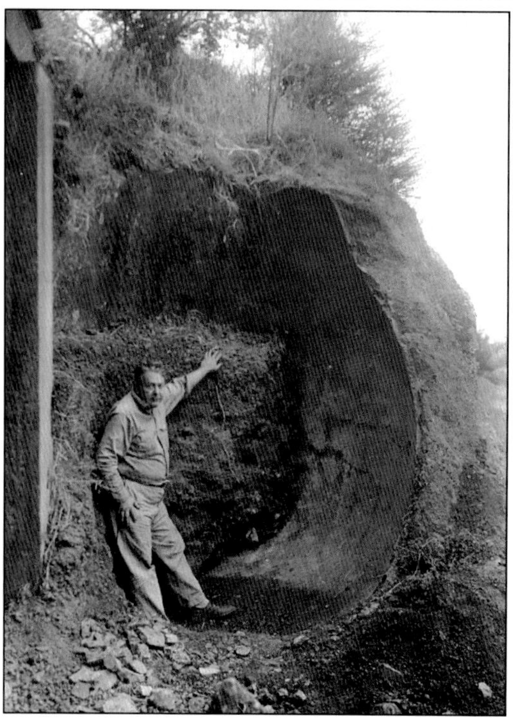

The only known wooden mortar still in existence and crafted by local Native Americans was found by accident in the Montezuma Slough off the Suisun Marsh. In 1969, contractor Bill Frost found it while he was operating a dragline. Historians Rod Rulofson and Bob Allen at the Peña Adobe carefully preserved the mortar. Carbon testing later performed by the US Department of the Interior dated the object to 1520 CE. (VHC.)

Historian Rod Rulofson examines the pear-shaped olla, or water cistern, found by workers at Thomasson Quarry near Cordelia. The olla was approximately eight feet across and 10 feet in depth and had been formed from cement consisting of sand, pebbles, and loosely ground seashells. The olla was likely used to irrigate crops under cultivation by Suisun neophytes associated with Santa Eulalia. (VHC.)

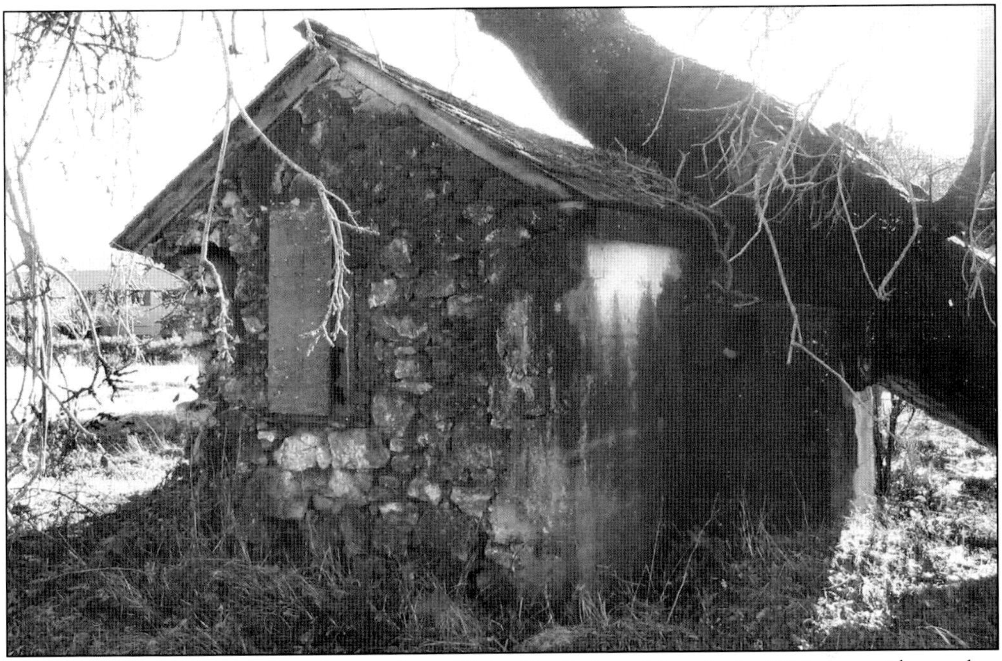

Santa Eulalia was an *asistencia* (outpost) established by Fr. Jose Altamira in 1824 to provide supplies to Mission San Francisco de Solano at Sonoma. In its own right, it was a mission on a smaller scale, complete with a chapel, *mayordomo* (manager) house, and outbuildings. It was built on land once known as Yul Yul, the Suisunes' village decimated earlier by small pox epidemics. The outpost was believed to have been long gone until 2007, when artist Daphne Nixon's inquiries into the building pictured here spurred an archeological study. As it turns out, strong evidence suggests the small rubble-stone building is the mayordomo house. A field trip to a neighboring parcel to examine the baptismal font below led researchers to discover that a building at the site, long used as a barn (and a speakeasy at one time), was actually the remnants of the chapel itself. The true identity of the oldest existing Solano County building was determined by the presence of a sacrarium fashioned from stone utilized to return unused sacraments back to the earth. (Both, ED.)

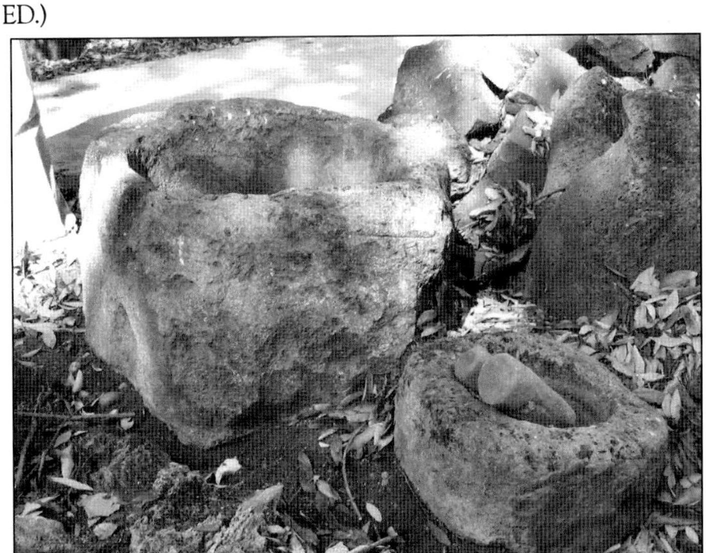

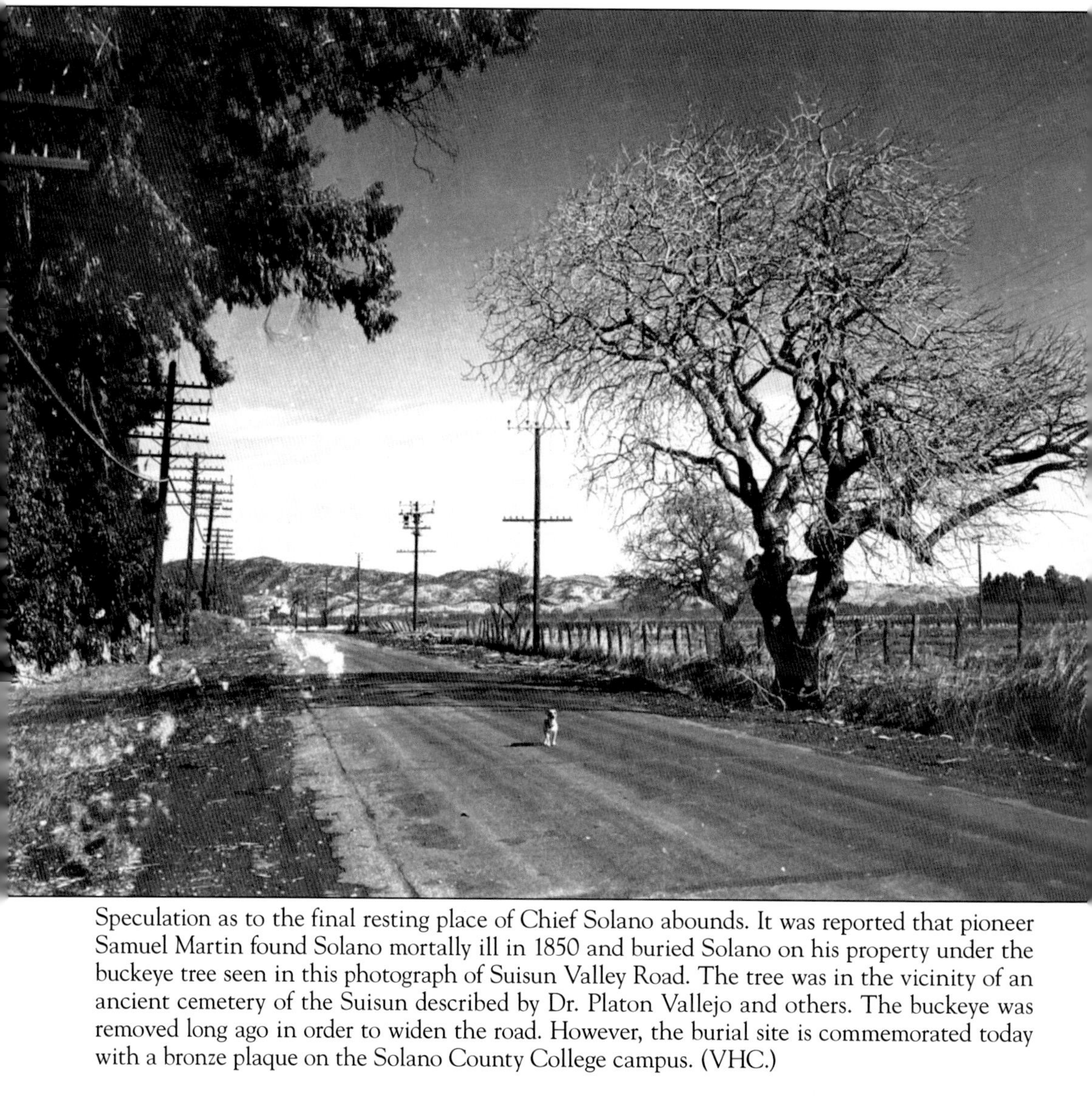

Speculation as to the final resting place of Chief Solano abounds. It was reported that pioneer Samuel Martin found Solano mortally ill in 1850 and buried Solano on his property under the buckeye tree seen in this photograph of Suisun Valley Road. The tree was in the vicinity of an ancient cemetery of the Suisun described by Dr. Platon Vallejo and others. The buckeye was removed long ago in order to widen the road. However, the burial site is commemorated today with a bronze plaque on the Solano County College campus. (VHC.)

Two

Birth of a Town

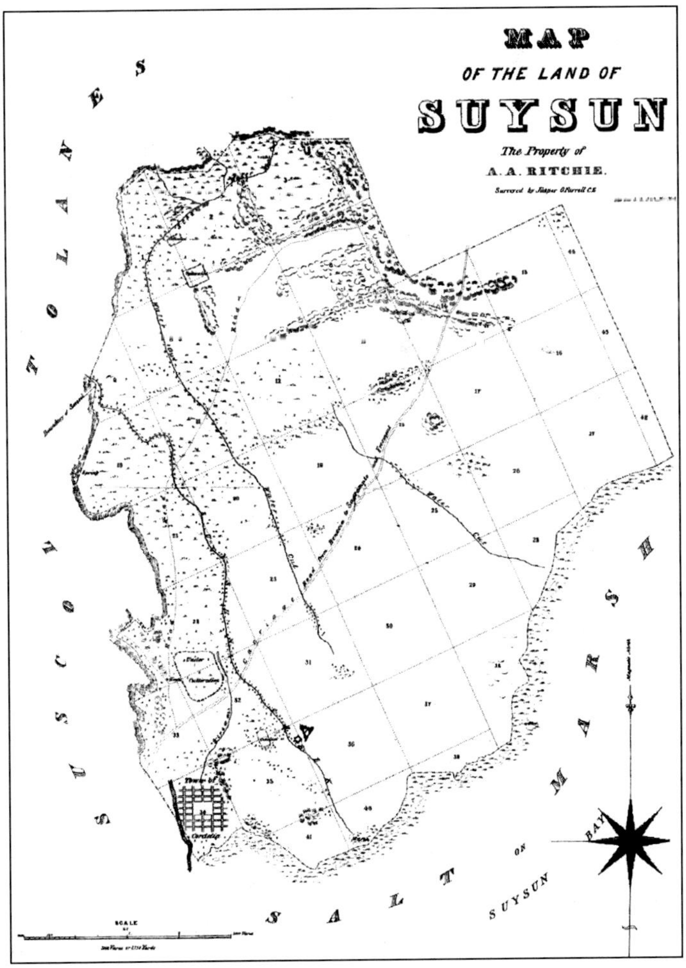

Identified as "Suysun," this map was drawn to delineate the Rancho Suisun property purchased by Archibald A. Ritchie, as surveyed by Jasper O'Farrell. It was submitted to the US District Court for the Northern District of California to help settle a title dispute. Notable is the exclusion of certain existing structures. The original *diseño* (map) filed on behalf of Chief Solano for the Rancho Suisun was lost when the Alcalde of Sonoma archives burned. Gen. M.G. Vallejo drew maps for testimony before the land court that included some of the structures excluded in the Ritchie Map. (SCHS.)

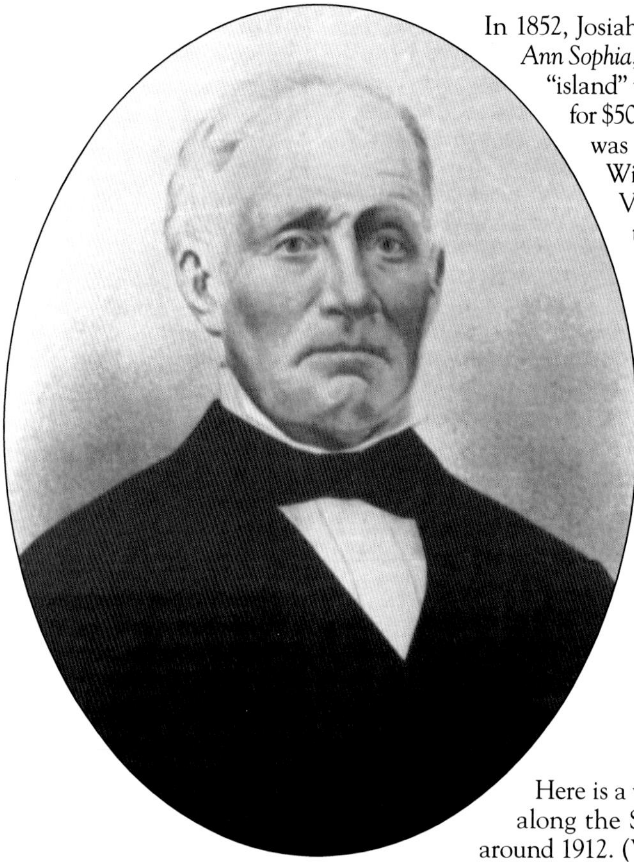

In 1852, Josiah Wing Jr., captain of the schooner *Ann Sophia*, arrived at Suisun and purchased the "island" with a tract of adjoining marshland for $500. It was Wing who observed Suisun was actually a peninsula at low tide, so Wing joined the "island" to the Suisun Valley shoreline with a plank way that later became known as Union Street. He then established a permanent wharf at Suisun and built a prosperous warehouse with sleeping quarters. Following that endeavor, he built a grand home for his family. (SCHS.)

Here is a view of the warehouses established along the Suisun waterfront at Suisun City around 1912. (VHC.)

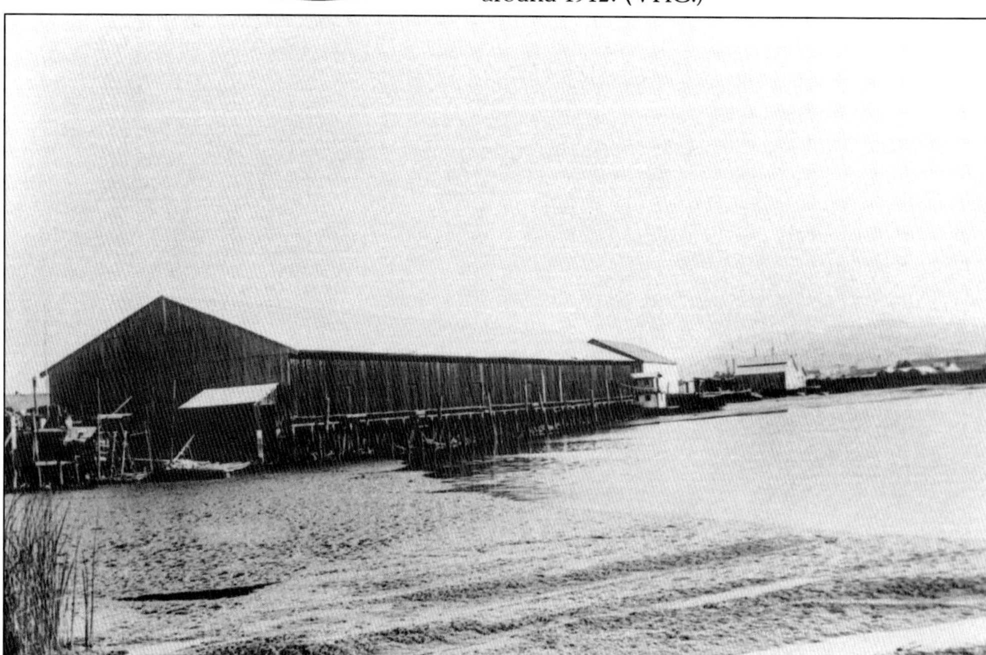

Wheat sacks are being loaded on the schooner *Champion* in the 1860s. Up to 50 wagons at a time would be lined up along the Suisun waterfront waiting to unload grain and produce for the San Francisco market. (VHC.)

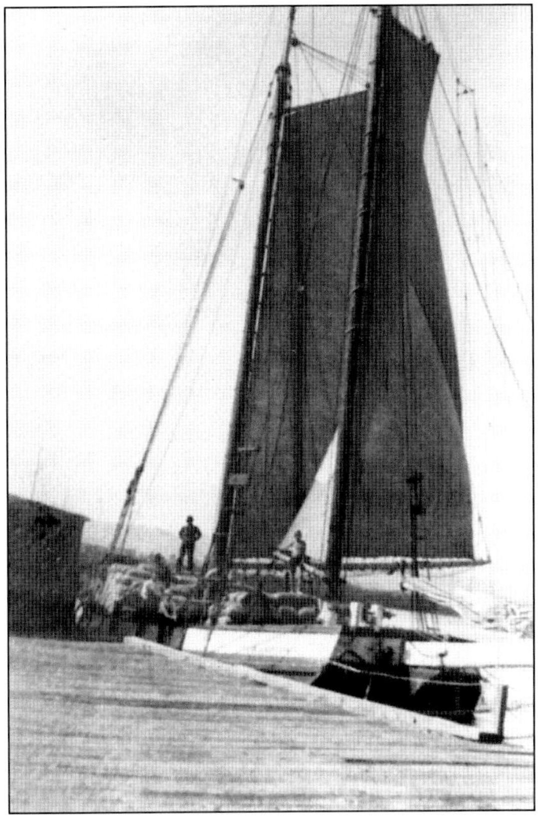

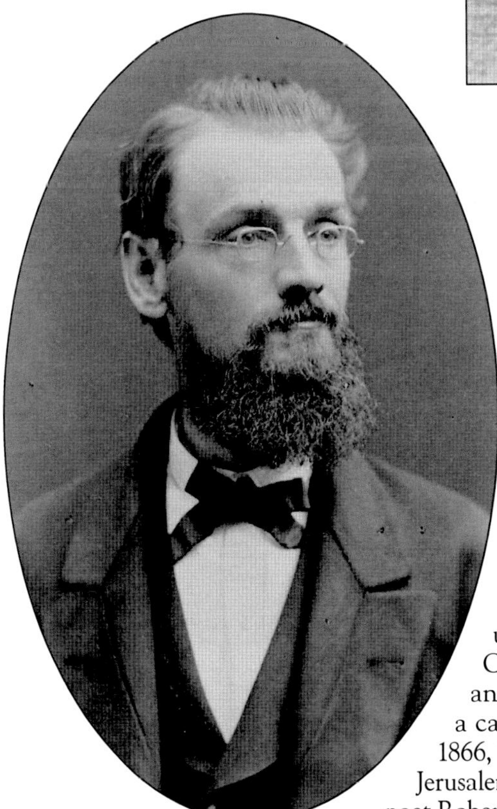

Arriving in 1849, John D. Doughty, a true renaissance man, started the first school in Cordelia at his store, served as school clerk for the Suisun District No. 4, ran as an Independent Whig and won a two-year term at the California State Legislature (where he introduced an unsuccessful bill to create a separate Suisun County), served as the county's district attorney, and was enlisted in the Suisun Light Dragoons, a cavalry mustered to protect Union interests. In 1866, Doughty became pastor of the Swedborgian New Jerusalem Church in San Francisco and later baptized the poet Robert Frost. (Courtesy of Paul Puente.)

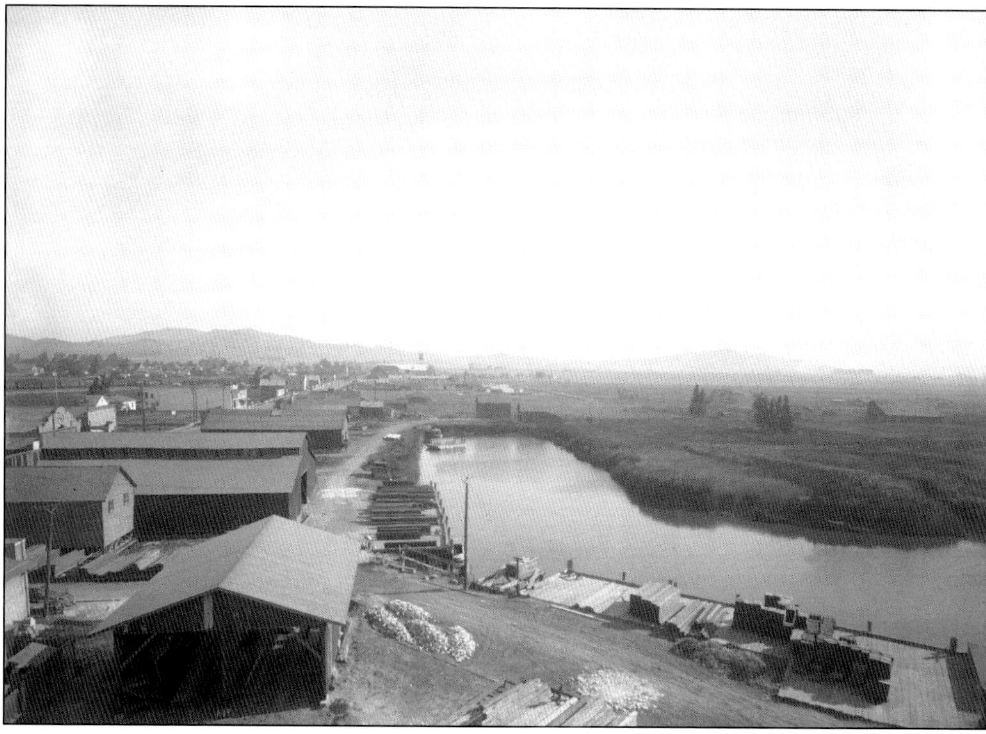

Here is a 1919 photograph of the Suisun lumberyard and slough. (VHC.)

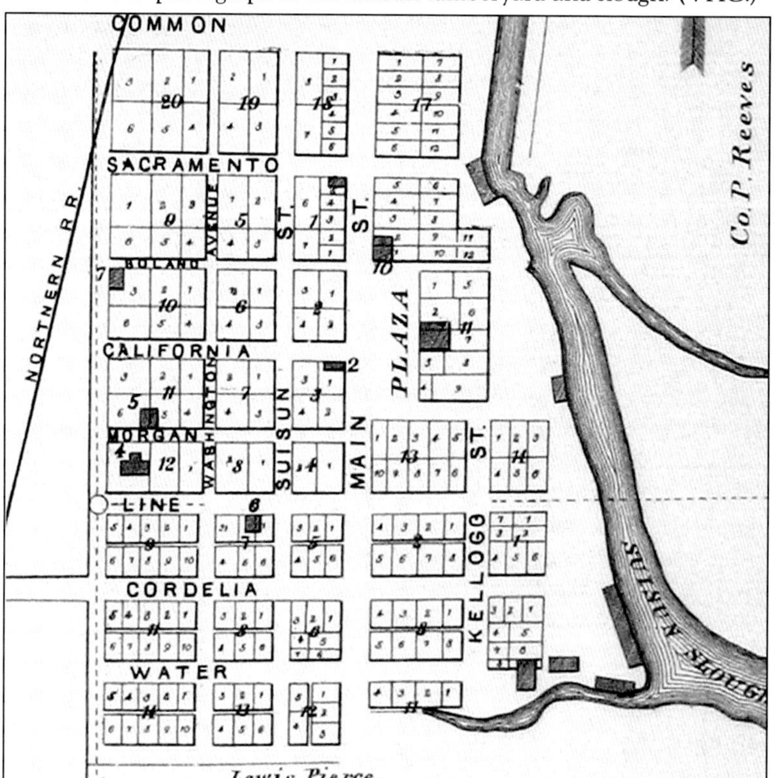

Capt. Josiah Wing, with the assistance of John W. Owens, drew up plans for the town of Suisun with street grids and lot subdivisions, as reflected in this detail of the 1878 map of Fairfield and Suisun published by Thompson and West of San Francisco. (SCHS.)

Three

Bounty of the Valley

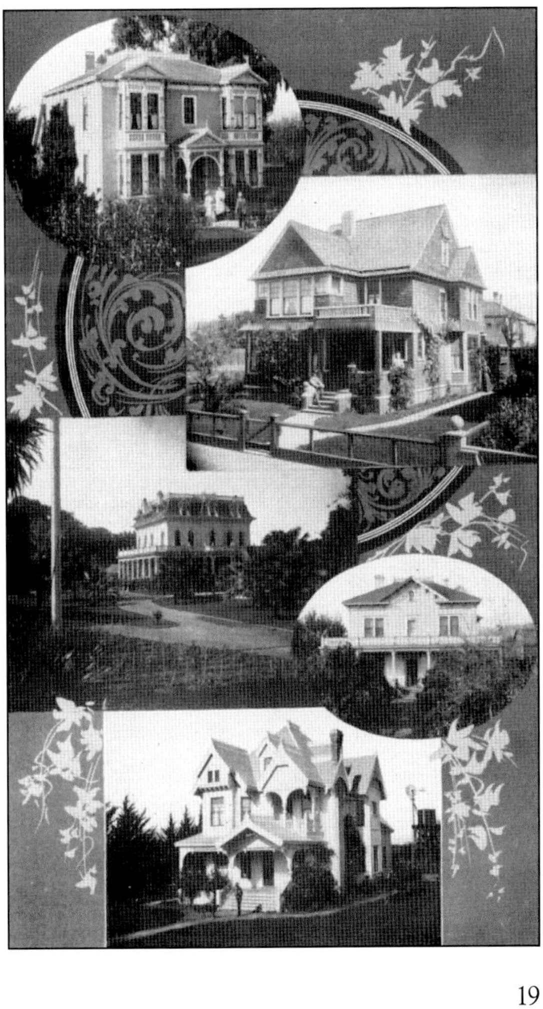

This page from the 1905 booklet *Solano County, California, the Land of Fruit, Grain, and Money*, issued by the Solano County Board of Supervisors, highlights the palatial homes that were built as a result of the booming agricultural industries of Suisun Valley. (SCHS.)

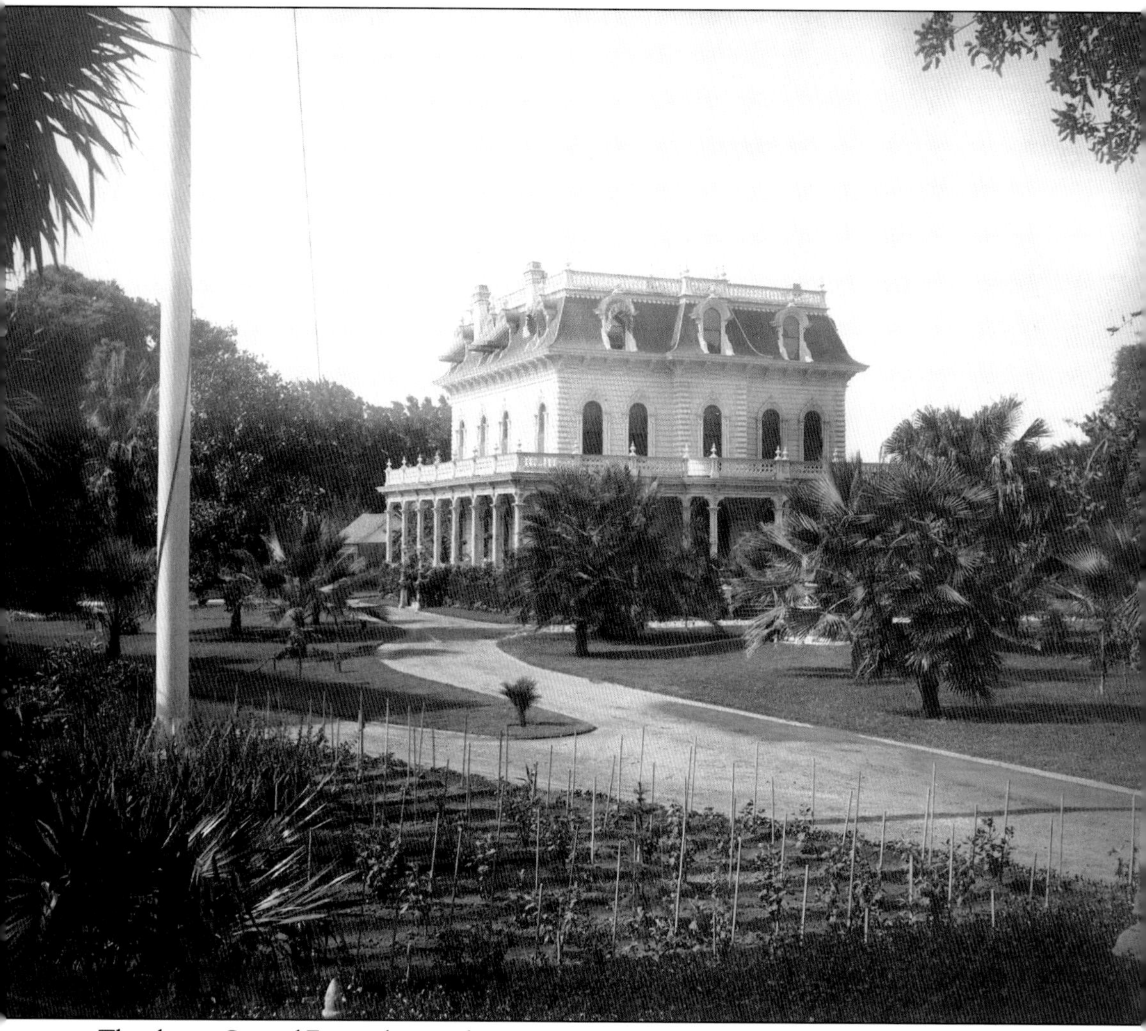

The elegant Second Empire home of pioneer Lewis Pierce was built in 1880. Pierce was orphaned at the age of 10. By the age of 15, he arrived at San Francisco, where he apprenticed as a baker for five years, saving enough money to settle in Suisun Valley, where he amassed his fortune cultivating grain. His son Judge William Pierce inherited the home and named it Willotta, a portmanteau of William and his wife's name, Lottie Mae. It stood just south of Rockville Road at Suisun Creek in what is now the neighborhood of Willotta Oaks. The grand home burned down in 1959. (SCHS.)

The widow of Lewis Pierce, Nellie Moulton, seated at the far right, is partaking in a typical affluent Victorian afternoon on the palatial grounds of her estate with her friends. (VHC.)

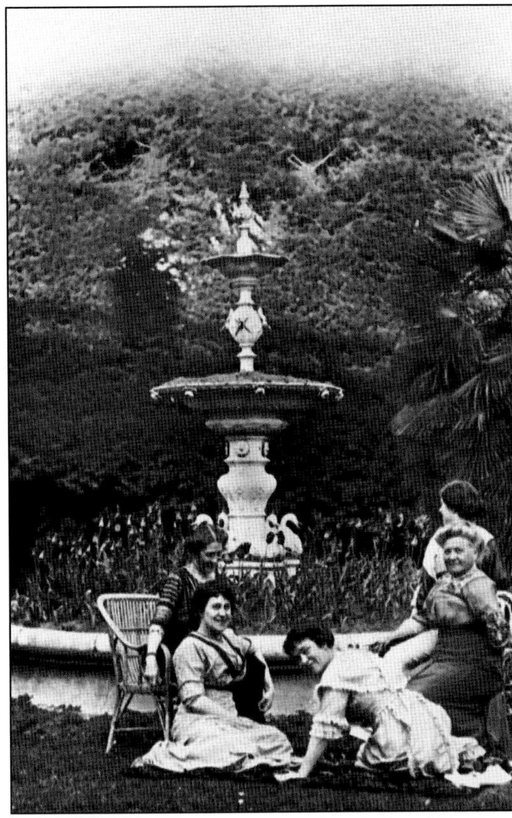

Nellie Moulton and her daughter Phyllis are enjoying a fashionable bicycle ride with all the accoutrements. (VHC.)

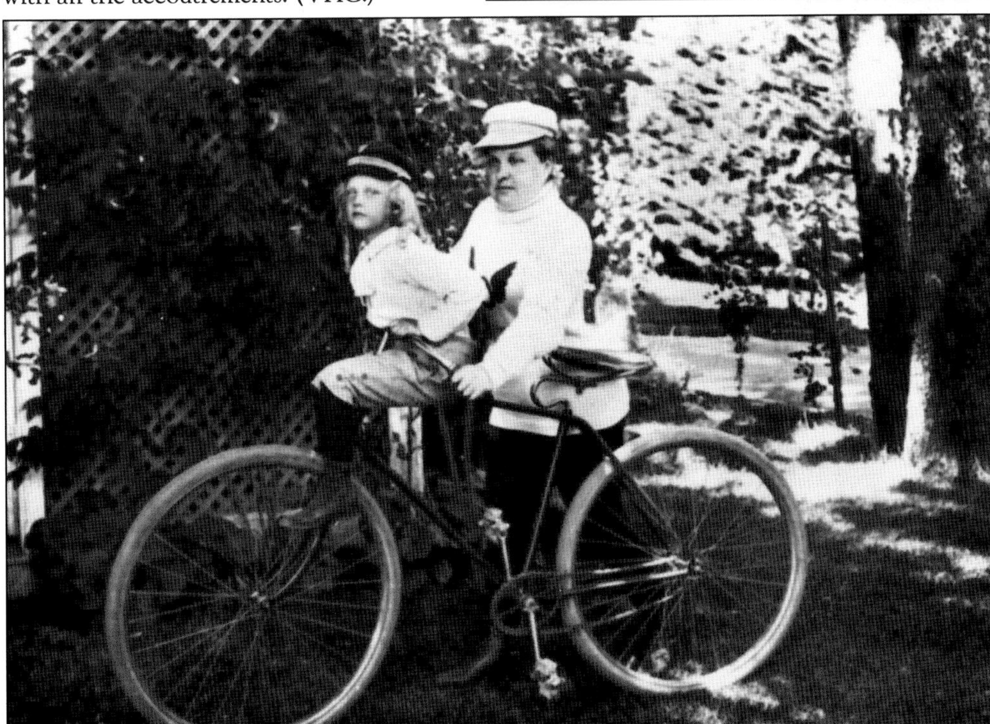

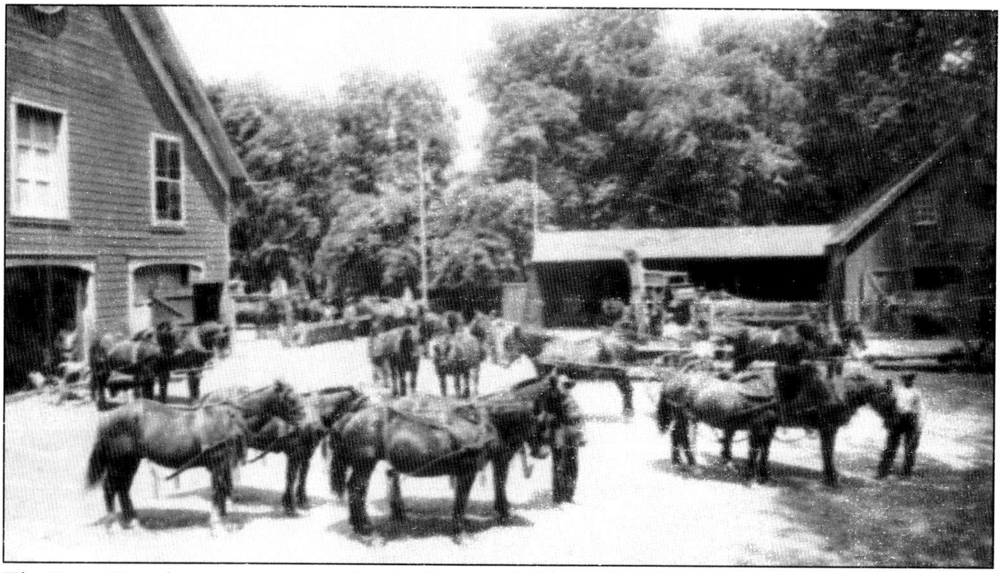

The Pierce Ranch, a vast expanse of orchards, grain fields, and cattle range, necessitated outbuildings and resources of an enormous scale. The barn to the left was located where the Iwama Market Building currently stands on Rockville Road. (VHC.)

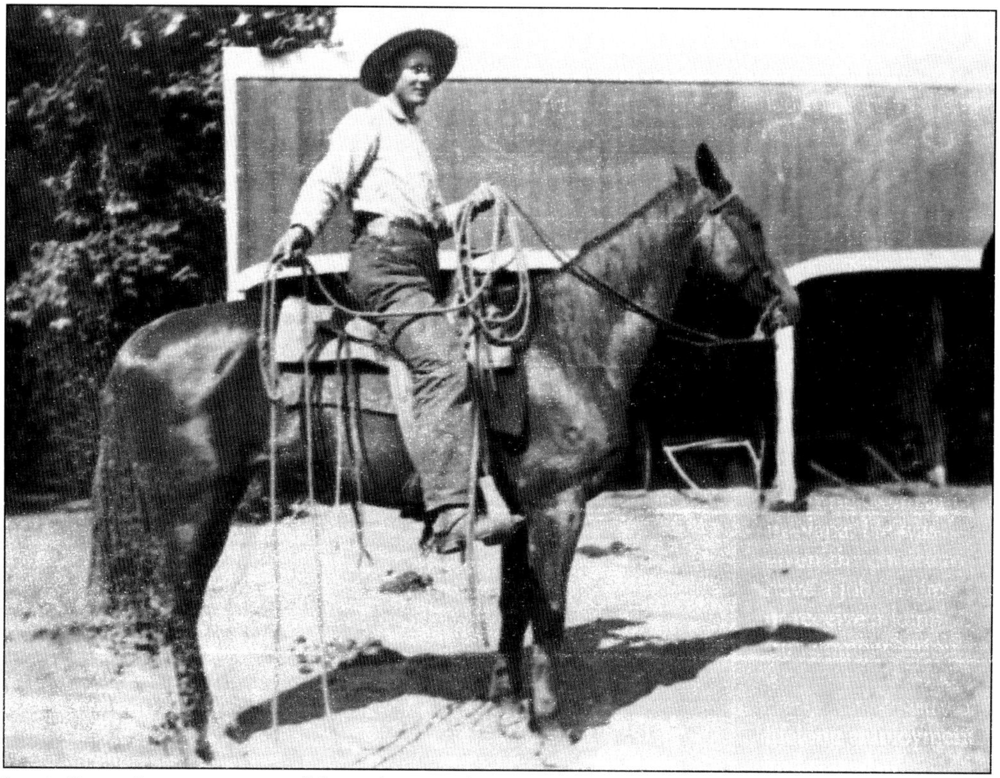

Lewis Pierce Jr. was a successful rancher, stock raiser, and horse breeder. Along with his brother William, he inherited the remarkable estate of his father, Lewis Pierce. Together the brothers continued the legacy. Lewis Jr.'s wife, Aline Mary Ford Pierce, lived to the ripe old age of 109 and was the first woman to serve on the Board of the National Cattlemen's Association. (VHC.)

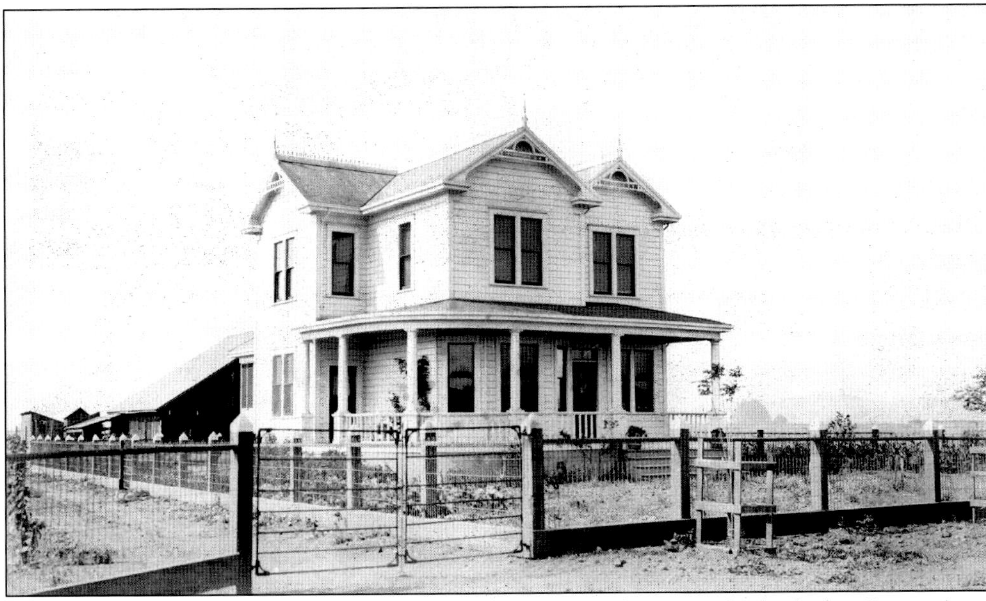

Originally residing on the Old Benicia Road, John and Katherine Siebe built this Queen Anne home in Suisun Valley in 1907 for their family. Soon after the house was completed, John fell ill with pneumonia, passed away, and, for the funeral, was laid in repose in the living room. Katherine was resilient and managed the operation of the ranch herself with the help of her children, Margaret and Harry. (DF.)

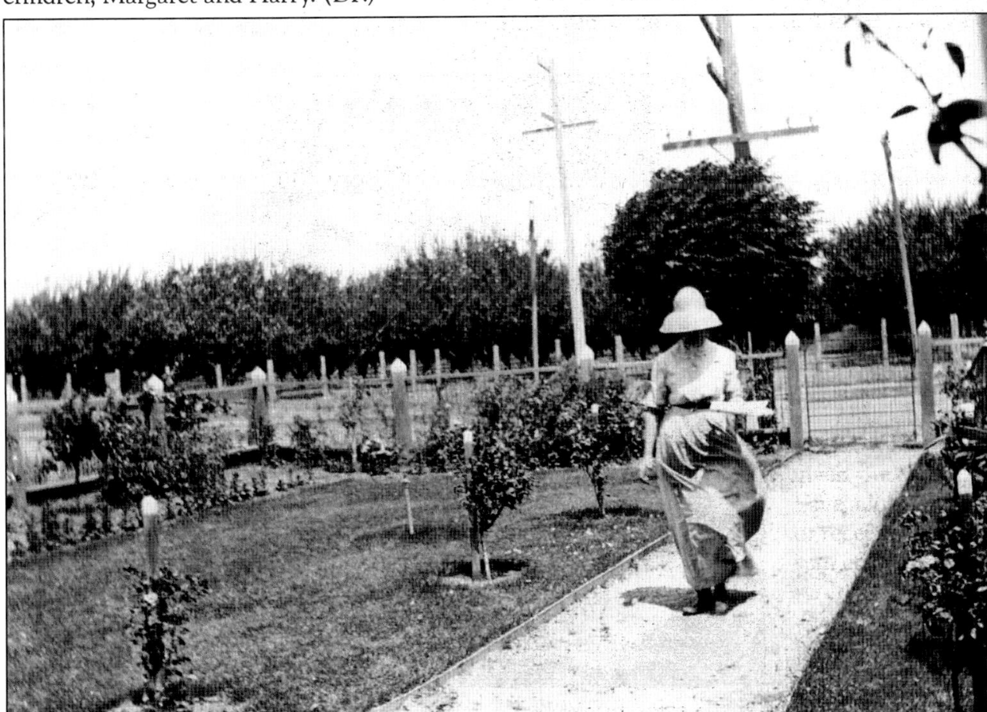

Katherine Siebe can be seen walking up the flower-lined path to her home, and the vast expanse of the neighboring Fred Chadbourne family's orchards can be seen in the background. (DF.)

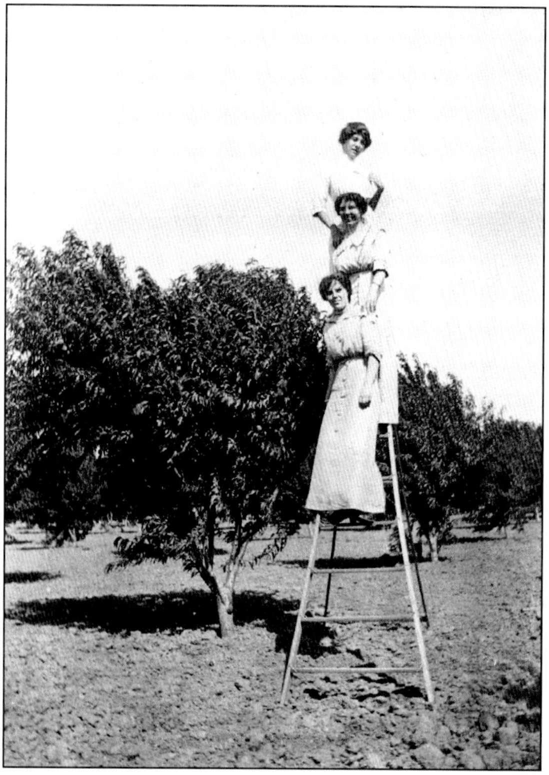

Margaret Siebe (top), Hattie Erickson (middle), and Bertha Schmidt (bottom) are posing on a ladder used for harvesting fruit at Katherine Siebe's ranch. (DF.)

From left to right, Hattie Erickson, Bertha Schmidt, and Margaret Siebe are seen in a precarious pose on the fruit packing shed at Katherine Siebe's ranch. The objects on the roof are not shingles; they are unassembled fruit crates. (DF.)

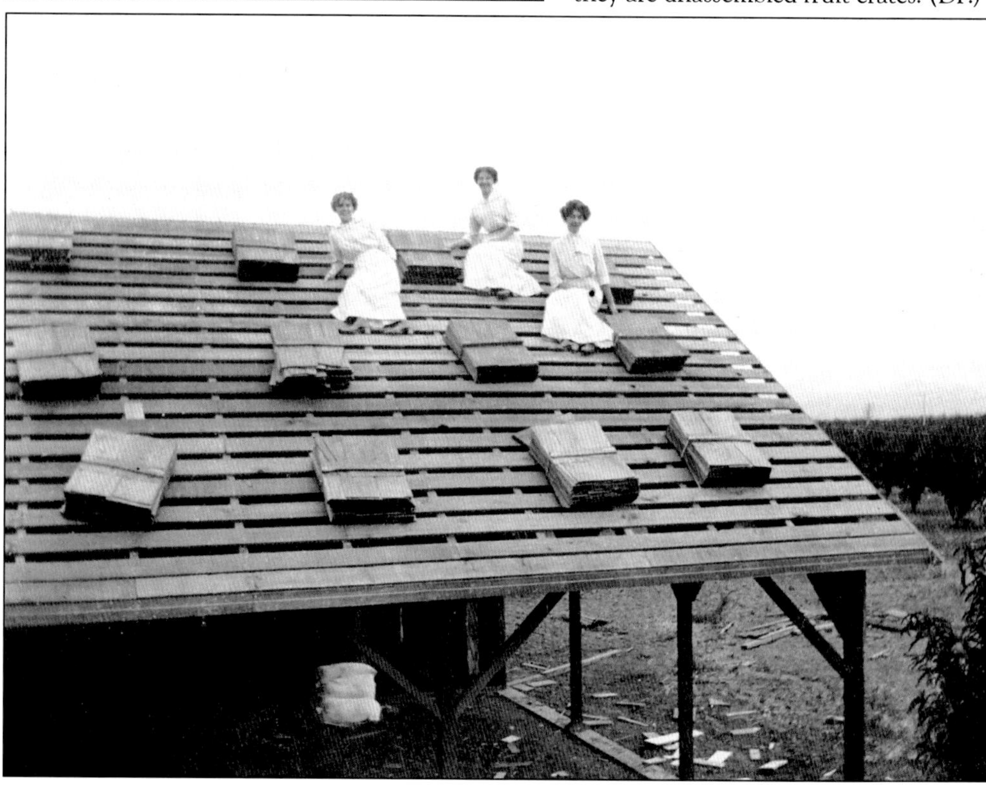

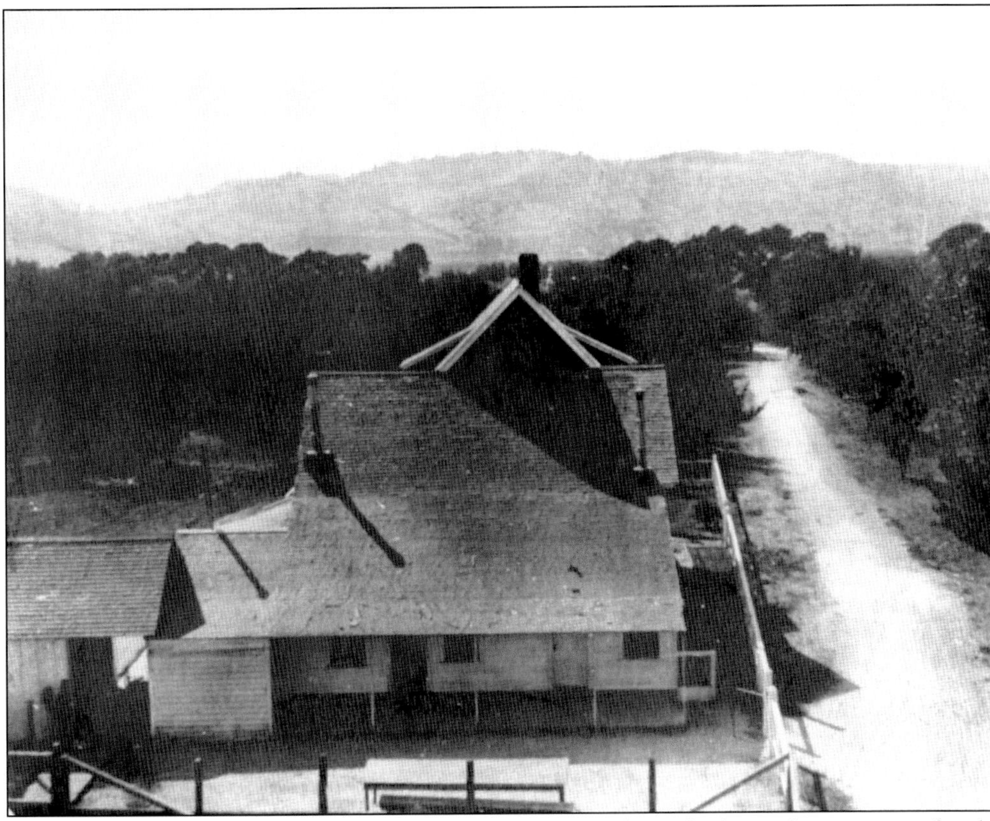

This view of the Morrison Ranch shows the additions made to the home for a growing family. These renovations were made possible by the lucrative fruit trade. Established in 1882 by William H. Morrison and his wife, Frances McEwen Morrison, the Morrison Ranch was one of the most fertile in Suisun Valley. Initially, the Morrisons started out raising stock, but they found horticulture to be more profitable. By 1900, they employed a workforce of nearly 60 people to service the extensive orchards and fields of grain. (DF.)

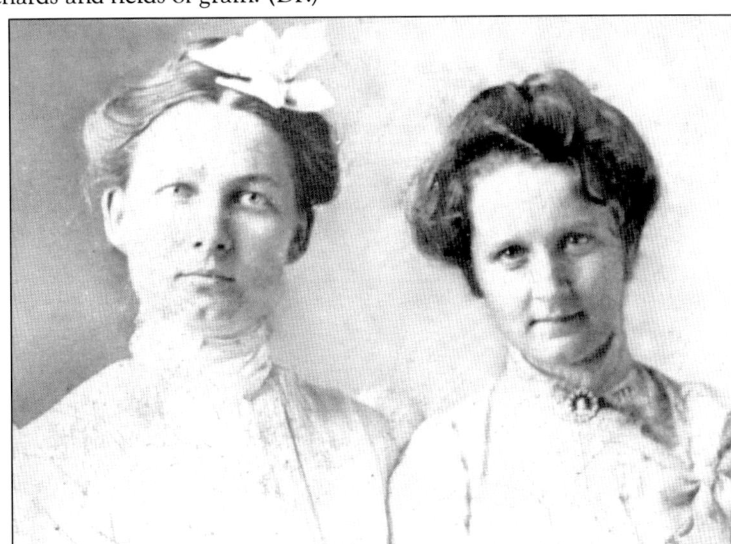

This is a well-loved photograph of Frances Julia McEwen Morrison (left) and Emma Vogel. The Morrisons and the Vogels were neighbors in the western valley and developed lifelong bonds. These bonds gathered strength upon the passing of Emma's mother, Lena Vogel. She died following the birth of her sixth child and namesake, Lena, in 1904. (DF.)

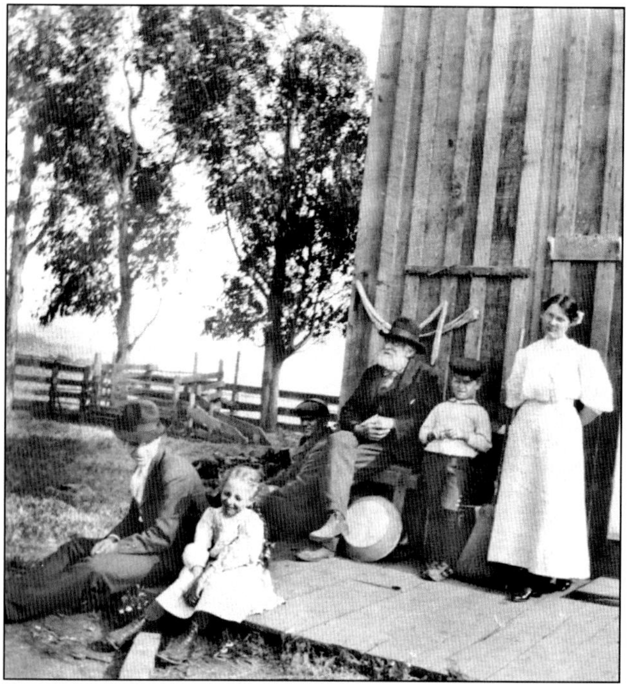

Members of the Morrison family are relaxing on the porch of the family barn around 1907. They are, from left to right, (first row) James Henry Morrison (son) and Gladys Elaine Morrison (daughter); (second row) William Henry Morrison (father); Josiah Zabriskie Morrison (grandfather), Julian Francis Morrison (son), and Bessie Edith Morrison (daughter). Josiah Zabriskie Morrison came to California in 1855 from Michigan. In 1859, his family came by steamer via the Isthmus of Panama route to join him. (DF.)

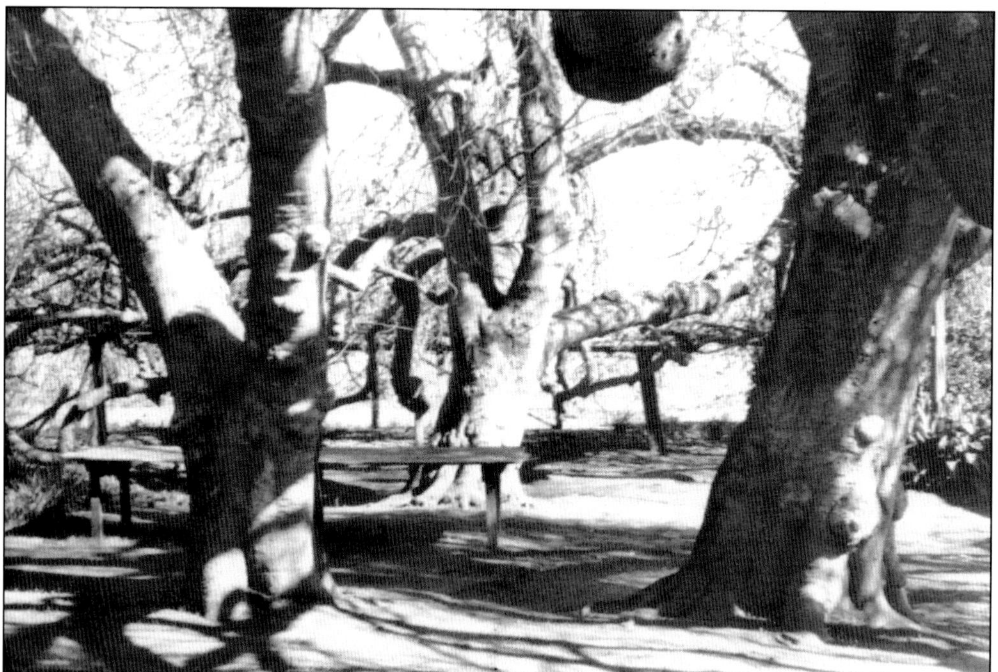

Over 150 years ago, Joe Capell found a whip made from a fig branch and broke it into three pieces, shoving them into the ground behind his house. From those pieces, three fig trees grew to become the oldest and largest fig trees in the world, at one point as tall as 75 feet with branches that spanned a third of an acre, as documented by *Ripley's Believe It or Not*. Long after the Capell Ranch was sold and the parcel divided, the trees remained and flourished in what became the backyard of the Peter L. Siebe home. (VHC.)

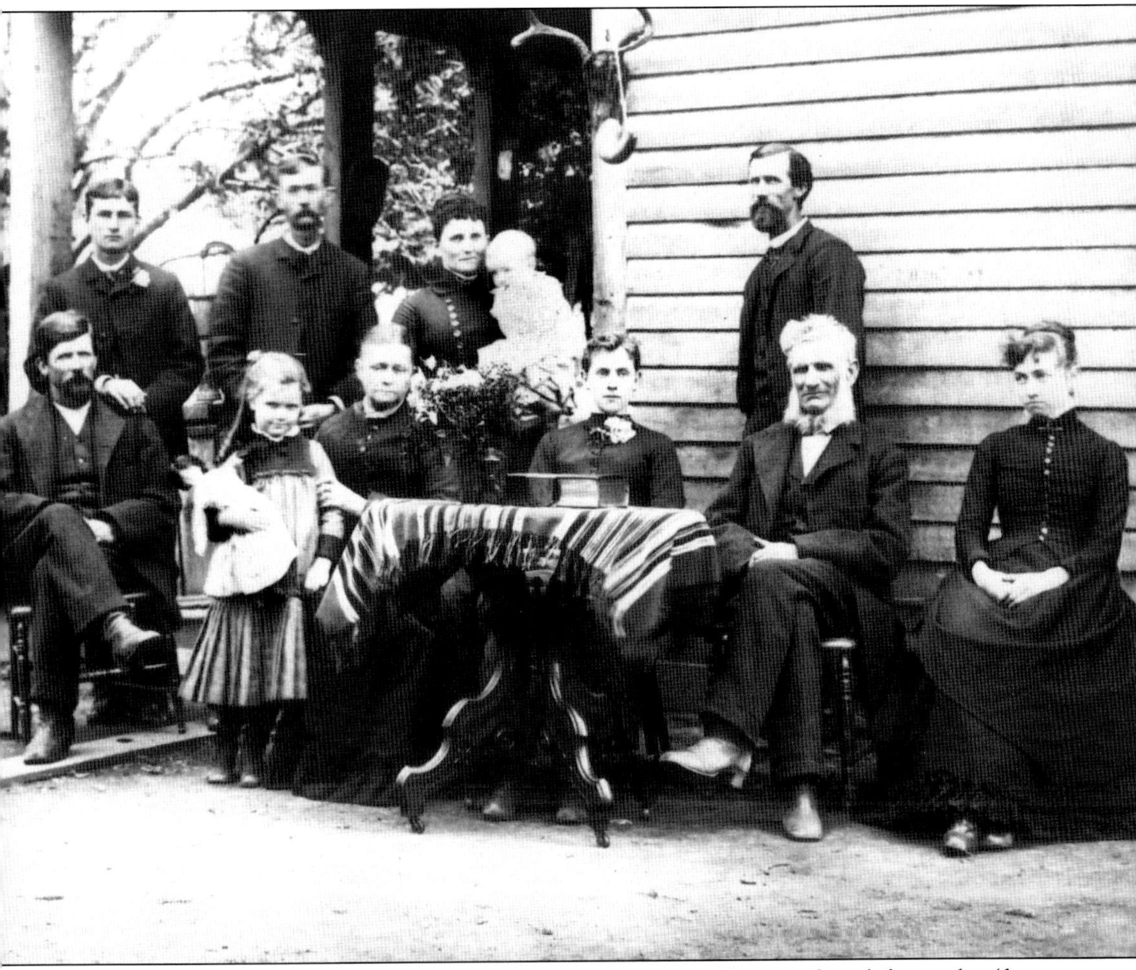

The family of Robert P. Williams poses for a photograph in 1892. They are, from left to right, (first row) Charles Williams (son), Grace Williams (granddaughter), Maria Ellard Williams (wife), Eleanor Bertha Williams (daughter), Robert Pearce Williams, and Mary Winifred Williams (daughter); (second row) Robert Francis Williams (son), William Henry Williams (son), Elizabeth Harkness Williams (daughter-in-law), Robert Duel Williams (grandson), and Thomas Pearce Williams (son). After crossing the Isthmus of Panama and suffering a couple of disasters, the Williamses' friend Capt. Josiah Wing persuaded the family to relocate to Suisun, where they resided with the Wings in their warehouse. There, Thomas Pearce Williams was born; he was the first Caucasian child born in Suisun. (DGS.)

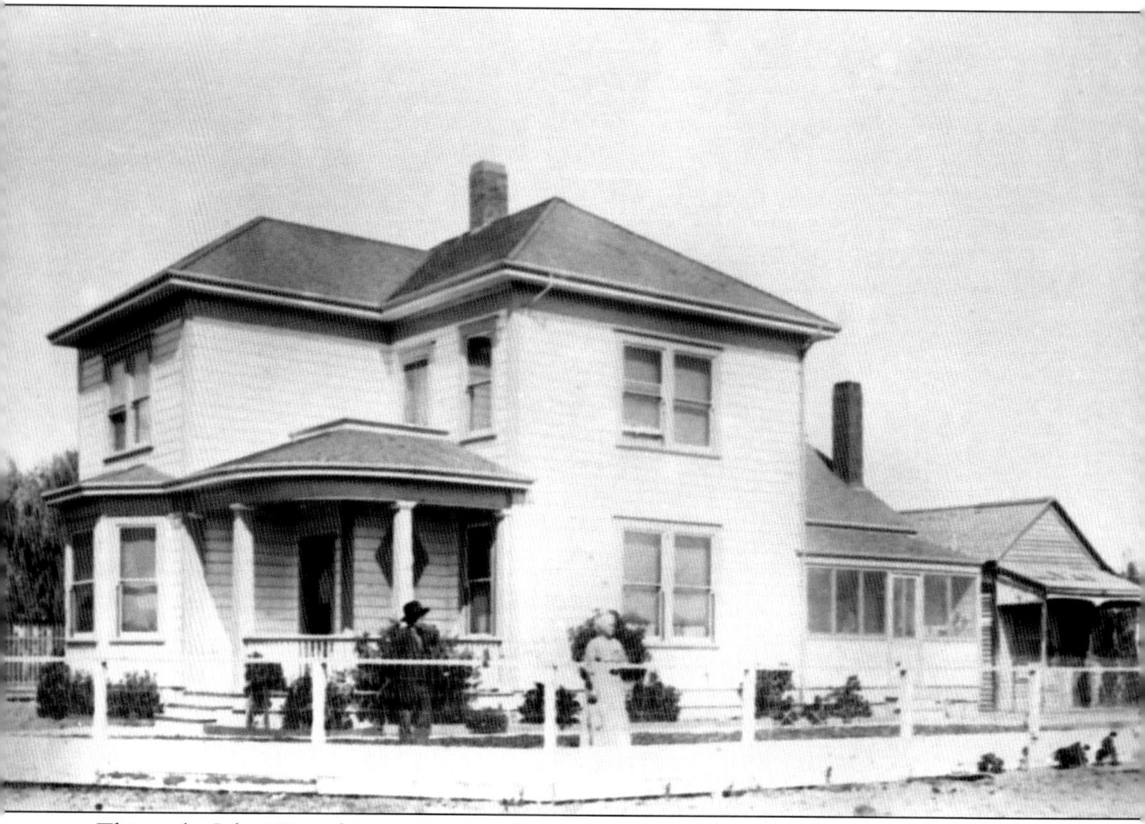

This is the John W. and Lovey Lambert home that was built in 1908 by Claus Siebe for $4,000. The original tiny ranch house can be seen behind the grander home. Siebe was a prolific carpenter in the area, and many of his homes still stand today. (VHC.)

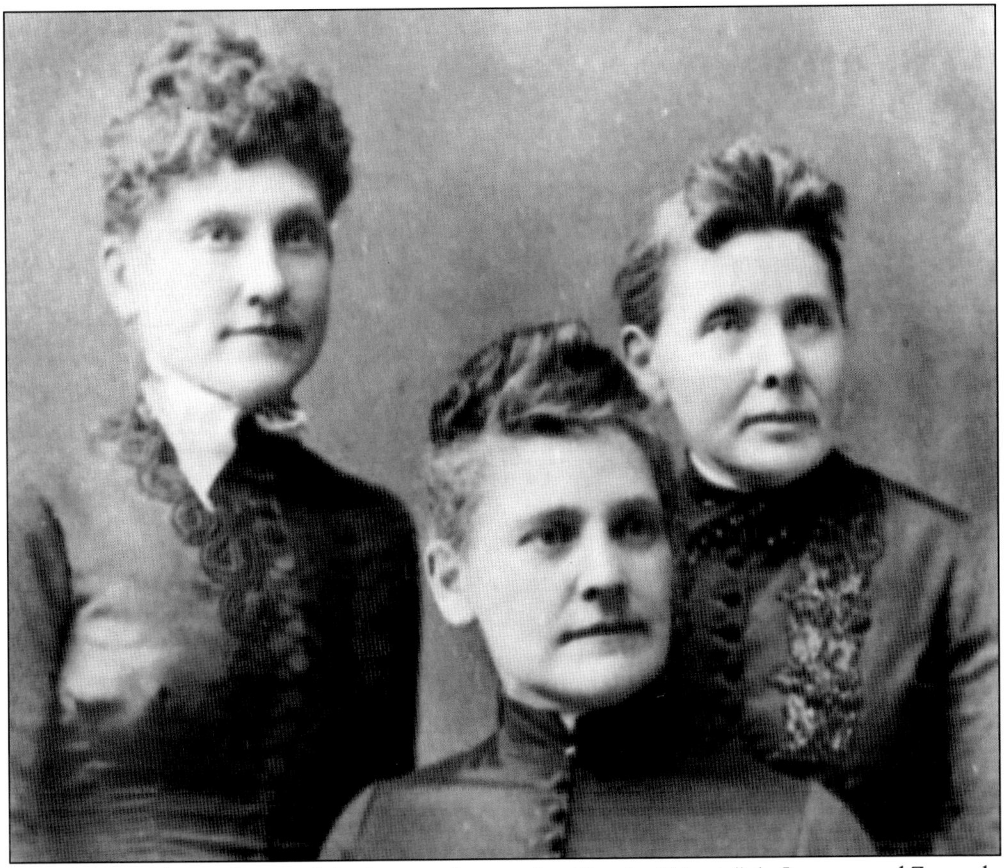

From left to right are Dennie May Lemon, her mother Harriet "Hettie" A. Lemon, and Zenendu ?. Dennie's father was John B. Lemon, the first postmaster in Suisun City, county treasurer for 10 years, and founder of the Suisun Detective Society, Solano County's only known vigilante group. It cost $5 to join the group formed to catch cattle rustlers. Dennie May Lemon married Edwin Hamilton Chadbourne, son of Ruth H. Chadbourne, in 1893, and they lived in the house pictured below. (Both, VHC.)

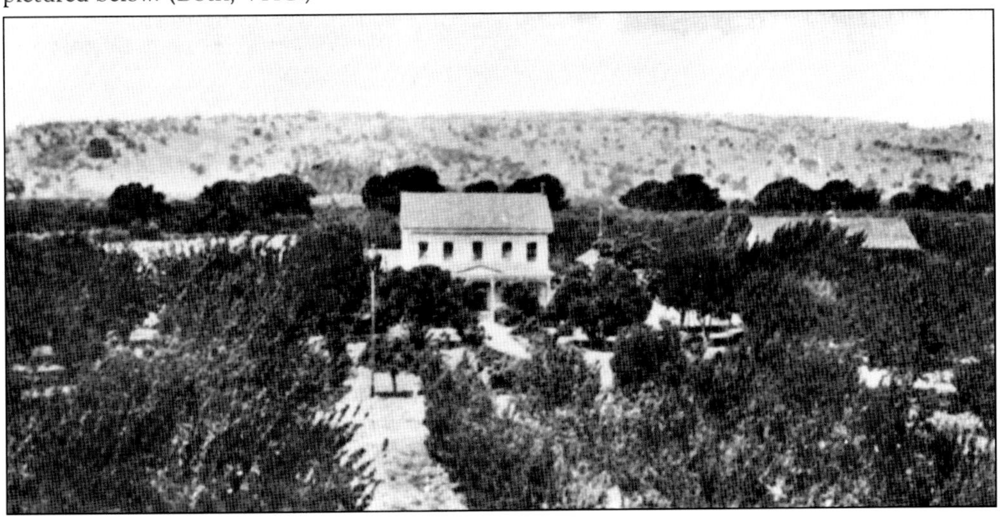

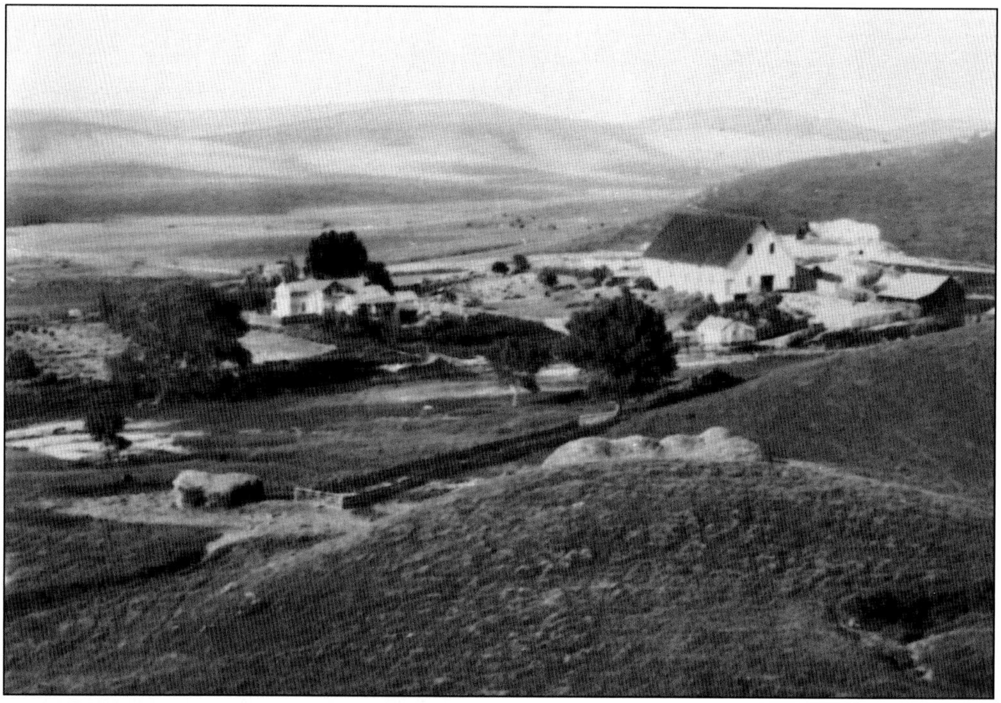

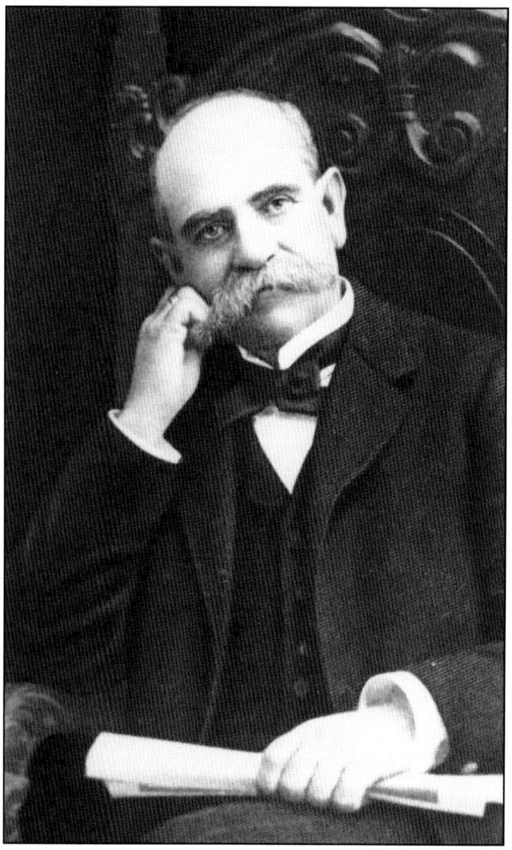

Hiram and Sarah Rush emigrated from Indiana in 1849, settling near Sacramento. Engaging in hotel keeping and stock raising, Hiram Rush began looking for areas to expand after a series of disasters struck Sacramento. With his sights on the Potrero Hills in Suisun, he started purchasing land and moved his family. The Rush Ranch, known to the family as the "tule ranch," is seen here at its height. Hiram Rush was killed when he was ejected from his buggy while inspecting the ranch. (VHC.)

From a young age, Benjamin F. Rush, pictured here, proved adept at managing the complexities of business, animal husbandry, and horticulture. He especially rose to the challenge upon the death of his father, when he was tasked with managing his family's extensive and diverse agricultural enterprises. Among his many endeavors, Rush served as Solano County sheriff, trustee of the Crystal School District, and state senator. As senator, he sat on the committees in charge of selecting and funding the sites that eventually became University of California, Davis, and the Veterans' Home in Yountville. (VHC.)

Pictured in 1929, Asanoma family members are, from left to right, (first row) M. Asanoma (father), Elaine (daughter), and Kusue (mother); (second row) George Onoda (step-son) and Frances Onoda (step-daughter). George, a top student at Armijo Union High School, went on to earn a degree from UC Berkeley. George married Ayako Yoshimua and had two children, Eleanor and George Jr. In 1942, Executive Order 9066, requiring their internment at Gila River, abruptly interrupted their lives. Despite that adversity, both of George's children went on to earn degrees from his alma mater. (VHC.)

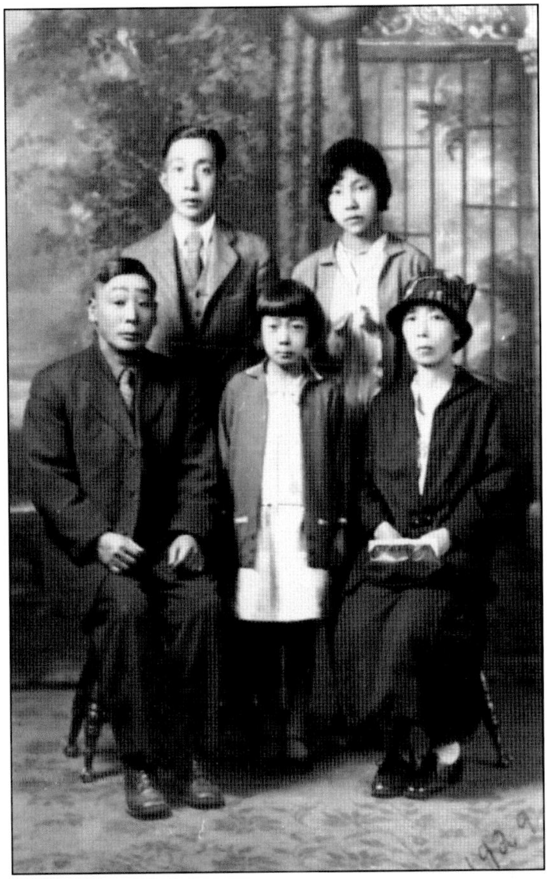

This Davisson family house was purportedly moved from California Street in Suisun City to John Russell Davisson's property on Rockville Road because the Davissons felt the city taxes were too high. The Davissons first arrived in Suisun Valley from Holt County, Missouri, in September 1854. The construction of the house is evocative of the Cordelia Hotel. (VHC.)

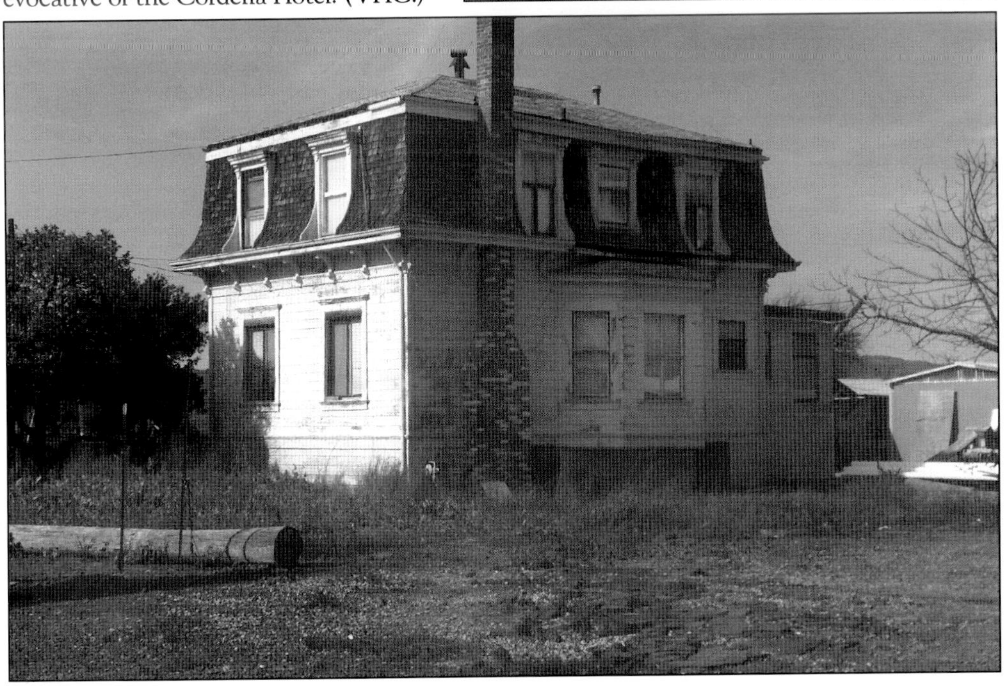

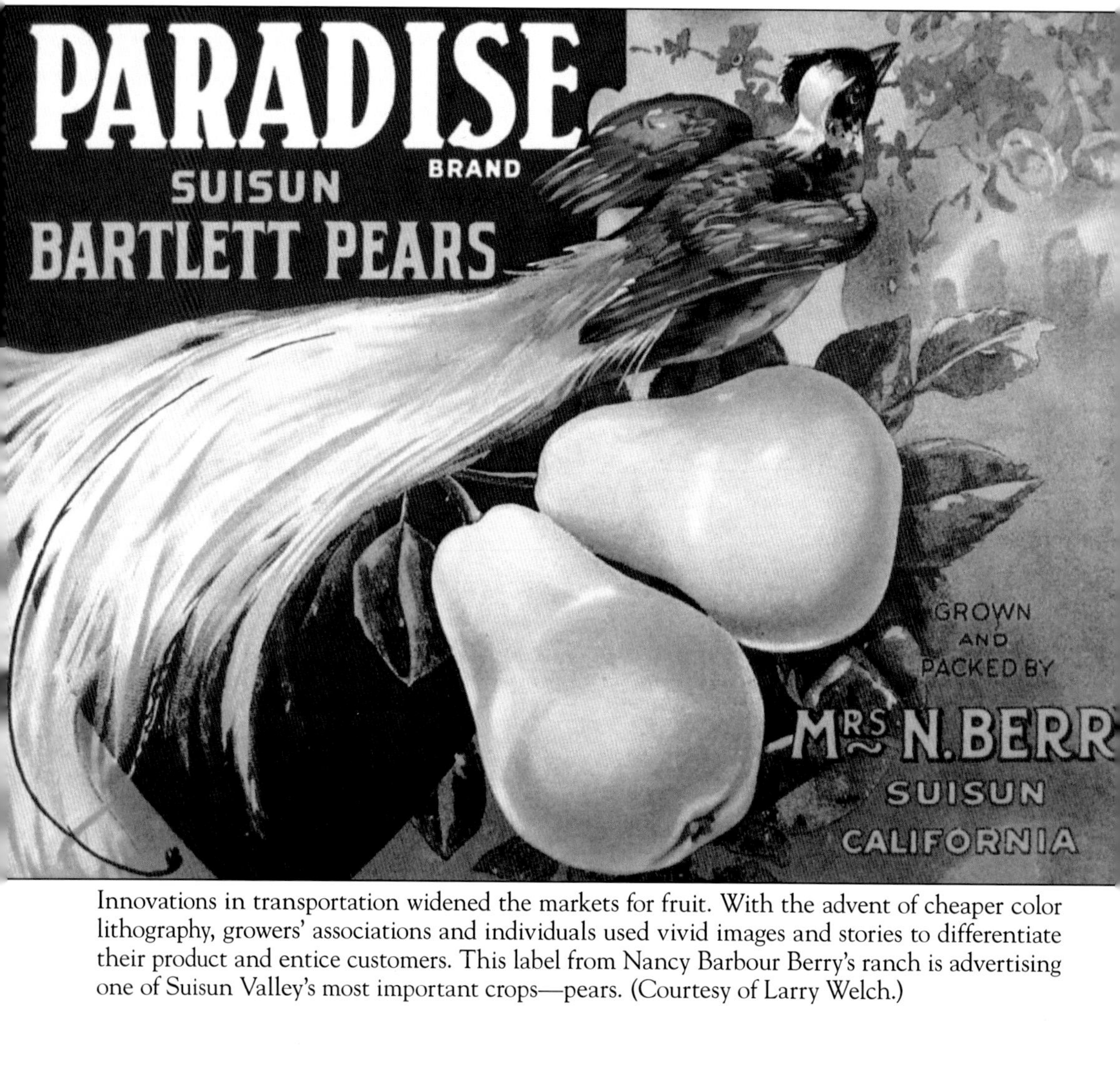

Innovations in transportation widened the markets for fruit. With the advent of cheaper color lithography, growers' associations and individuals used vivid images and stories to differentiate their product and entice customers. This label from Nancy Barbour Berry's ranch is advertising one of Suisun Valley's most important crops—pears. (Courtesy of Larry Welch.)

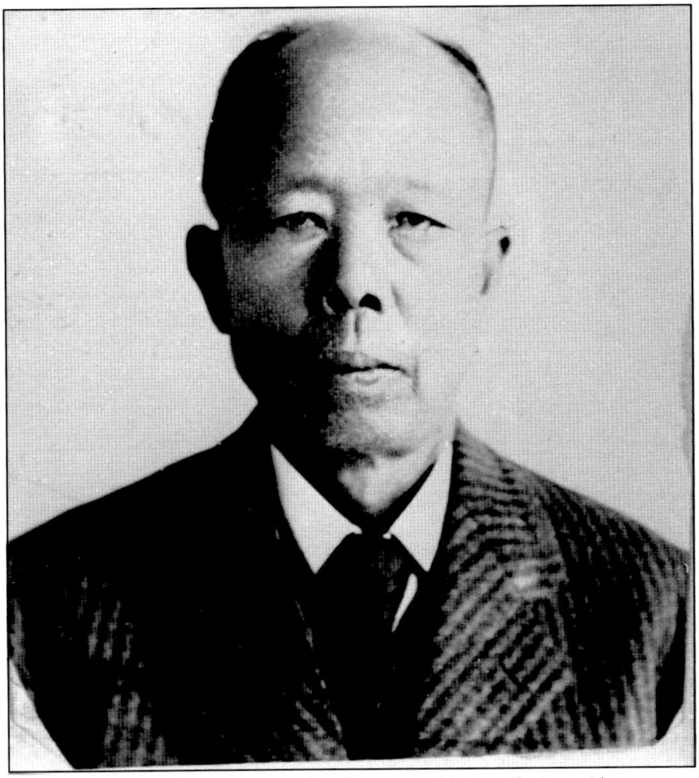

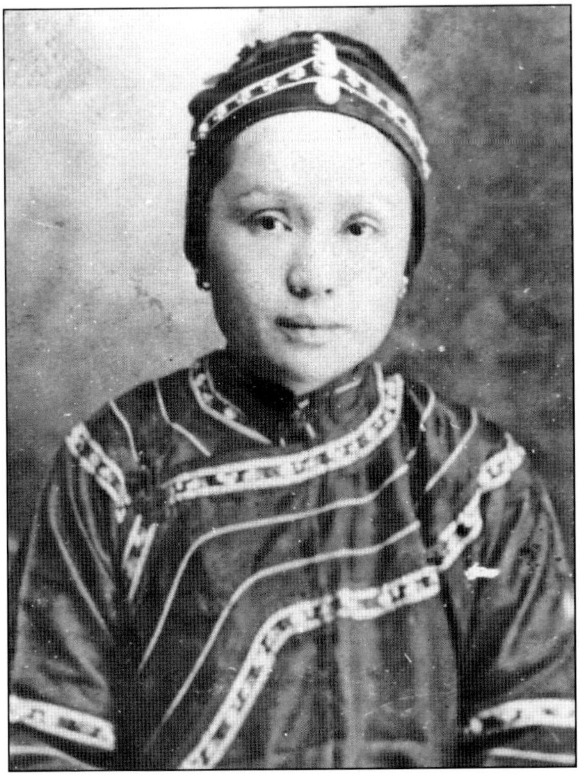

Go Long and his wife, Lee Shee, exemplify success in spite of adversity. Go Long emigrated from China in 1872, at first working for the railroads. Later, he moved to Suisun Valley and started farming. A series of economic setbacks contributed to anti-Chinese sentiment, which inspired a series of laws that severely curtailed immigration, employment, and property rights of Chinese. Suisun's isolated and shrinking Chinese population was typical for Chinese rural communities throughout the state. Despite this, Go Long met and married Lee Shee in 1898. Together, they had 16 surviving children. Barred from owning land, the Longs rented a fruit ranch and gained the respect of their fellow orchardists. Eventually, the laws barring Chinese from owning land relaxed, and Go Long purchased a ranch in Yolo County. Some of their children remained in Suisun Valley. (Both, VHC.)

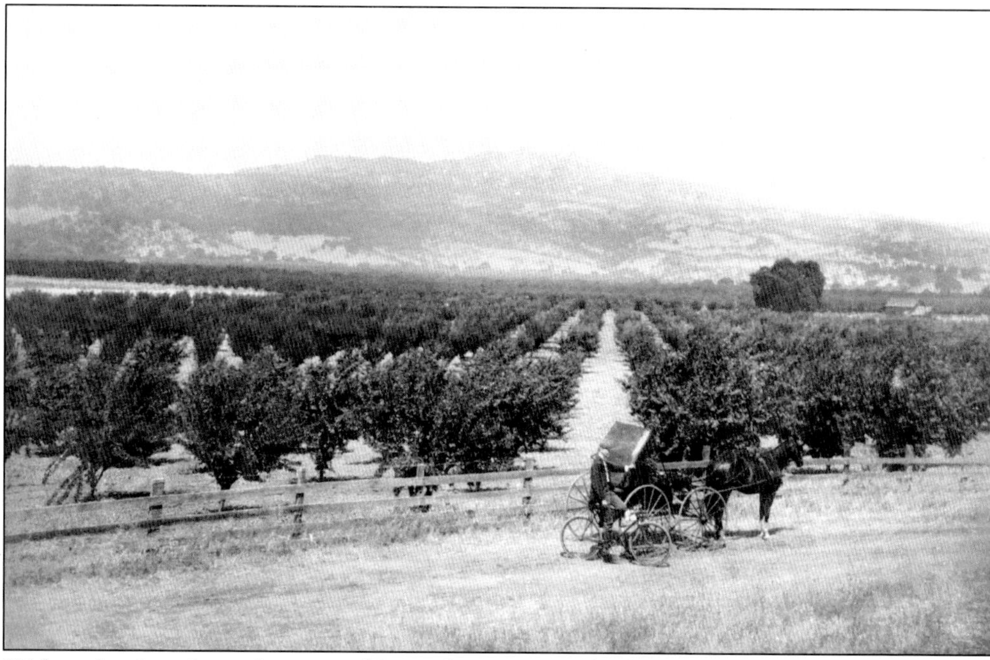

With orchards as far as the eye could see, cherries were the first crop of the year. They were the most difficult. A rainstorm just before harvest could ruin much of the crop. If the cherries got wet they would split, and those that did would have to be sorted out. The apricots and plums would ripen next. Finally peaches were the last of the spring crops. Summertime was pear time. In the fall, walnuts, almonds, and other nuts were harvested. (VHC.)

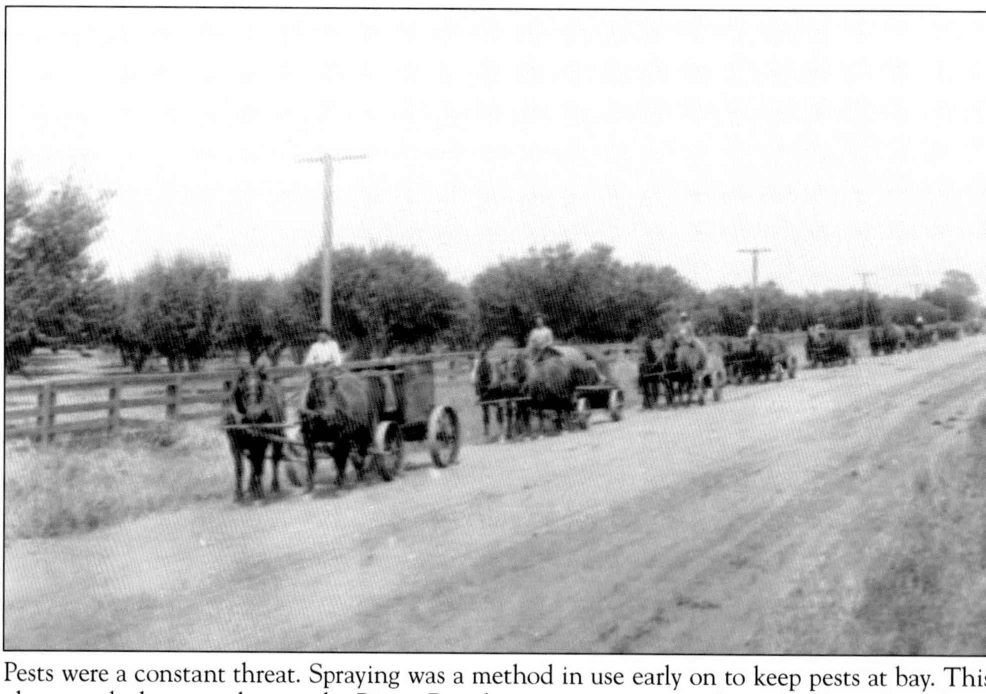

Pests were a constant threat. Spraying was a method in use early on to keep pests at bay. This photograph shows workers at the Pierce Ranch preparing to spray the orchards with tanks of spray pulled by teams of horses. (VHC.)

By the 1940s, mechanical sprayers, such as this one, had been developed that could apply spray to a larger area with less manpower and less outlay in equipment. (MD.)

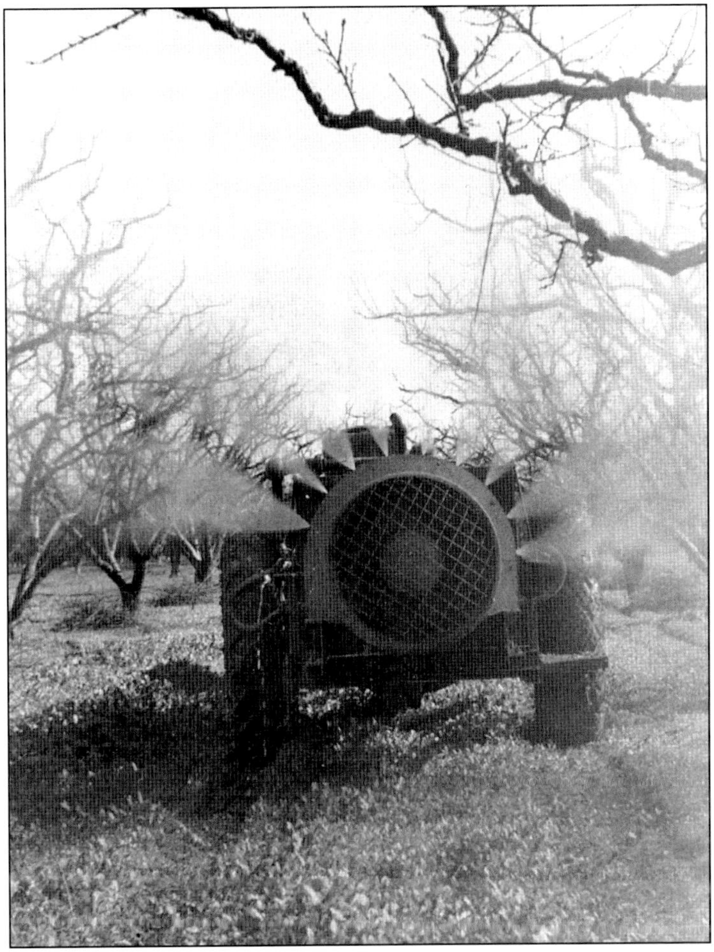

On smaller farms, harvesting the fruit from the orchards was a multigenerational family affair. Here, members of the Siebe family surround their crop of peaches. Bessie Siebe is in the center of the photograph, seventh from the right. (DF.)

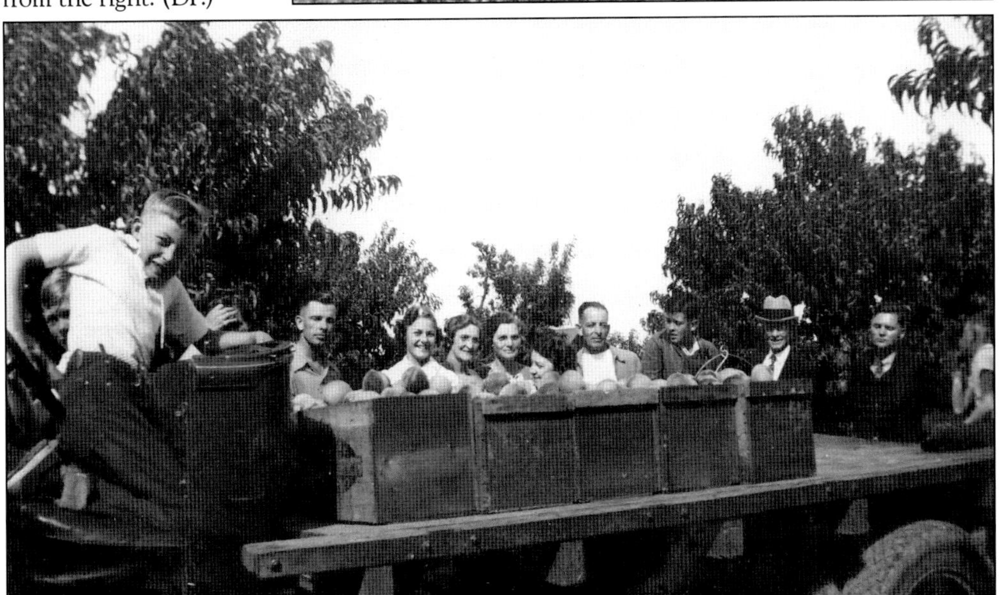

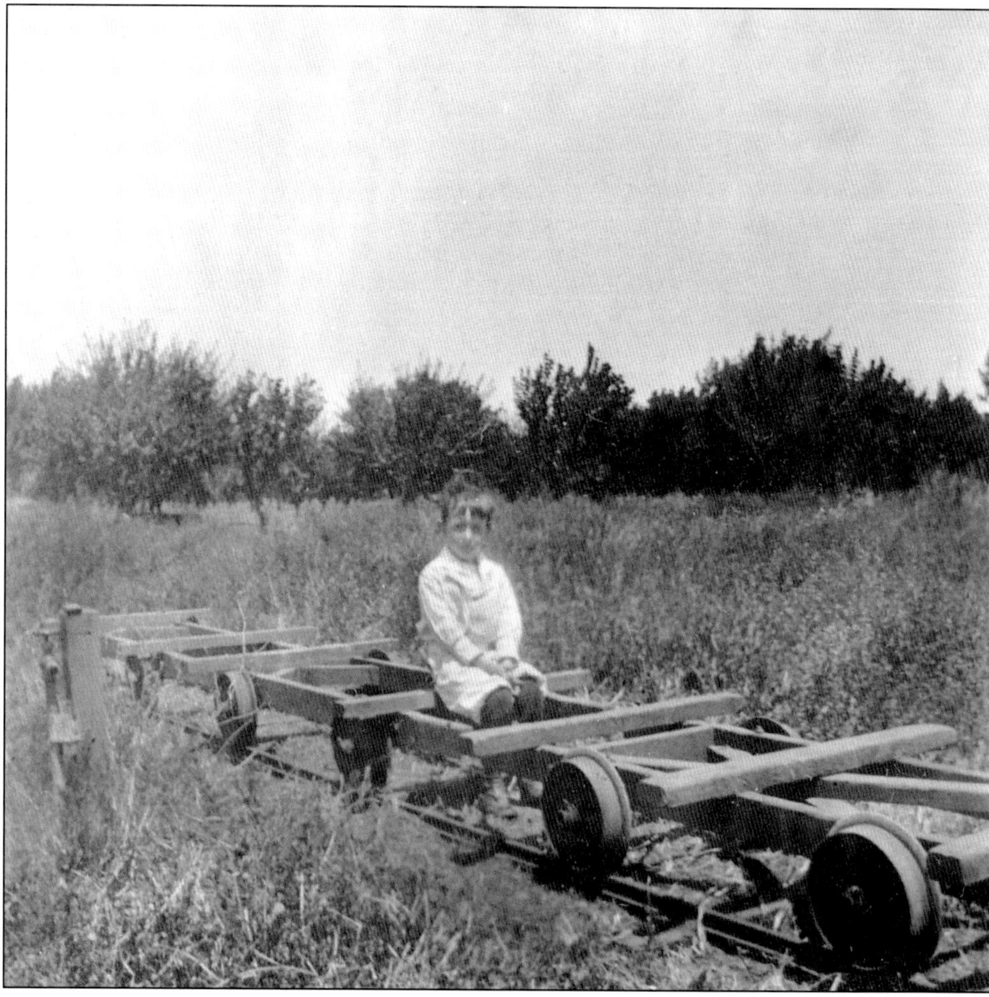

The orchards in Suisun Valley were planted before the advent of tractors. For efficiency, tracks would be laid in the rows to be picked that day. Handcarts would be loaded with boxes or trays of fruit and be pushed by hand to wagons or pulled by horse to the farm's fruit shed. Young Andreas Schmidt, pictured here, is sitting on a classic example of one such cart. Local children sometimes used the carts as transportation from home to school. (DF.)

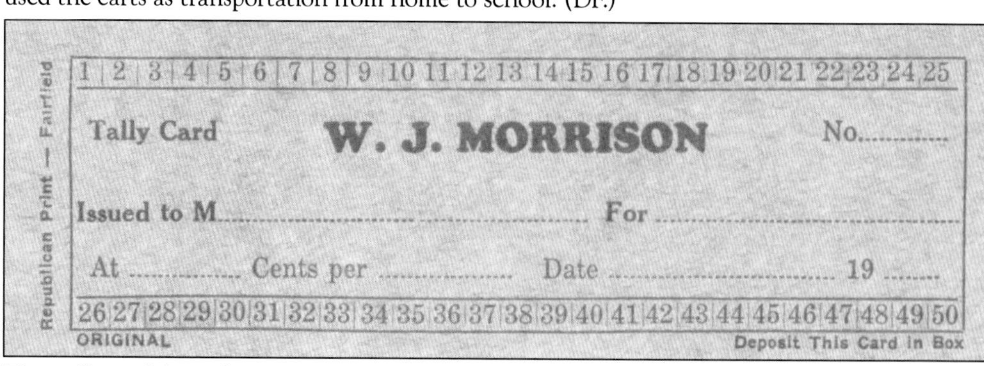

1 2 3 4 5 6 7 8 9 10 11 12 13 14 15 16 17 18 19 20 21 22 23 24 25

Tally Card **W. J. MORRISON** No............

Issued to M.. For ....

At .... Cents per .... Date .... 19 ....

26 27 28 29 30 31 32 33 34 35 36 37 38 39 40 41 42 43 44 45 46 47 48 49 50

ORIGINAL Deposit This Card in Box

Republican Print — Fairfield

This tally card from the W.J. Morrison ranch exemplifies the method that was used to calculate the wages for the fruit cutters. Workers were paid by the box, tallied with a hole punch. (MD.)

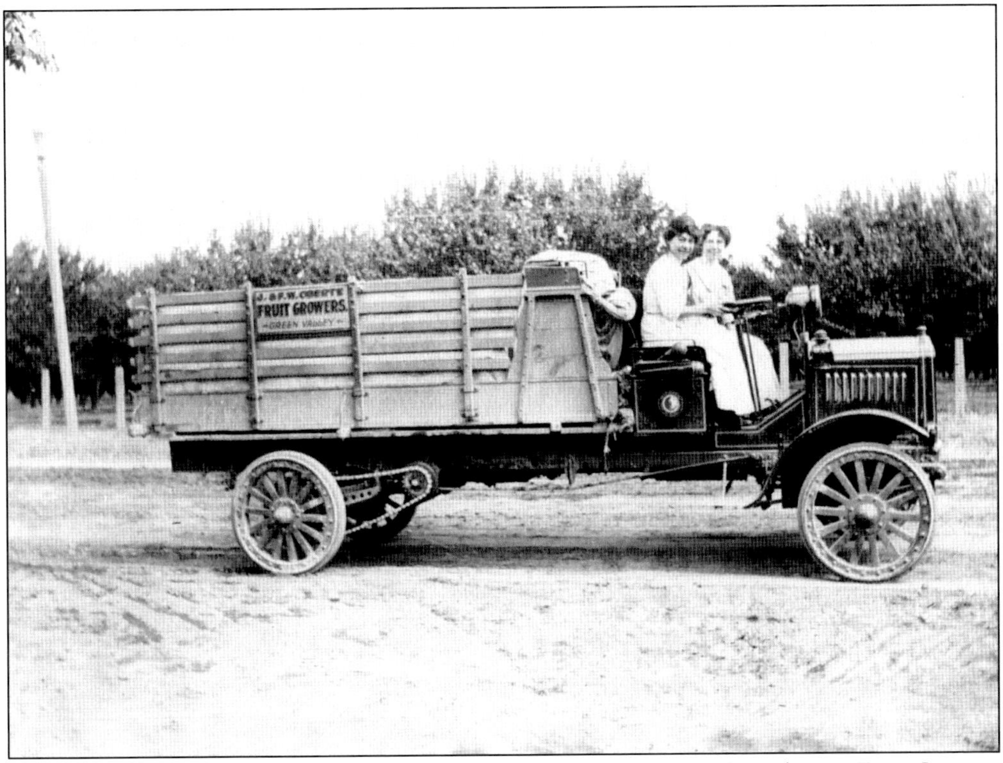

Margaret Siebe is driving Hattie Erickson on Joseph and Frank Wesley Oberte's Fruit Growers truck, manufactured by the Wichita Falls Motor Truck Company. (DF.)

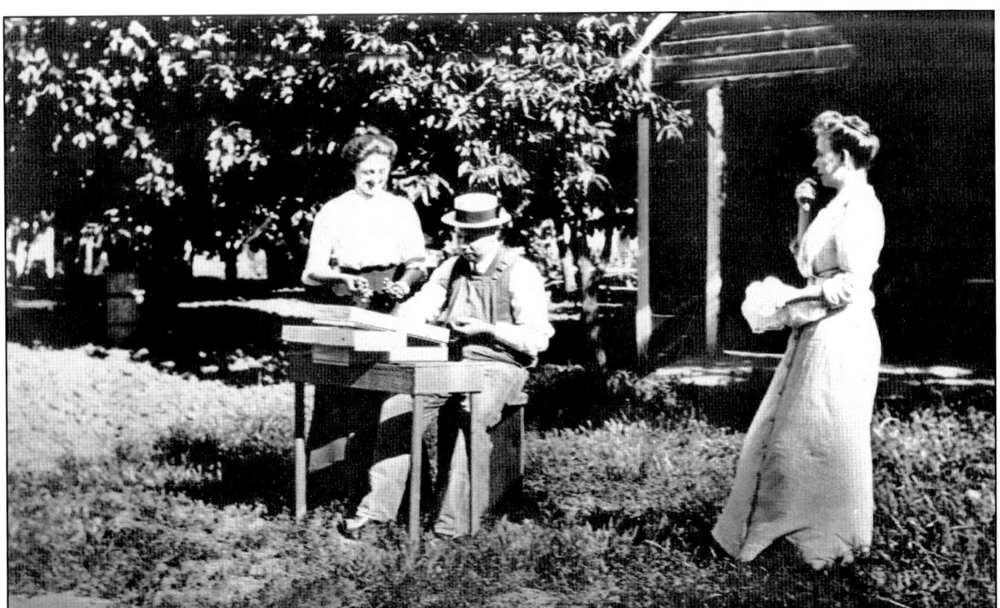

Members of the Morrison family look on as William H. Morrison grades fruit from the cherry harvest. (DF.)

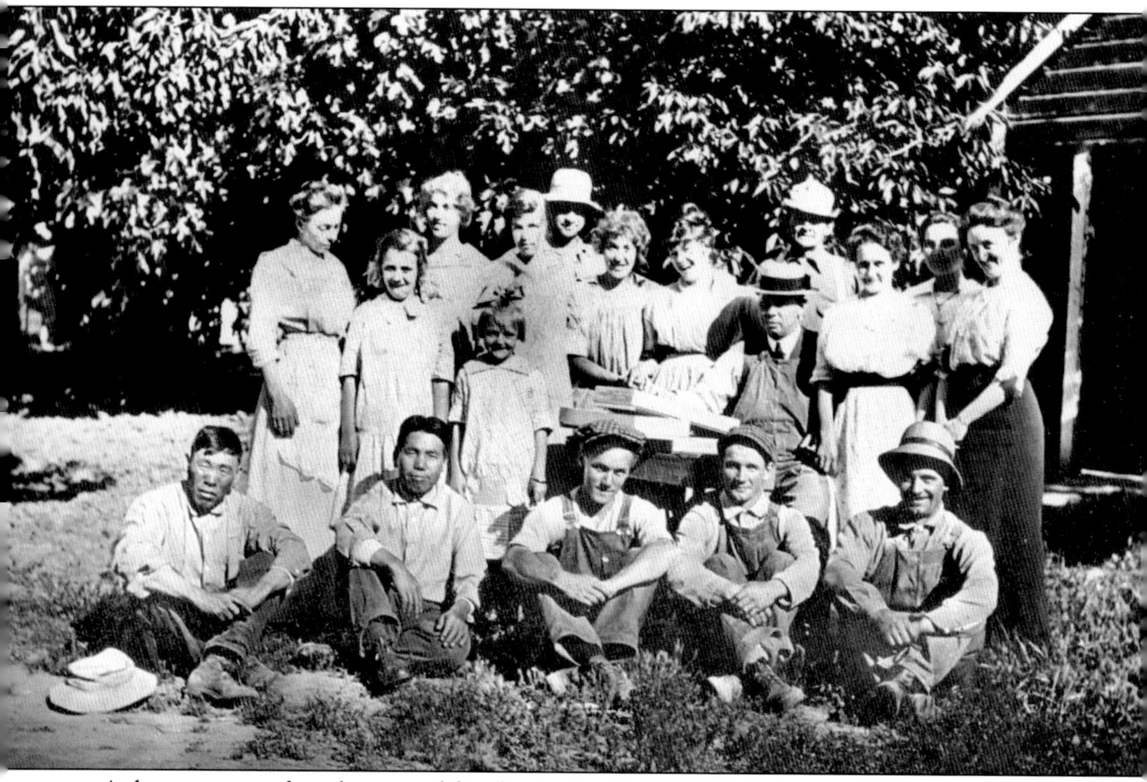

A diverse group of employees and family members alike all worked to gather the harvest, as can be seen in this photograph of the Morrison family and farmhands. From left to right are (first row) all unidentified; (second row) Gladys Elaine Morrison, unidentified, William H. Morrison (seated), Emma Vogel, and unidentified; (third row) Frances Morrison, six unidentified people, and Bessie Edith Morrison. (DF.)

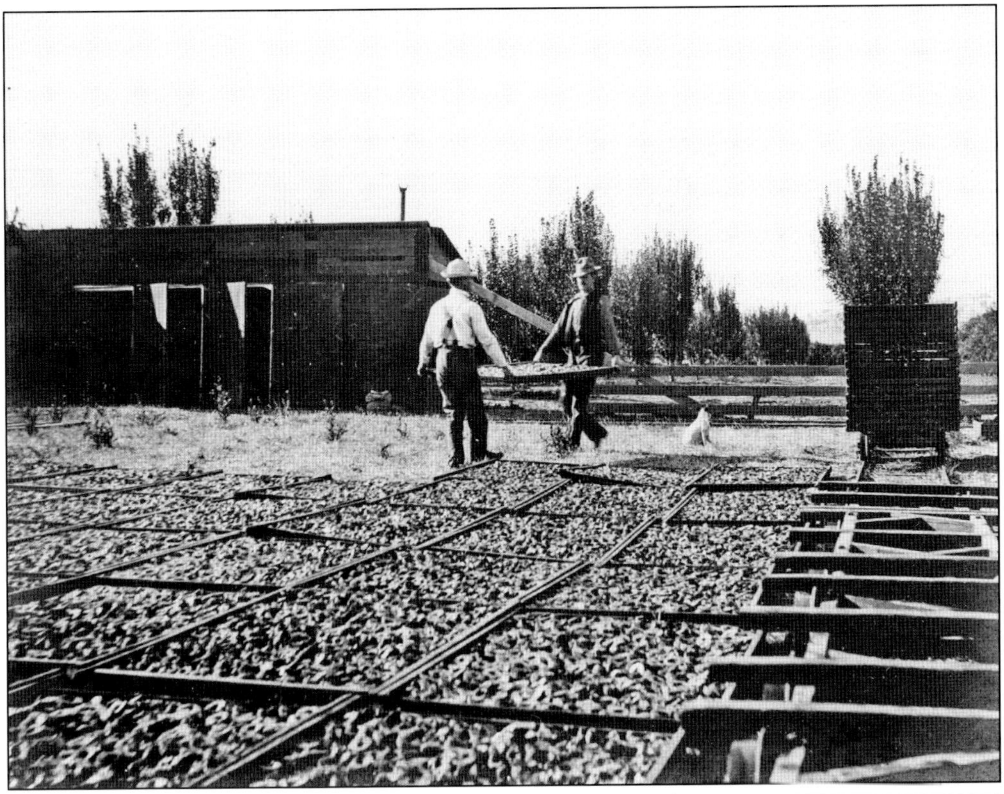

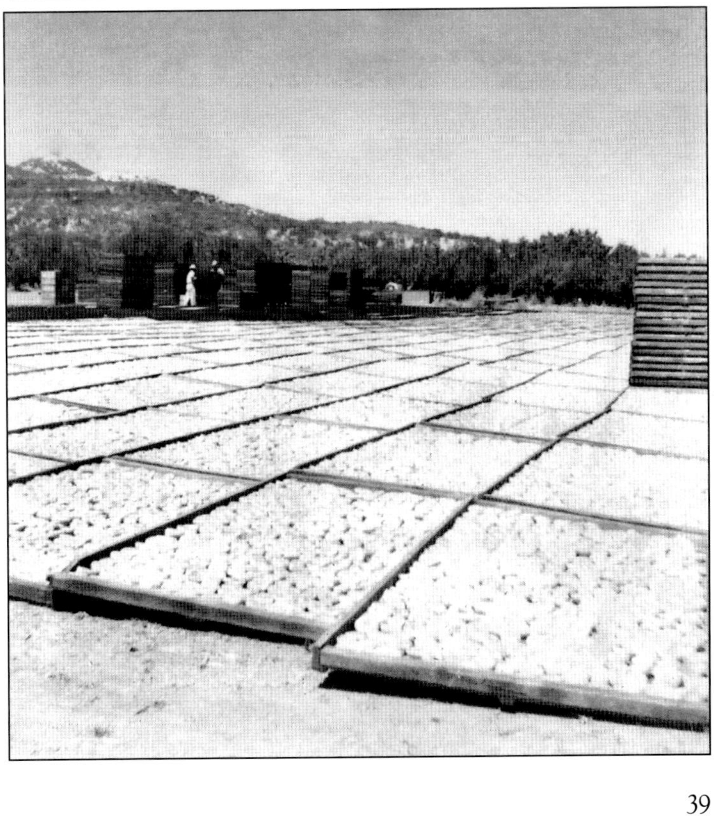

Once the fruit was harvested, the next step would be to take the fruit for dipping in large lug boxes by box cart. First, the fruit was dipped in lye and then dipped in water to rinse the lye away. Once dipped, the fruit was placed in the sun to dry on large wooden trays and turned regularly, as seen in the early image above taken in the late 1890s. If there was any chance of rain, the trays had to be stacked and covered with canvas. As can be seen in the image to the right from the 1940s, little has changed since the late 1890s in the methods used to dry and pack fruit. (Above, DF; right, MD.)

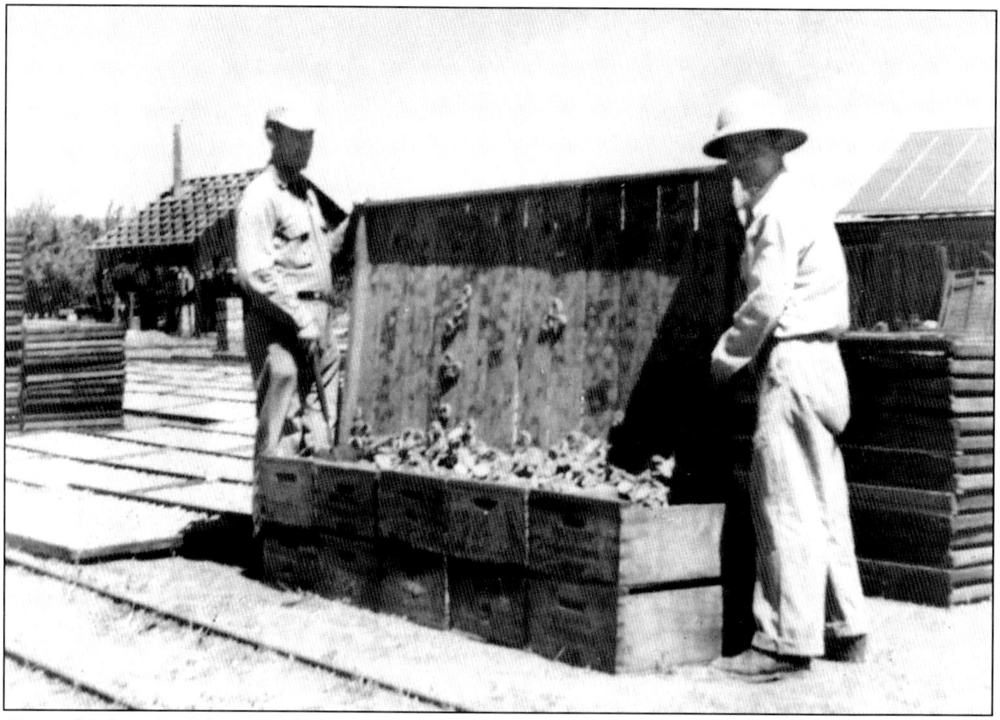

Once the fruit had dried in the sun for several weeks, it would be taken to sweat and cure on the pine floors of the drying sheds. In order to ensure even curing, the fruit had to be turned daily with a large shovel. The dried fruit was then packed in 100-pound sacks. (MD.)

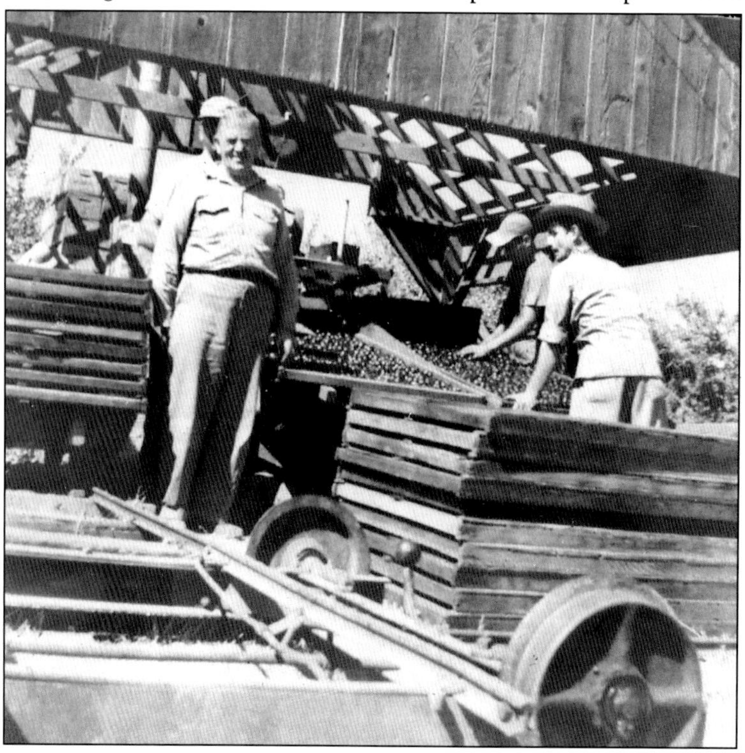

Franz Micheal "Mike" Knecht is overseeing the cherry harvest from beneath the Marlowe Oberti ranch packing shed. Mike lost his arm in a machinery accident at the Sawyer Tanning Company in Napa. He was given the choice to have a job for life or receive a lump sum compensation for his injury. Mike chose the security of lifelong employment and stayed at the tannery as a watchman for the rest of his working days. (MD.)

CLARENCE E. MONEZ TRUCKING SERVICE

P. O. Box 79 — SUISUN, CALIFORNIA — Phones: HA 5-3936

Delivered To:

Freight Charges As Follows:

DATE	SHIPPER	DESCRIPTION	QUANTITY	RATE	AMOUNT

Many valley farmers diversified to augment their farming incomes. The Monez families farmed in Gordon and Suisun Valleys. Manuel Monez and his children built the Icehouse and fruit stand at Rockville Corners. From there, his son Clarence and his family operated a trucking business in addition to their farm in Gordon Valley. The Clarence Monez Trucking Co. carried other valley farmers' produce to the commission markets in Oakland and San Francisco. Clarence's wife, Lois, would also take produce to the farmers' market in San Francisco. At that time, it was located on Duboce Avenue, in view of the US Mint. (Both, courtesy of the Monez family.)

FRESH FRUITS And VEGETABLES Eat Fruit for Health

CLARENCE E. MONEZ

PRODUCER AND WHOLESALER

FRUITS AND VEGETABLES

PHONE HAR. 5-3936

SUISUN VALLEY, CALIF., ____________ 195__

DATE	DESCRIPTION	CHARGES	CREDITS	BALANCE

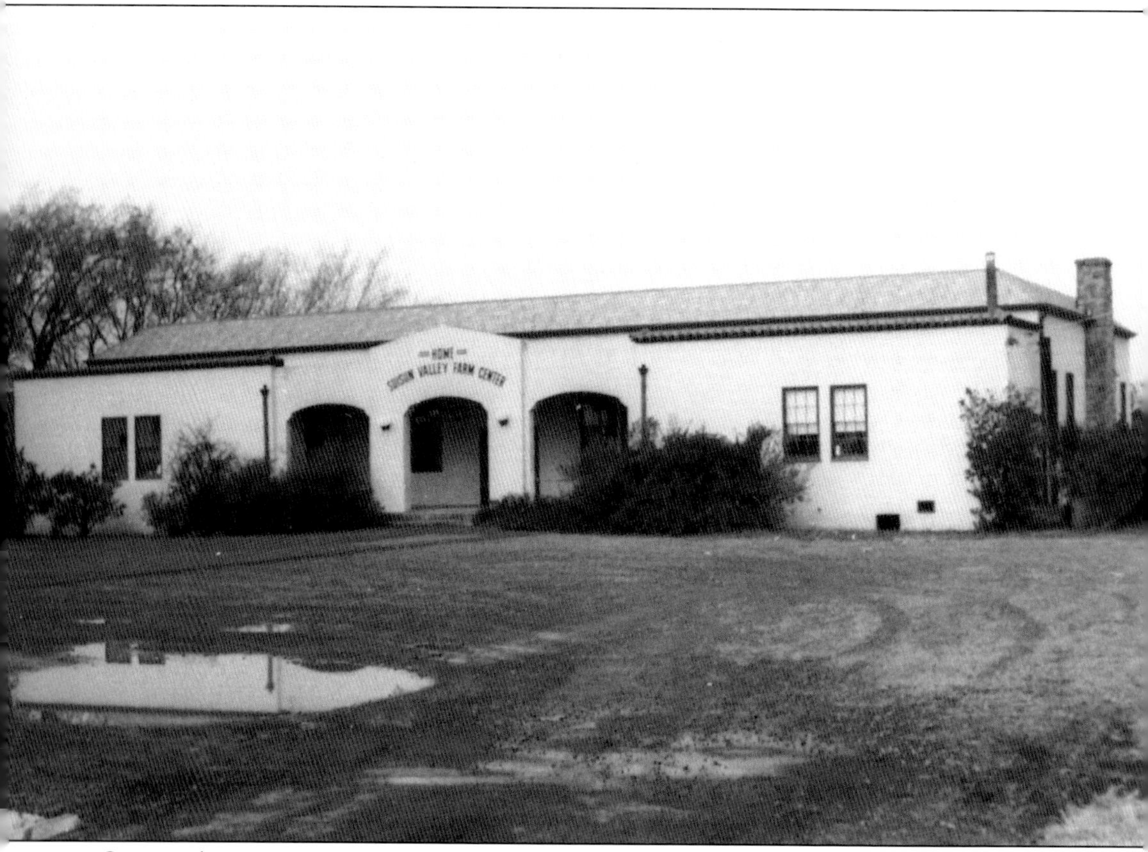

Organized in 1916 as a result of the Smith Lever Act of May 1914 and the subsequent establishment of the University of California Agricultural Cooperative Extension Service, the Suisun Valley Farm Center was created to facilitate the transfer of scientific research to rural residents. William J. Morrison, Fred A. Chadbourne, and William G. Davisson established the Suisun Valley Farm Center itself with funds raised from social gatherings held on the dance floor that had been installed in the loft of Joseph R. Chadbourne's barn. The Bank of Suisun aided financing. Despite the Depression of the 1930s, the debt was paid in full by the membership of over 300 valley farmers. Among the services provided by the Suisun Valley Farm Center were disease troubleshooting, demonstrations of new farming techniques, and addressing the labor shortages caused by World Wars I and II. (VHC.)

Four

A Bustling Town

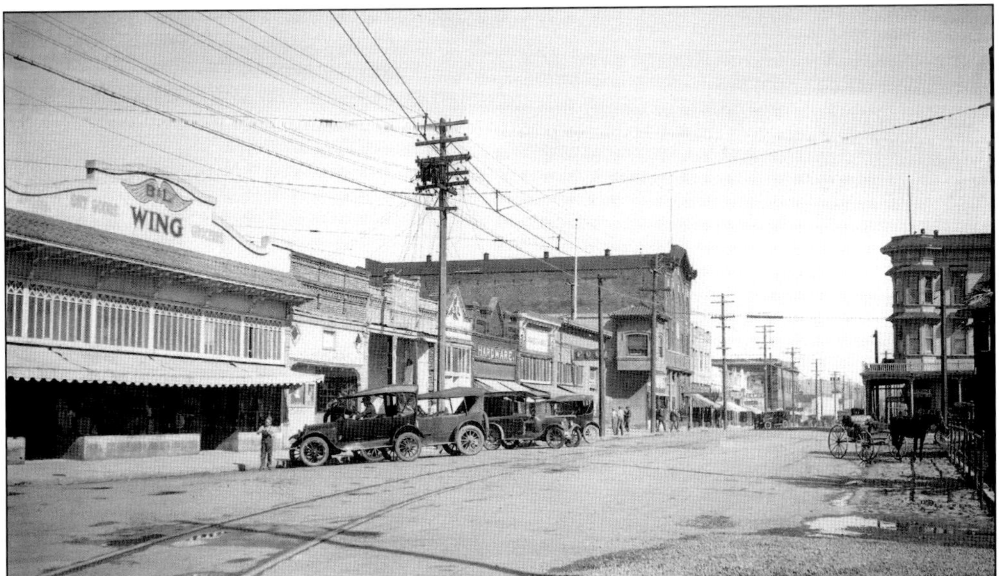

Looking north towards Fairfield, this early photograph of Main Street highlights the various modes of transportation that were in use in the early 1900s, including horse and buggy, automobiles, and railcars. One may wonder why there is a small child standing in the street unattended among the hustle and bustle of downtown. Perhaps hc wandered away from his mother while she was shopping at B&L Wing Dry Goods and Groceries, "Dealers in Fancy and Staple Groceries." (VHC.)

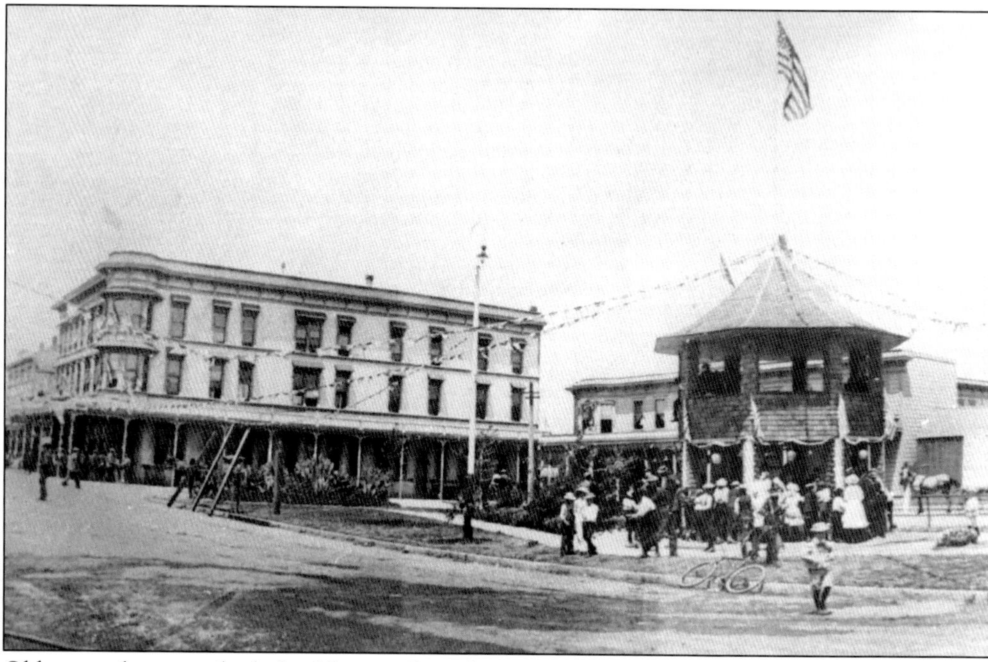

Old town plaza was the hub of Suisun City. At its center was a bandstand where city functions and events, such as parades and dances, were held. There were concerts on Sundays featuring local bands such as the Speedy Swift Orchestra. The Arlington and Union Hotels can be seen in the background of this photograph of Fourth of July revelers of the early 1900s. (VHC.)

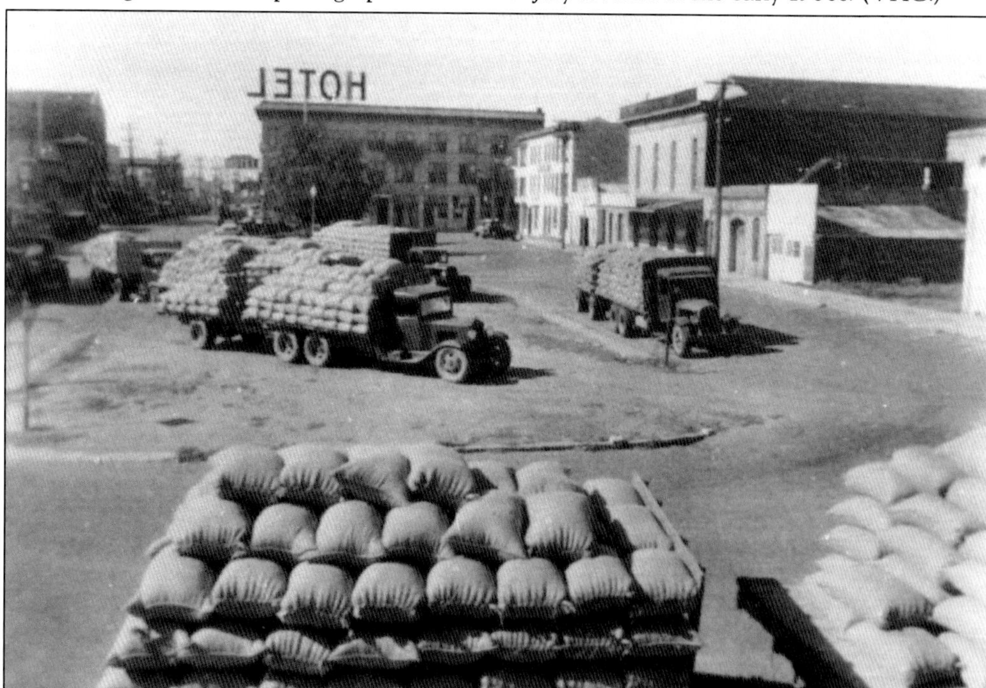

Grain trucks are lined up in Suisun City Plaza. Arlington and Union Hotels can still be seen in the background, but the bandstand is long gone. (VHC.)

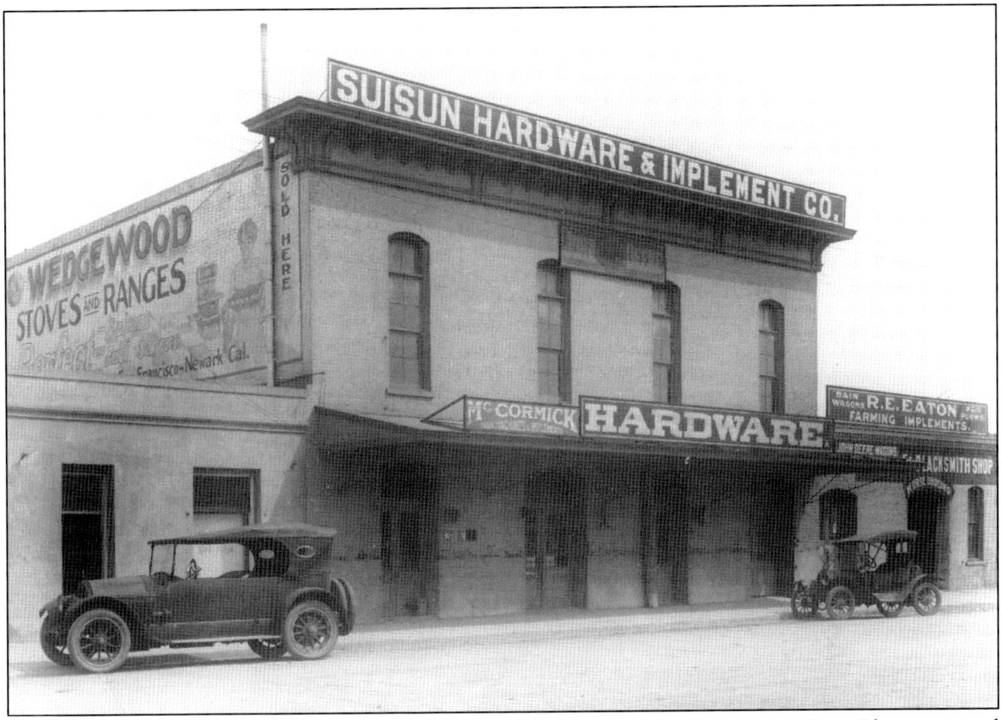

The Suisun Hardware and Implement Co. was located in the Suisun City Plaza around 1920. (VHC.)

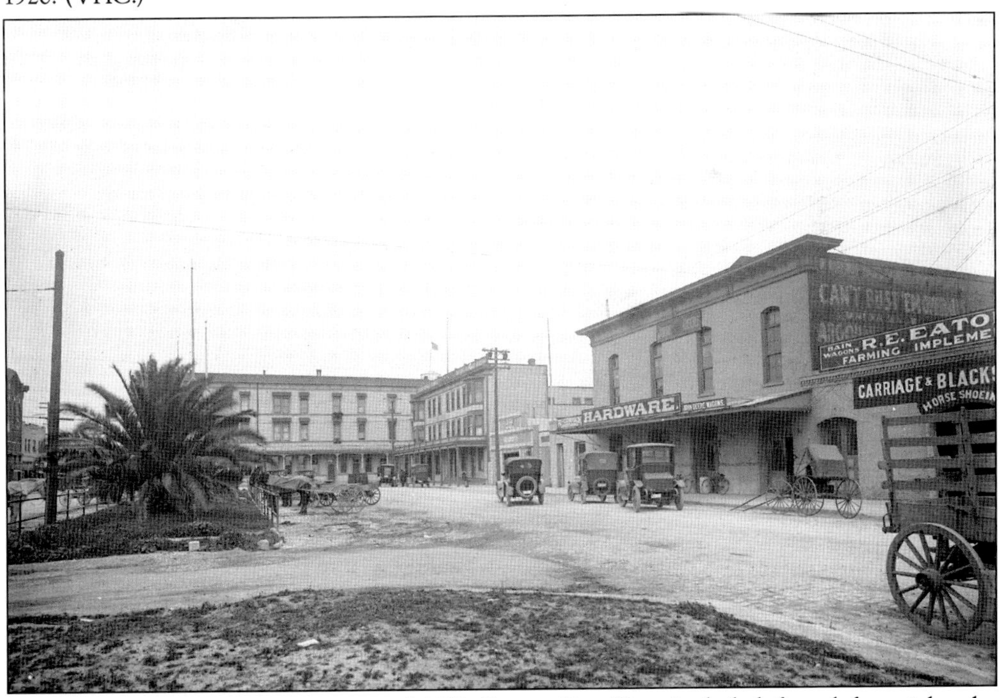

As viewed from Morgan Street around 1919, Suisun City Plaza included, from left to right, the Masonic Hall, Arlington Hotel, Union Hotel, Wilson's Garage, Suisun Hardware and Implement Company, and R.E. Eaton's Carriage and Blacksmith's Shop. (VHC.)

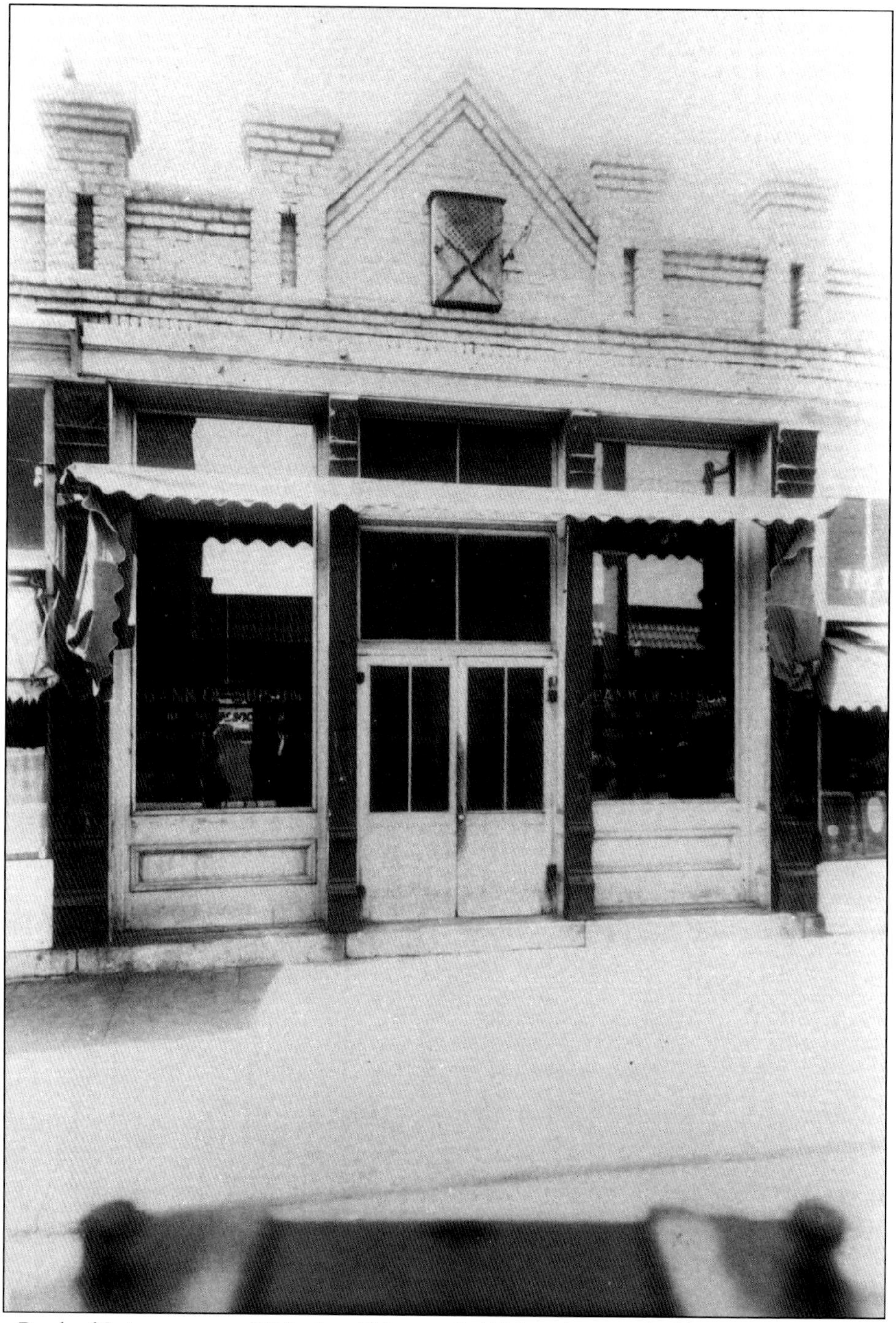

The Bank of Suisun was established on February 7, 1876, with capital of $100,000. R.D. Robbins served as president, with W. Wolf as cashier, and the directors were R.D. Robbins, C.F.D. Hastings, E.P. Hilborn, W.H. Turner, and J.B. Hoyt. Much of the town's development can be directly attributed to capital provided by the Bank of Suisun. From the humble beginnings of his first job in Solano County driving a team to haul bricks from the waterfront to the site of the Fairfield Methodist Church, R.D. Robbins amassed great wealth and influence over the course of his life. (VHC.)

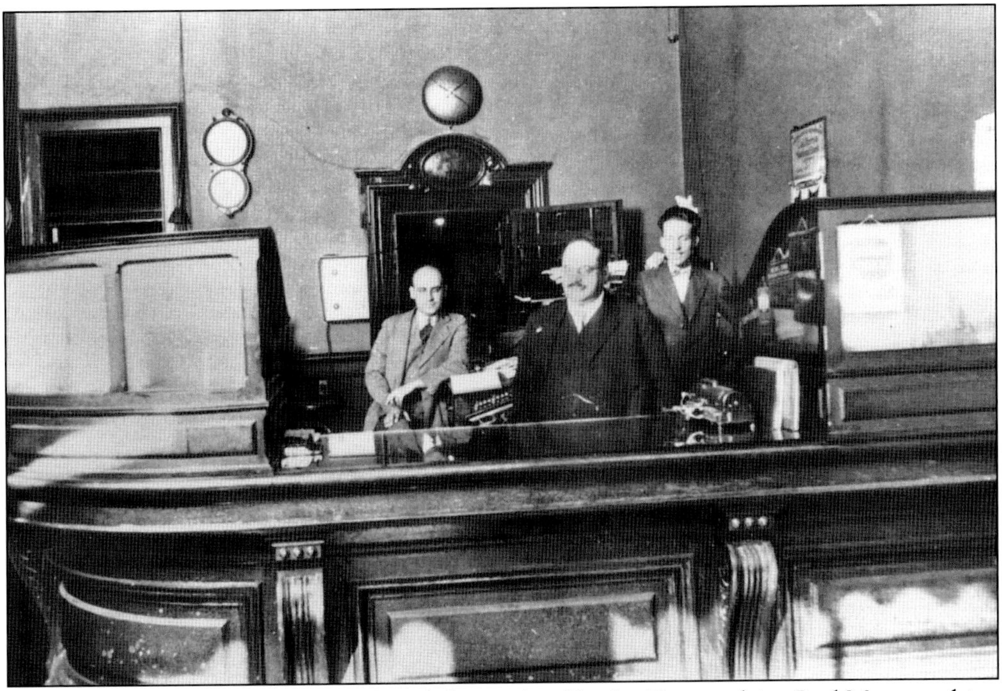

Bank of Suisun staff members are, from left to right, Charles Torp, cashier; Paul Mertz, cashier; and John Kinloch, assistant cashier. (VHC.)

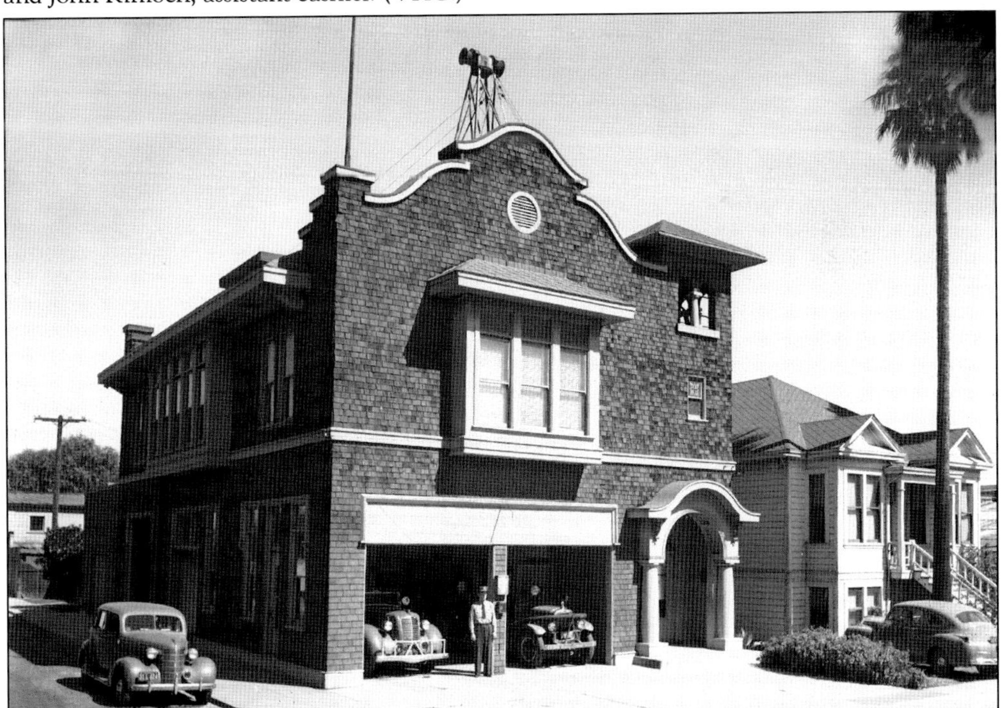

This is a photograph of the former Armijo Club Building after it was repurposed by Suisun City as a firehouse and city offices. The Suisun Improvement Association originally constructed it in 1901 as a social center and clubhouse. (VHC.)

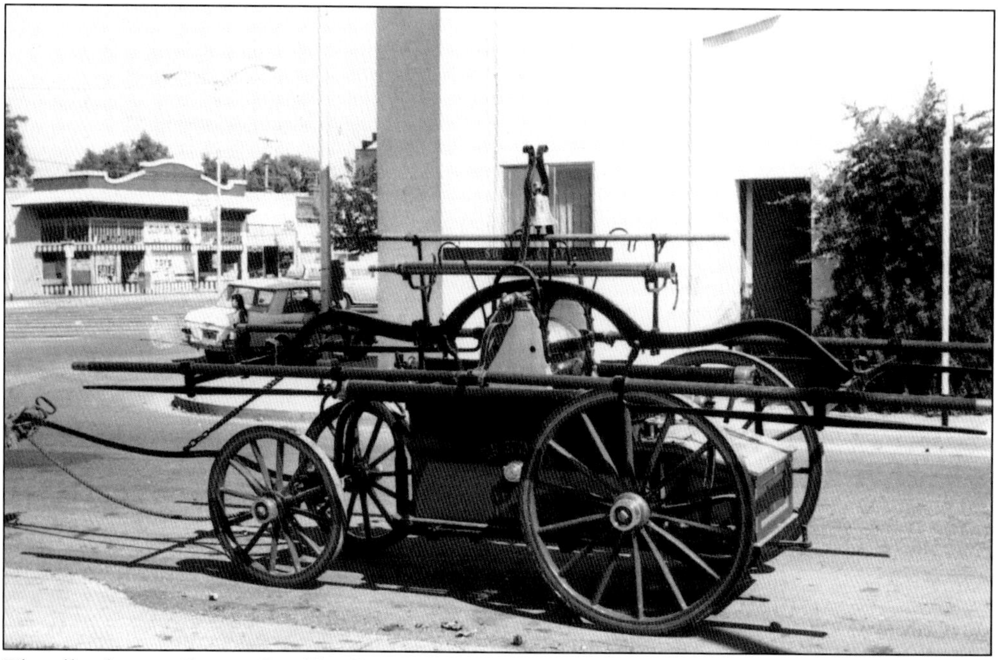

The all-volunteer Suisun City Fire Department was formed on April 27, 1861. This is a photograph of the S.R. Spinney No. 14 fire engine acquired by the brigade that same year. Made in 1857, the engine was shipped around the Horn and first used by the San Francisco Fire Department. Its heavy design and cumbersome operation were not compatible with the hills of San Francisco. Suisun City lore has it that funds were raised through fines levied at the town's brothels. (VHC.)

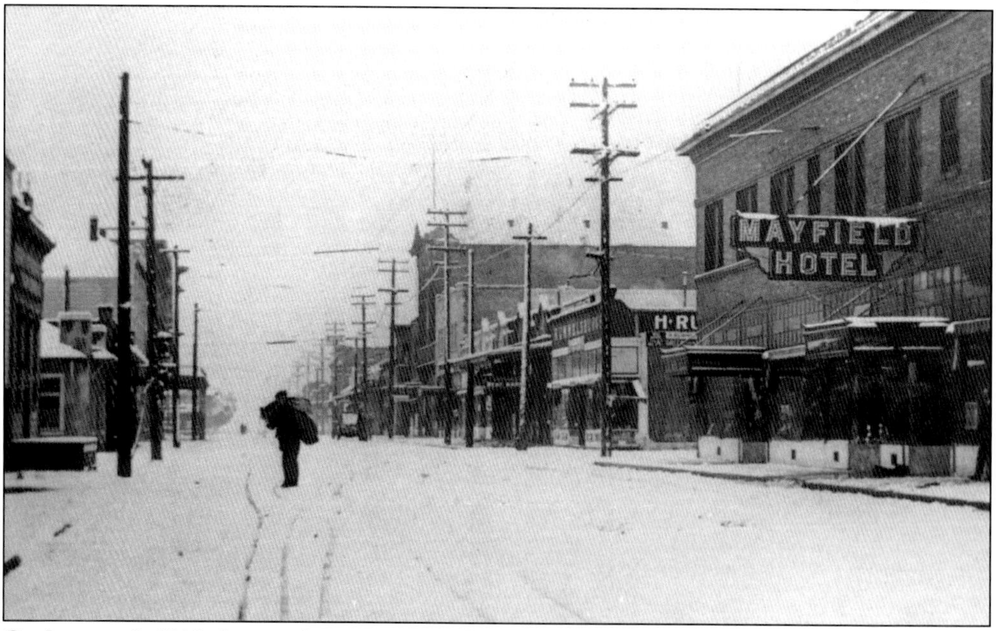

On January 9, 1913, Suisun City experienced a rare snowstorm (the last severe snowstorm had happened 45 years earlier). To the right is the Mayfield Hotel, built in 1910 by Charles Mayfield, on the corner of Main and Sacramento Streets. The three-story building farther up the street on the same side is the Masonic Hall, built in 1888. (VHC.)

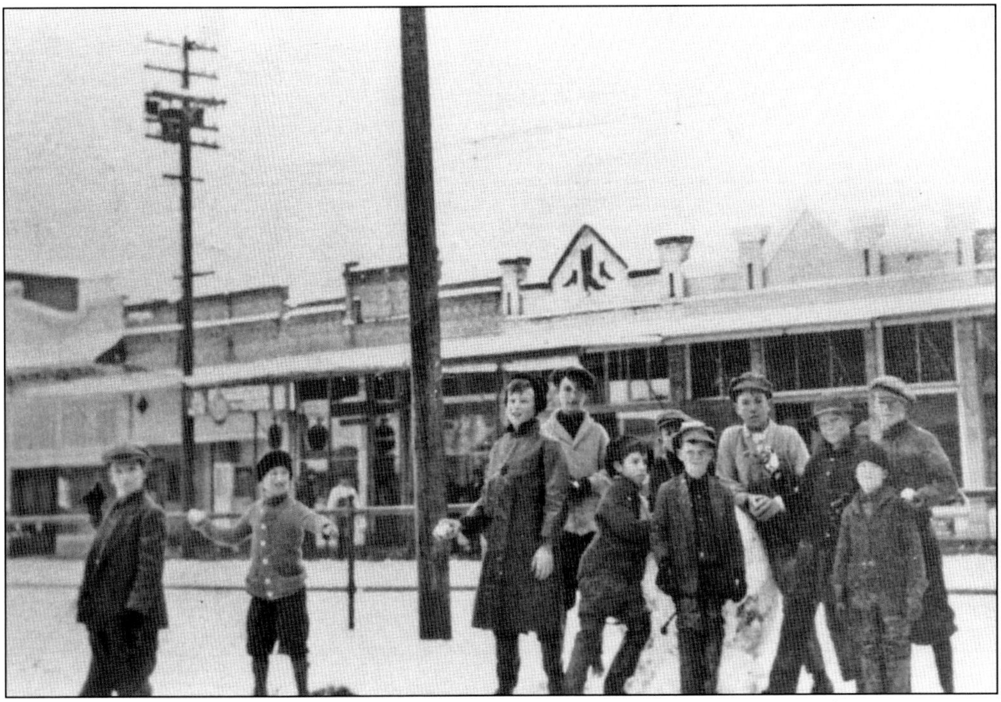

At least these boys were enjoying the inclement weather. There was even enough snow on Main Street to create a gigantic snowball. From left to right are George Wilson, Lorenzo "Premo" Maltagliati, Herbert Roland, Harold W. Loomis, Ellie J. Mullen, Gaines Dinkelspiel, unidentified, Harold Nelson, John W. Kinloch, W. Robie Chrisler, and Clemence J. McGinty. (VHC.)

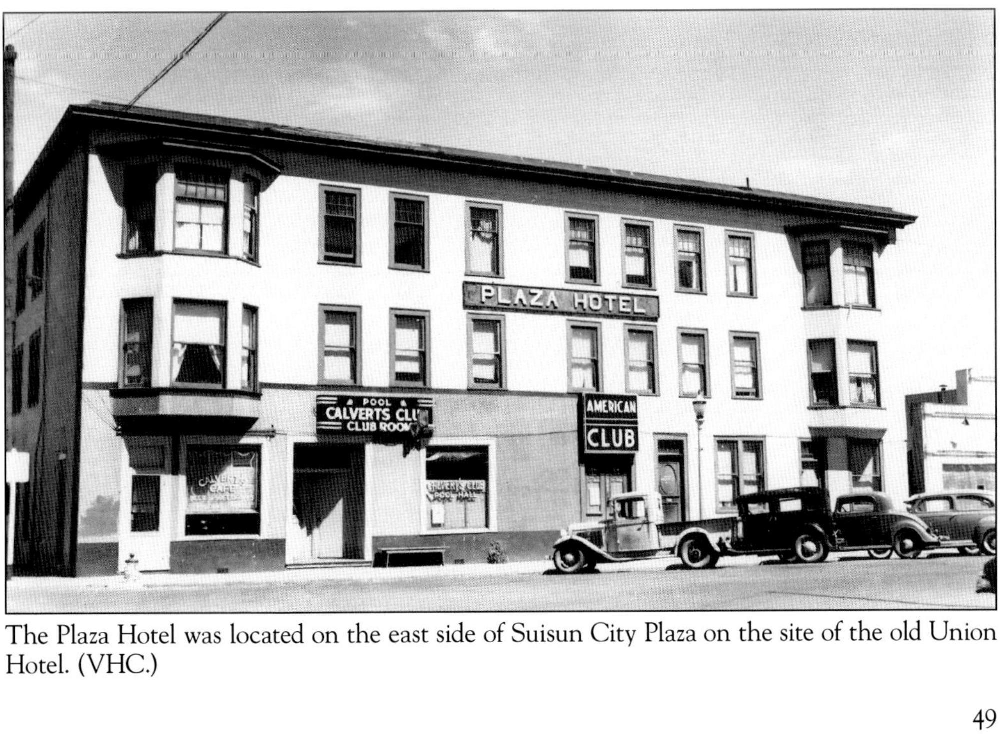

The Plaza Hotel was located on the east side of Suisun City Plaza on the site of the old Union Hotel. (VHC.)

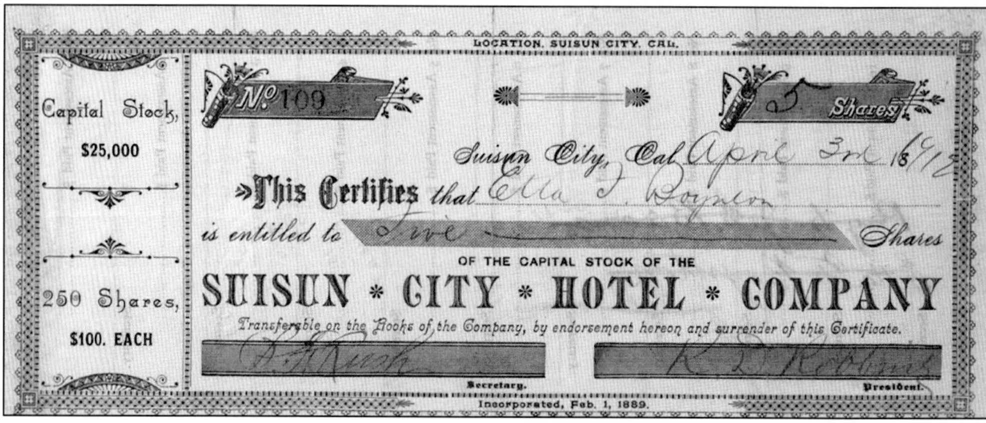

LOCATION, SUISUN CITY, CAL.

Capital Stock, $25,000

250 Shares, $100. EACH

No. 109

Shares

Suisun City, Cal. 18

»This Certifies that

is entitled to Shares

OF THE CAPITAL STOCK OF THE

SUISUN * CITY * HOTEL * COMPANY

Transferable on the Books of the Company, by endorsement hereon and surrender of this Certificate.

Secretary. President.

Incorporated, Feb. 1, 1889.

Following the devastating fire of 1888 that destroyed downtown, there was a pressing need to raise funds to rebuild local businesses. This stock certificate was issued to raise funds for construction of what would become the new Arlington Hotel, located on the north side of the plaza. (VHC.)

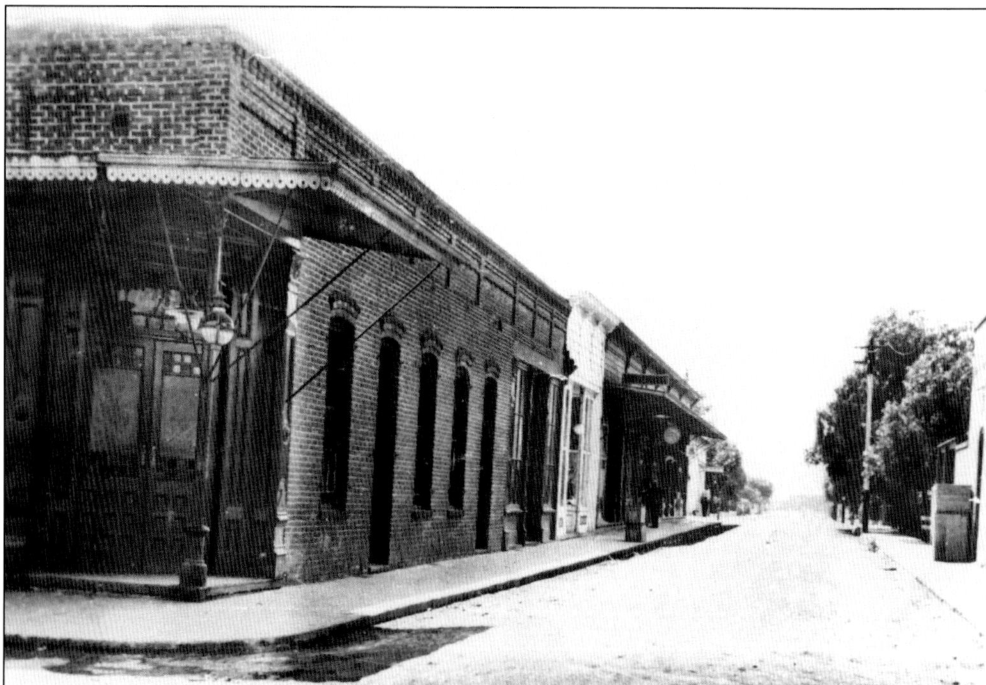

Located on the corner of Solano Street and Main Street, the Oriole Saloon was an elite barroom with an attached reading room that operated from 1888 until 1914. Early proprietors included C.T. Canfield, S.S. Suits & Company, and Robbins & Woods. In 1896, Thomas H. Wood became sole proprietor of the establishment. Thomas H. Wood was the uncle of Wood Young, a founding member of the Solano County Historical Society. (VHC.)

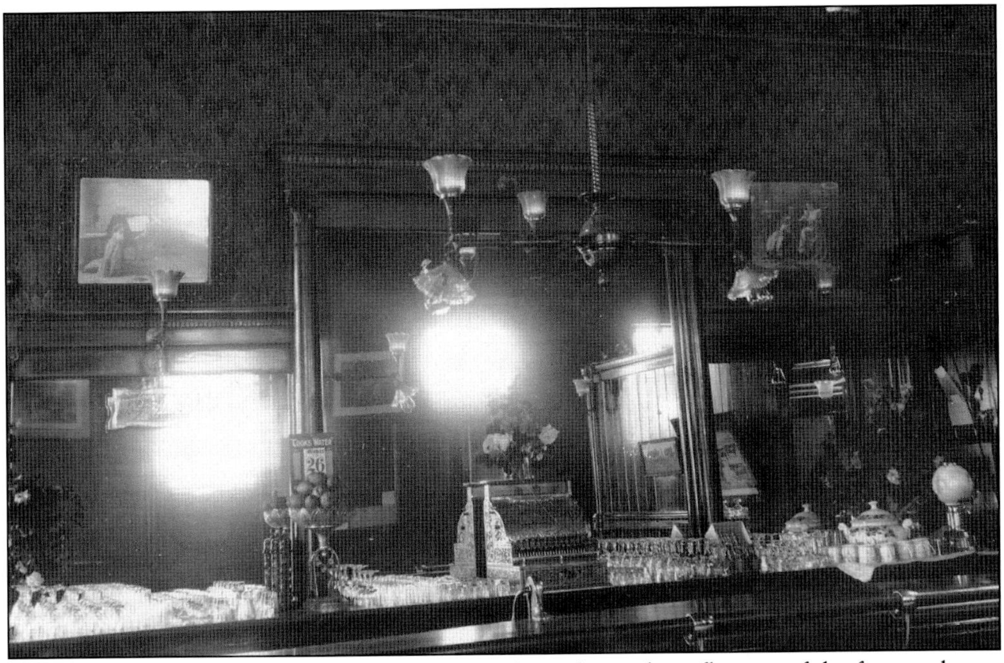

This photograph of the interior of the Oriole Saloon shows the reflection of the first gas lamps in use in the city. The gas for the lamps was provided by the nearby Rochester Oil Company well. (VHC.)

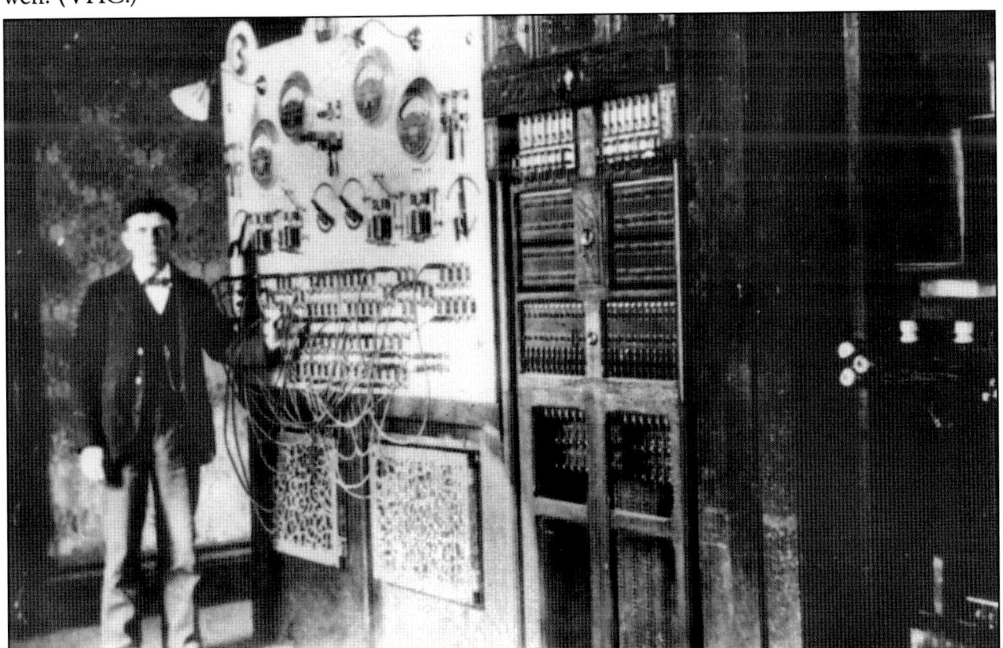

Suisun City's first telephone switchboard was installed when Sunset Telephone & Telegraph established telephone service in the 1880s. In 1898, Edgar E. Long, druggist at Miller's Drugstore and later county assessor, was the company's agent in Suisun. In that year, there were only 17 phone numbers. The board of supervisors was the first and only Fairfield number served by the Suisun exchange in that year. (VHC.)

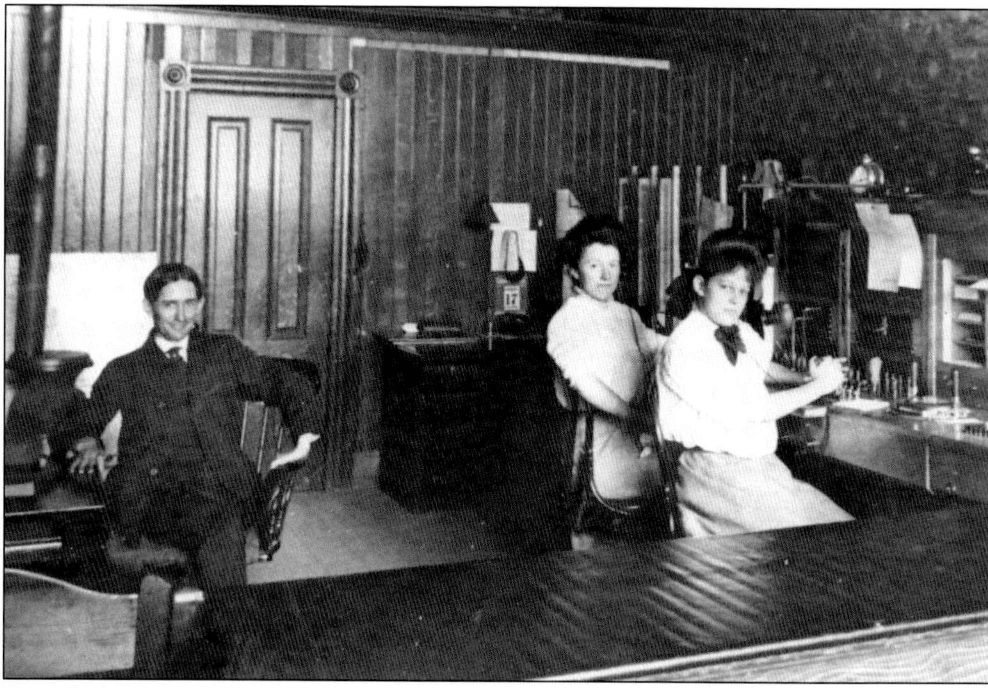

Two telephone operators are sitting in front of their plug boards ready to assist their callers' needs. In the pigeonholes are toll tickets to keep track of the length and parties of each call. In 1918, it could take 15 minutes to complete a long-distance connection. (VHC.)

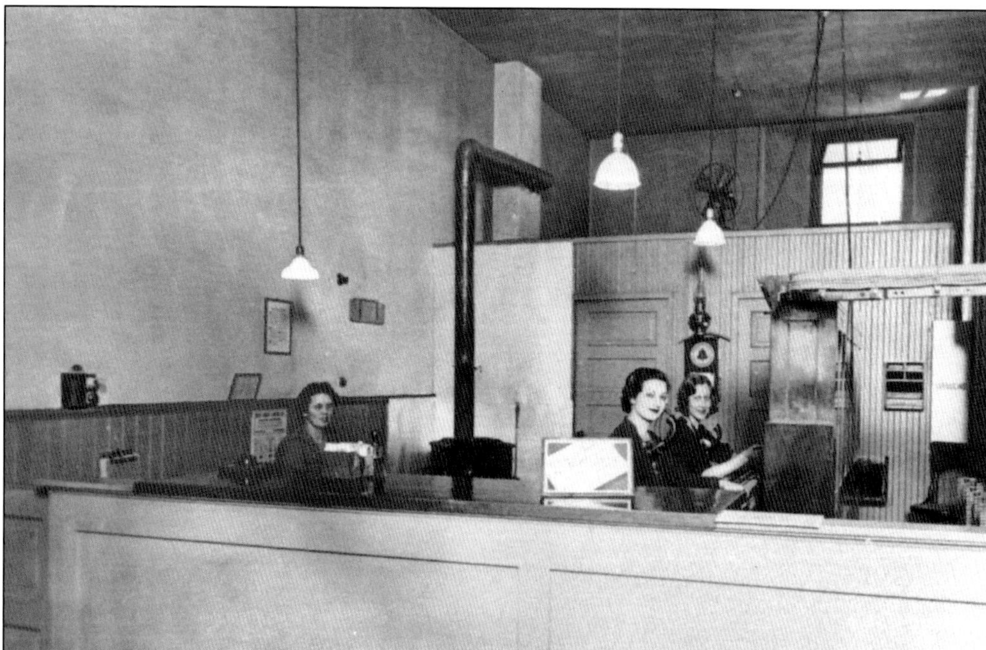

By the 1930s, Pacific Telephone & Telegraph had absorbed the Sunset Telephone & Telegraph Company. Still only two operators and their supervisor were servicing Suisun-area callers. However, the average time to make a long-distance call improved to less than two minutes. (VHC.)

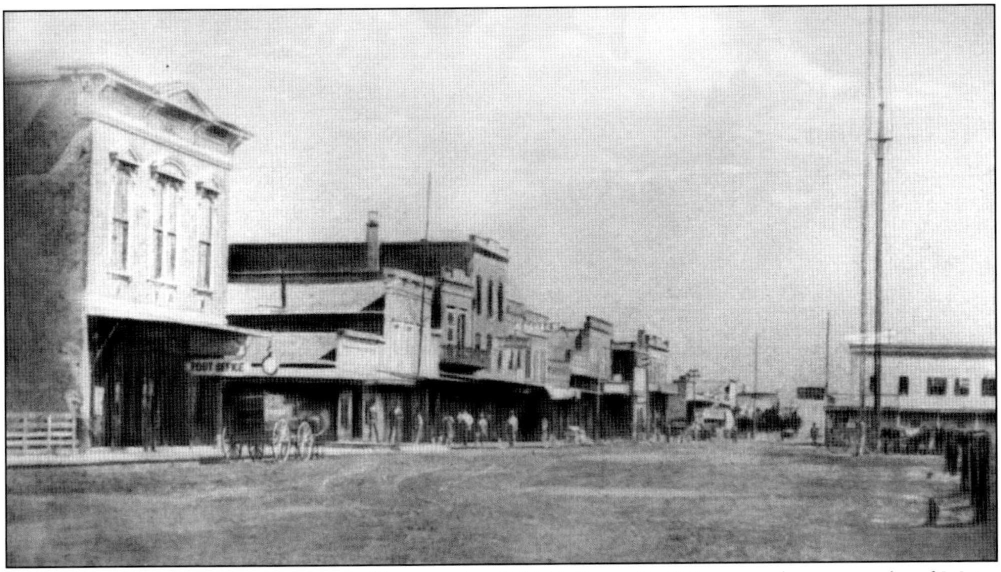

This photograph shows the post office in the Odd Fellows Building on the west side of Main Street before the devastating fire of 1888. The Pacific Hotel, later the Roberts House and the Arlington, can be seen to the far right. (VHC.)

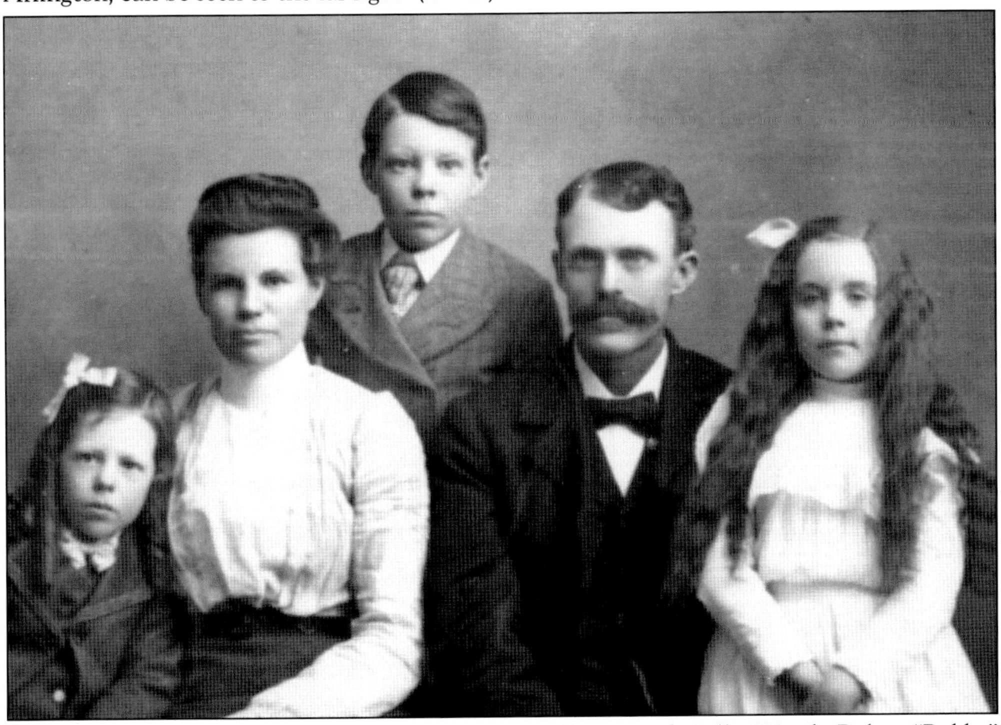

The Woods family members are, from left to right, Wilbur Woods, Lillie Woods, Robert "Bobby" Woods, Warren Woods, and Inez Woods. Warren Woods was appointed to serve as postmaster of Suisun, first by Pres. Theodore Roosevelt on February 23, 1903, and then upon reappointment on March 8, 1912, by Pres. William H. Taft. In keeping with 19th-century custom, Wilbur had not yet had his first haircut. Son Bobby would grow up to become clerk of Solano County Bank. (VHC.)

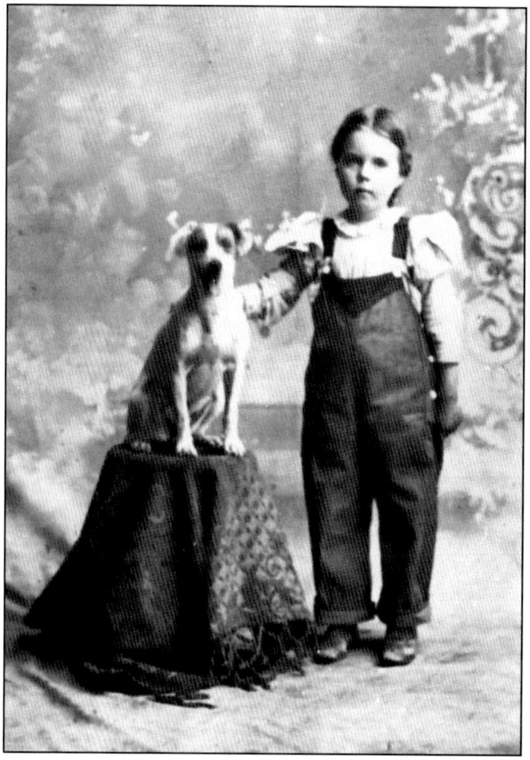

Solemn little Inez M. Woods posed in an unusual photograph with her spry terrier. For the period, it was unusual for girls to pose in a formal portrait wearing pants. Perhaps it was an homage to her father who, at one time, was a livery stable keeper prior to being appointed postmaster. Sadly, Inez succumbed to diphtheria on July 2, 1904, at 10 years old. (VHC.)

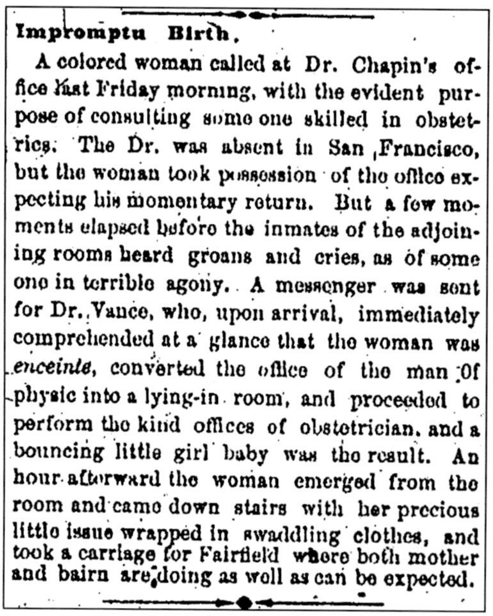

Impromptu Birth.

A colored woman called at Dr. Chapin's office last Friday morning, with the evident purpose of consulting some one skilled in obstetrics. The Dr. was absent in San Francisco, but the woman took possession of the office expecting his momentary return. But a few moments elapsed before the inmates of the adjoining rooms heard groans and cries, as of some one in terrible agony. A messenger was sent for Dr. Vance, who, upon arrival, immediately comprehended at a glance that the woman was *enceinte*, converted the office of the man of physic into a lying-in room, and proceeded to perform the kind offices of obstetrician, and a bouncing little girl baby was the result. An hour afterward the woman emerged from the room and came down stairs with her precious little issue wrapped in swaddling clothes, and took a carriage for Fairfield where both mother and bairn are doing as well as can be expected.

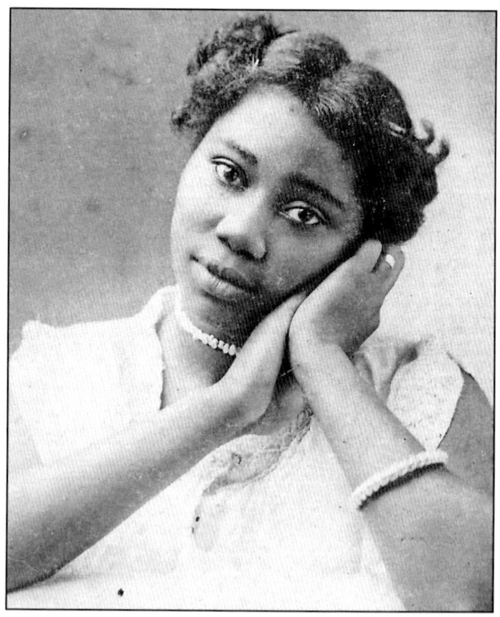

Mary Lenore (Hazel) Fann made quite the grand entrance into the world, as seen in this March 22, 1877, *Weekly Solano Republican* article. This photograph was taken at the time of her marriage in 1893 at the age of 16 to David Armstead Sinclair, with whom she had two children, Raymond and Ralph. Hazel was the niece of Adam Willis, a former slave. Having gained his freedom, Willis cooked for Josiah Wing and taught those skills to Hazel. (Both, courtesy of the descendants of Sarah Grey Thompson.)

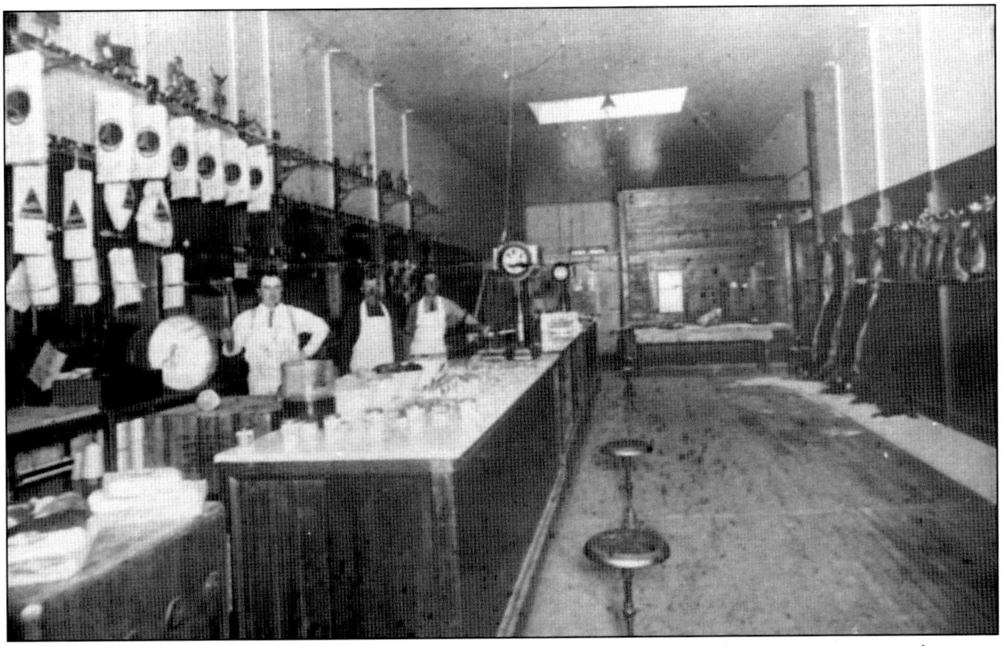

In 1915, Ellie Buzzini, pictured on left, and John W. Lambert, pictured at center, operated a meat market on Main Street. Ellie Buzzini had previously been a clerk at the B&L Wing market. Charles Lambert, son of John Lambert and Lovey Chadbourne Lambert, is on far right. (VHC.)

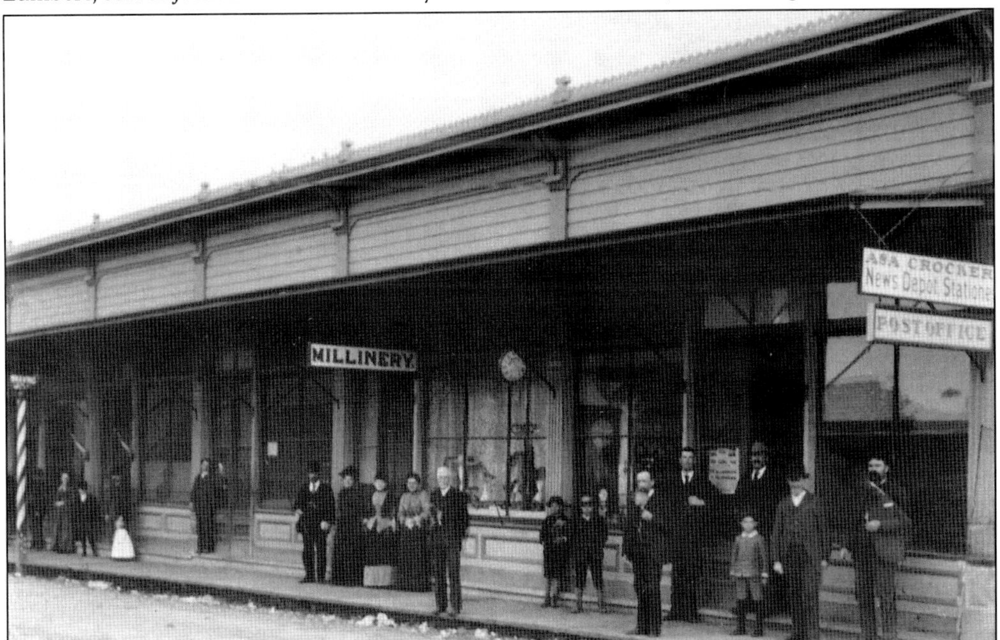

This 1884 photograph shows the businesses on the south corner of California Street at Suisun Street. The businesses in view include the barbershop of William A. Ames, a millinery store, E. Korr Smith Jewelry Store, and Asa Crocker's News Depot, Stationers, and Post Office. Asa Crocker was the pilot of Capt. Josiah Wing's schooner *Ann Sophia.* The poster in the window advertises a game at Suisun Baseball Park on April 2, 1884, between the Brakemen and the Suisuns. (VHC.)

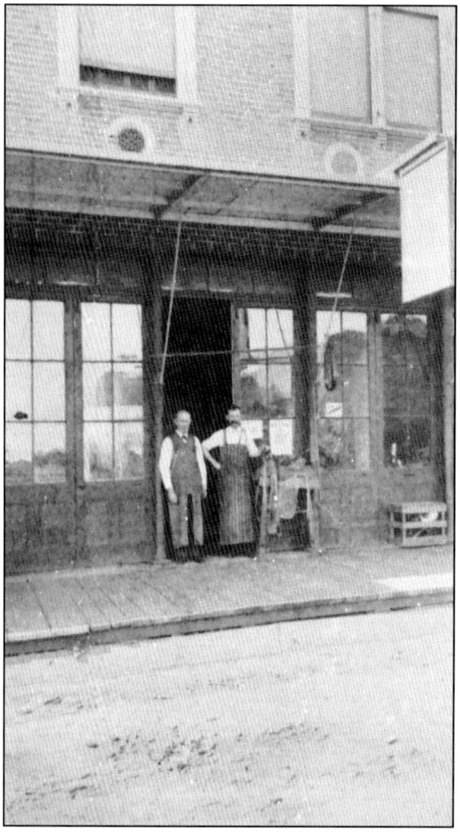

Alexander C. Wood (left) and his son John H. Wood are pictured in front of their saddle and harness shop, established in Suisun City in 1875. A popular fixture of the Woods' shop was a stuffed dapple-gray horse on display. Suisun City children would stare at it in wonder after they were told its mane and tail continued growing after its demise. (VHC.)

Edgar E. Long, third from the left, and companions stand in the doorway of the drugstore he operated in Suisun for James Miller, who owned and operated a second branch in Vacaville. Long was also the agent for Sunset Telephone & Telegraph Company. He would later work as Solano County assessor. (VHC.)

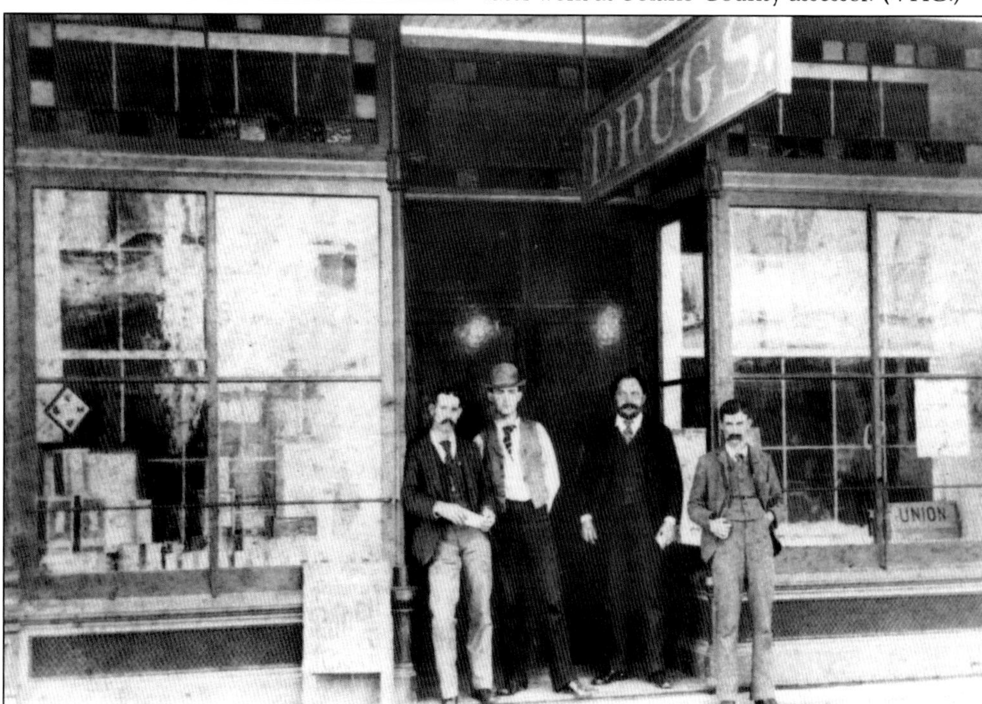

The Elite Saloon, seen here about 1888, was located on the south side of Solano Street, near the railroad tracks. The publishing office of the *Solano Republican* was located to the left out of view of the photograph. (VHC.)

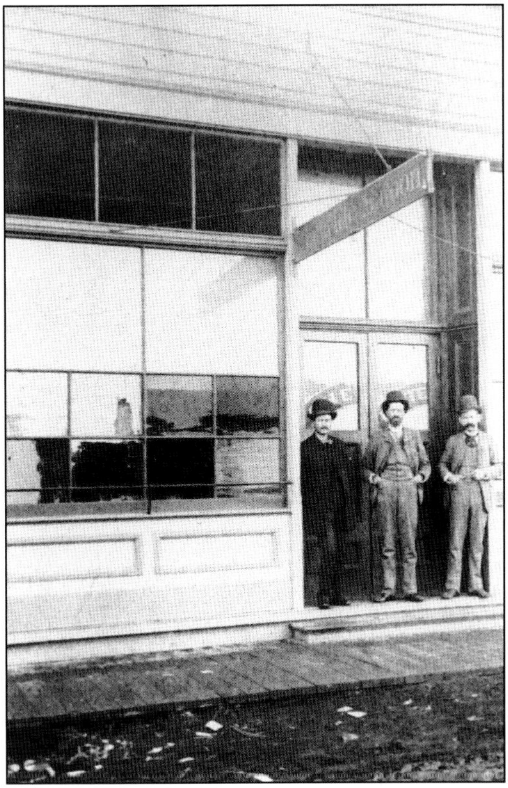

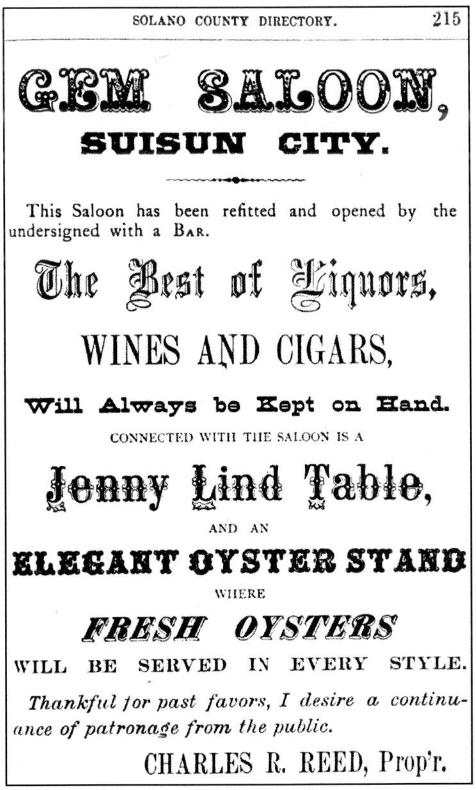

SOLANO COUNTY DIRECTORY. 215

GEM SALOON,

SUISUN CITY.

This Saloon has been refitted and opened by the undersigned with a BAR.

The Best of Liquors,

WINES AND CIGARS,

Will Always be Kept on Hand.

CONNECTED WITH THE SALOON IS A

Jenny Lind Table,

AND AN

ELEGANT OYSTER STAND

WHERE

FRESH OYSTERS

WILL BE SERVED IN EVERY STYLE.

Thankful for past favors, I desire a continuance of patronage from the public.

CHARLES R. REED, Prop'r.

Here is an advertisement for the grand reopening of the Gem Saloon, a favorite watering hole for the distinguished and refined. (SCHS.)

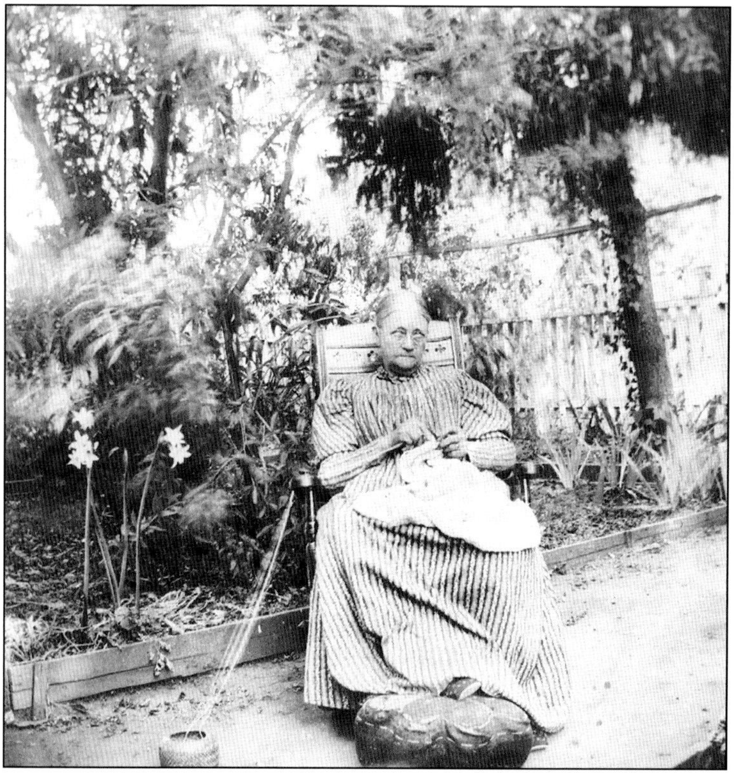

Maria Ellard Williams was born in London, England, on February 27, 1828. She witnessed the coronation parade of Queen Victoria in 1837. Maria immigrated to St. Louis, Missouri, where she married Robert Pearce Williams. In 1852, the Williamses made their way to California via the Isthmus of Panama, which was quite an undertaking for a young mother with a toddler and another on the way. Later, Maria reflected that she would not make that trip again for all the gold in California. (DGS.)

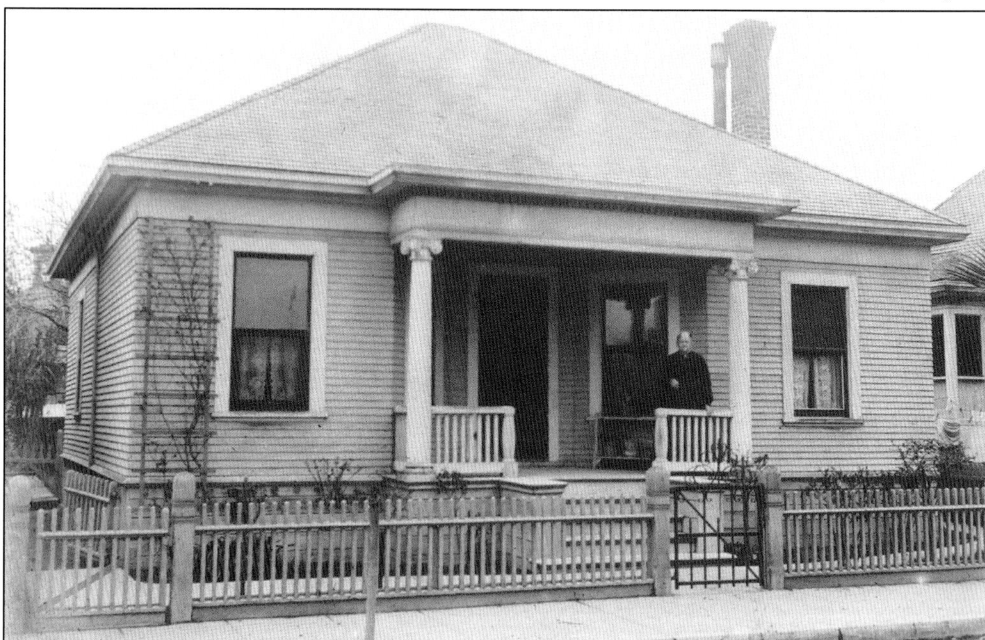

Several years after the death of Robert Pearce Williams, Maria Ellard Williams had this home built on Suisun Street in 1900. There, she lived with her daughter Mary Winifred Williams until her death on December 11, 1914. Maria's sons Thomas P. and Robert "Frank" Williams took over management of the ranch in Upper Suisun Valley. (DGS.)

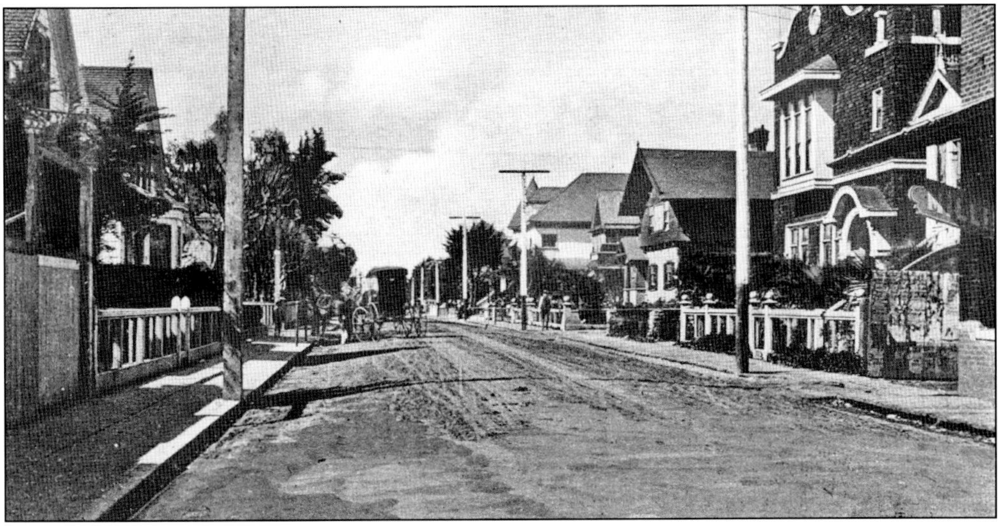

This view is of California Street looking west from Main Street. The Armijo Club is in the foreground (right). The Buzzini house is pictured at the center with the cupola. (VHC.)

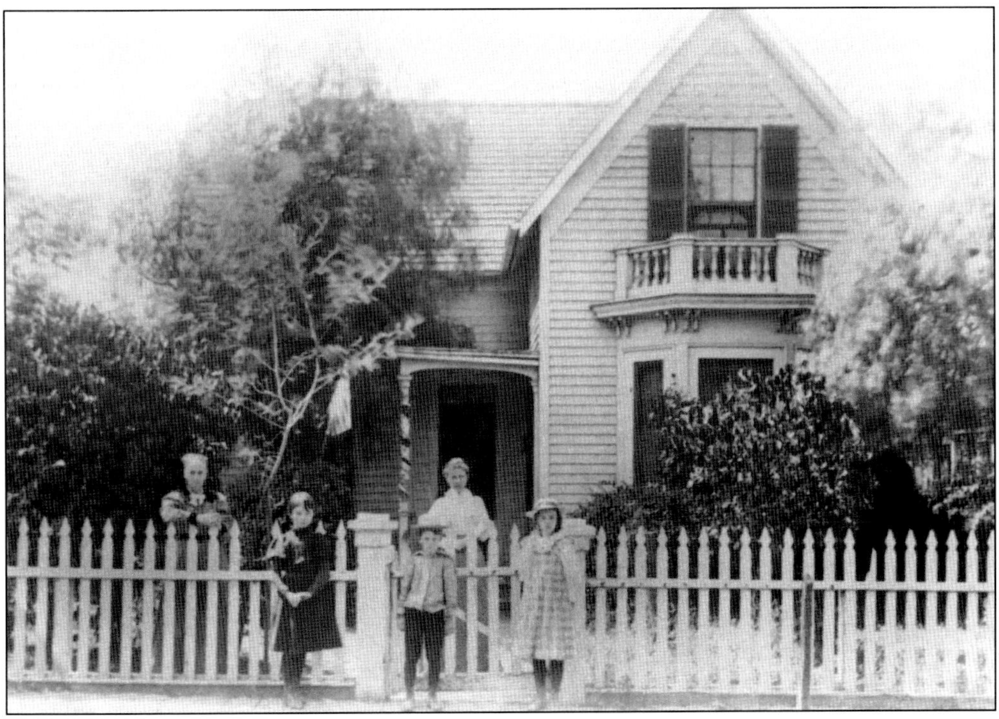

This house at 1012 School Street belonged to Kate Richardson, the sister of famed orchardist Eliza P. Buckingham of Vacaville. Pictured around 1900 are, from left to right, (first row) Bell Bowen (Richardson's granddaughter), Charles Harvey Ostrander, and Annis Myrtle Ostrander; (second row) Kate Richardson and Alice E. Dunnell. The Ostranders were children of Dr. Jasper Annis Ostrander, who passed away in 1900. (VHC.)

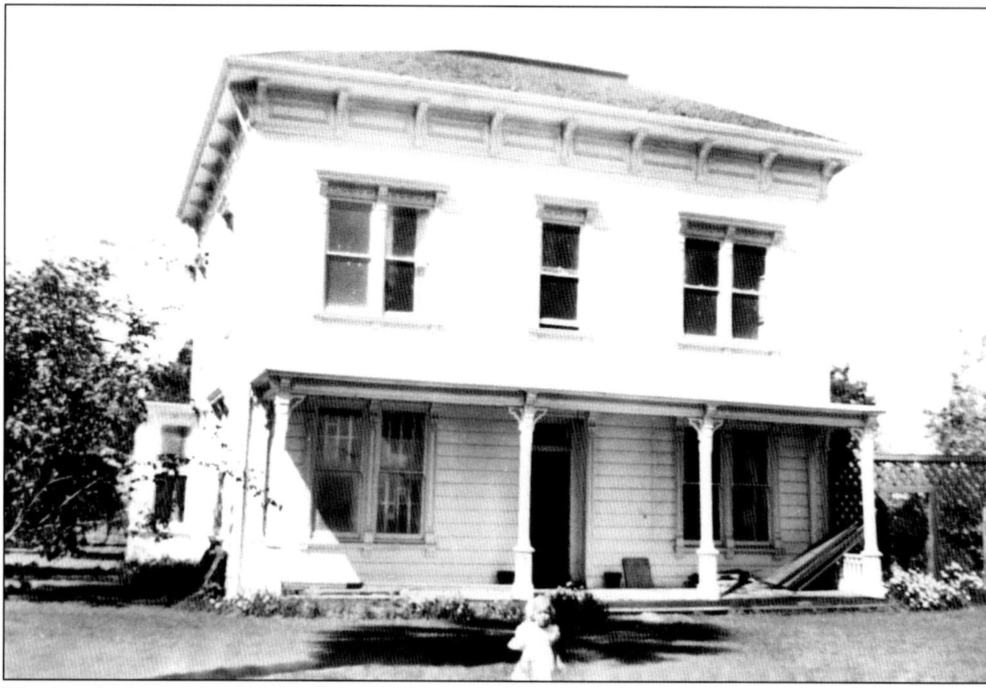

The Lawler house, built in 1857, is depicted here before its 1979 move across Suisun Slough by Bob Klemmedson and Clarence Richards and relocation next to the former site of the Suisun City Plaza. Mary Higham, Jean Marcuzzo, and Debbie Woodruff of Preserve All Solano's Treasures (PAST) spearheaded its rescue when threatened with destruction. PAST volunteers camped out at the house during negotiations to ensure its safety from vandals. Today, it houses the Lawler House Gallery and the Solano History Exploration Center. (SCHS.)

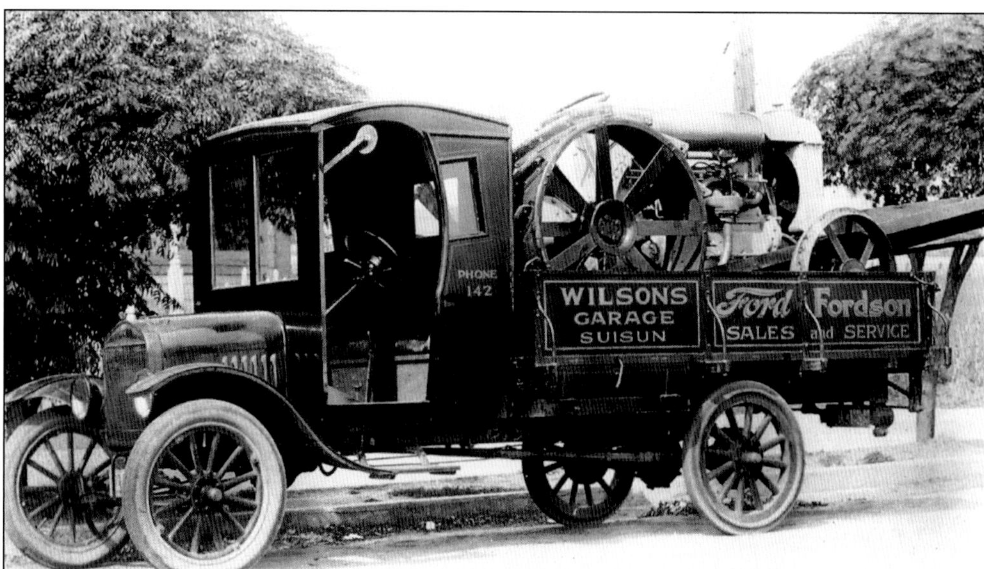

Wilson's Garage, formerly the Sparks & Robie Garage, was located on the east side of the Suisun City Plaza between the Union Hotel and the Suisun Hardware and Implement Co. (SHEC.)

This 1940s photograph is of Frederick J. Klusman's service station. He had various jobs as a farm manager, switch operator for Pacific Gas & Electric, and salesman for a grocery prior to owning and operating his service station. (VHC.)

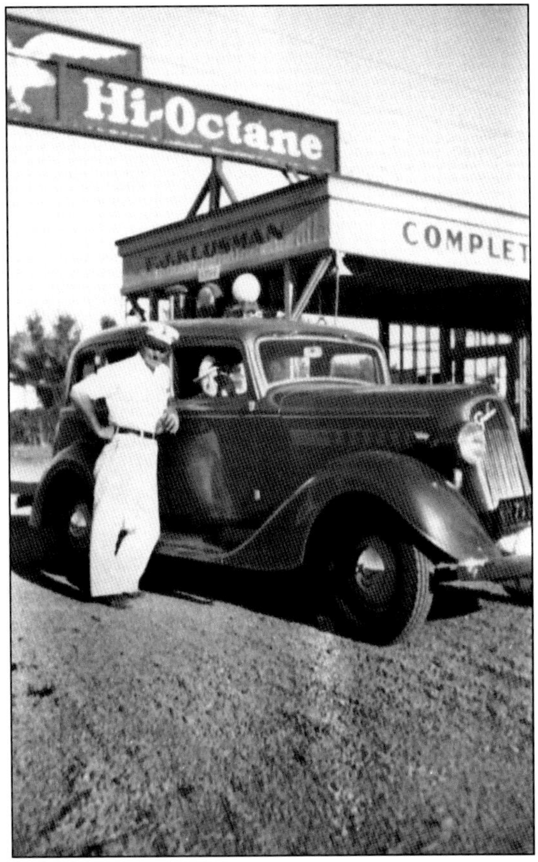

This photograph of the Suisun Junior Chamber of Commerce, taken in the 1930s, includes, from left to right, (sitting) Richard Dinkelspiel and Peter Bennett; (standing) Carl Kelly, William C. Robbins Jr., and John Kinloch. (VHC.)

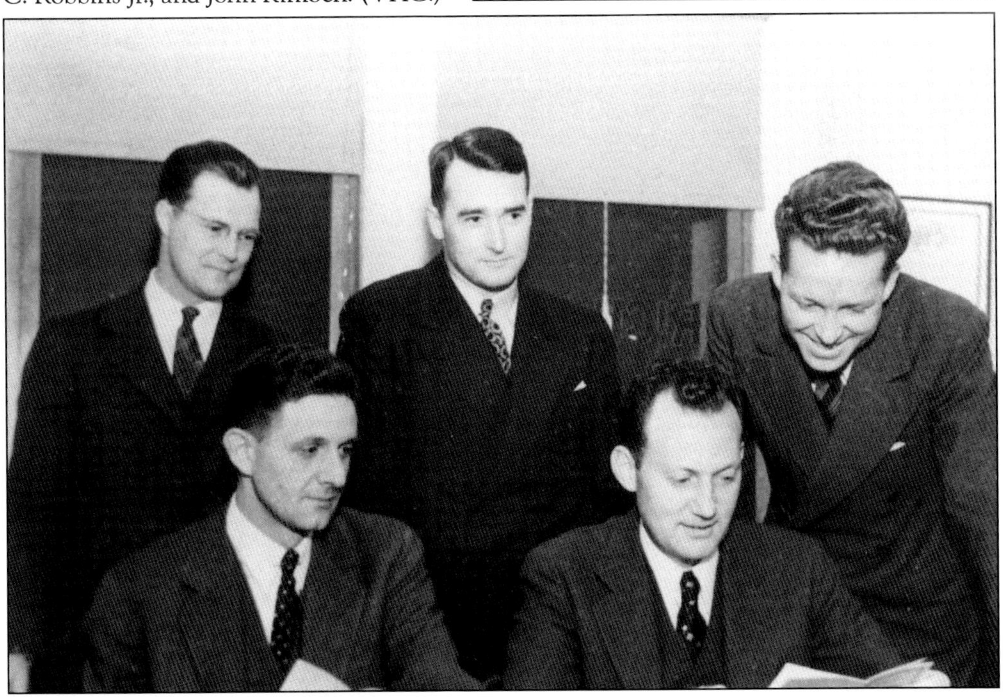

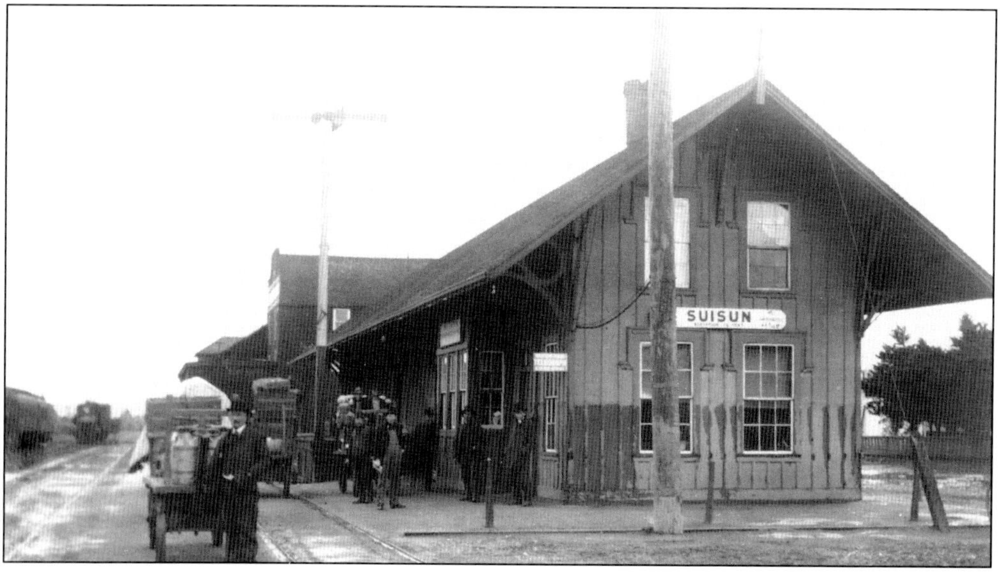

Suisun City had rail service starting in 1869. The Suisun station in the top photograph was built after the great fire of 1888 and was located at the end of Solano Street. The depot survived the San Francisco 1906 Earthquake but was destroyed later that same year when a quarter of the city's residential area was devastated by a fire sparked by a passing train. As a temporary measure, a boxcar was outfitted with siding and converted to serve as a depot until a permanent structure could be rebuilt. The repurposed boxcar can still be seen today. After contentious debate between the two sister cities, the Suisun-Fairfield depot, seen below, was relocated closer to Fairfield in 1914. (Both, VHC.)

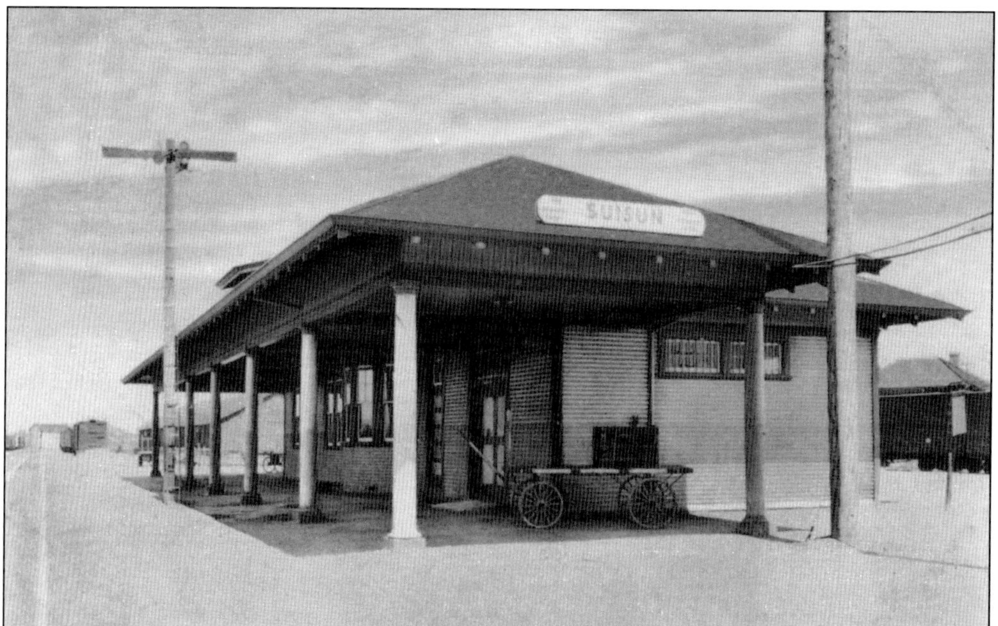

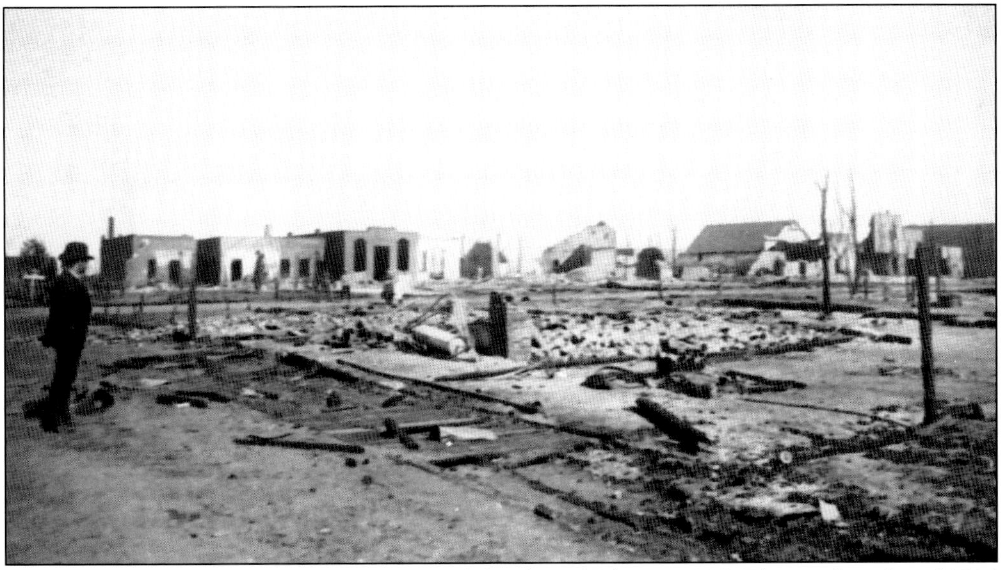

A gentleman looks upon the devastation of the fire of July 24, 1906. The earthquake of 1906 spared Suisun City, but it was not so lucky when sparks from a passing train ignited the Armsby Fruit Packing House. Save for a few lucky houses, everything west of Suisun Street was destroyed. All told, over 40 structures were lost at a value of $200,000. (VHC.)

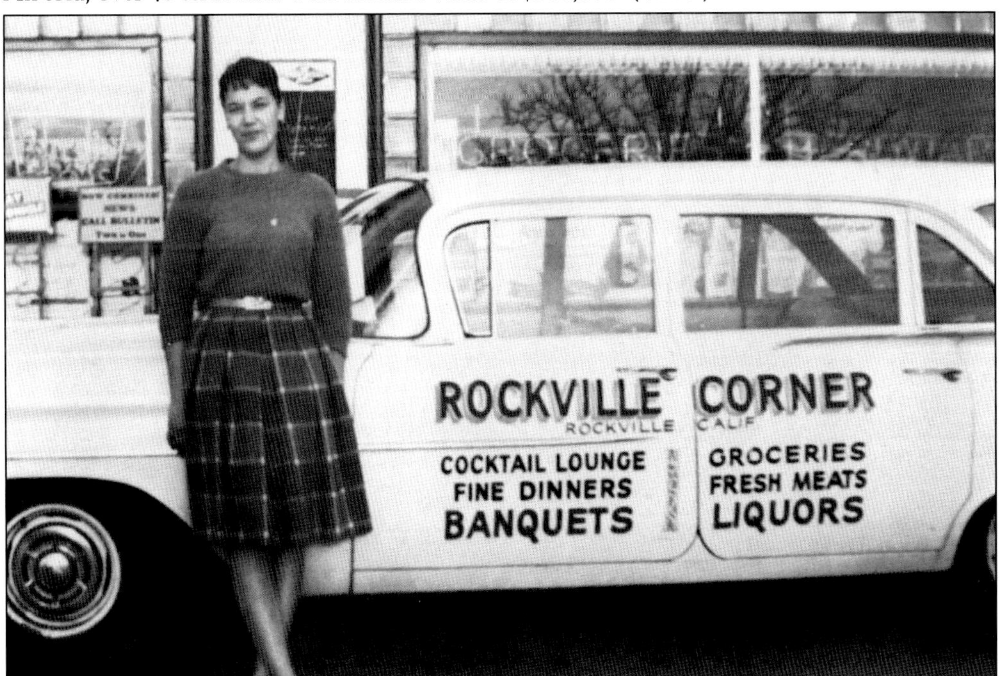

Rockville was a center of commerce long before this photograph of Judy Baucom standing next to an advertisement for the predecessor of the Rockville Inn was taken. The northern border of the Suisunes' extensive Yul Yul village was located here along an early Native American trading route. The Old Fremont Trail, used by early travelers coming from the east to Sonoma and beyond, passed right through Rockville Corners. Stage routes from Benicia and Sacramento and on occasion the Pony Express later followed the trail. (VHC.)

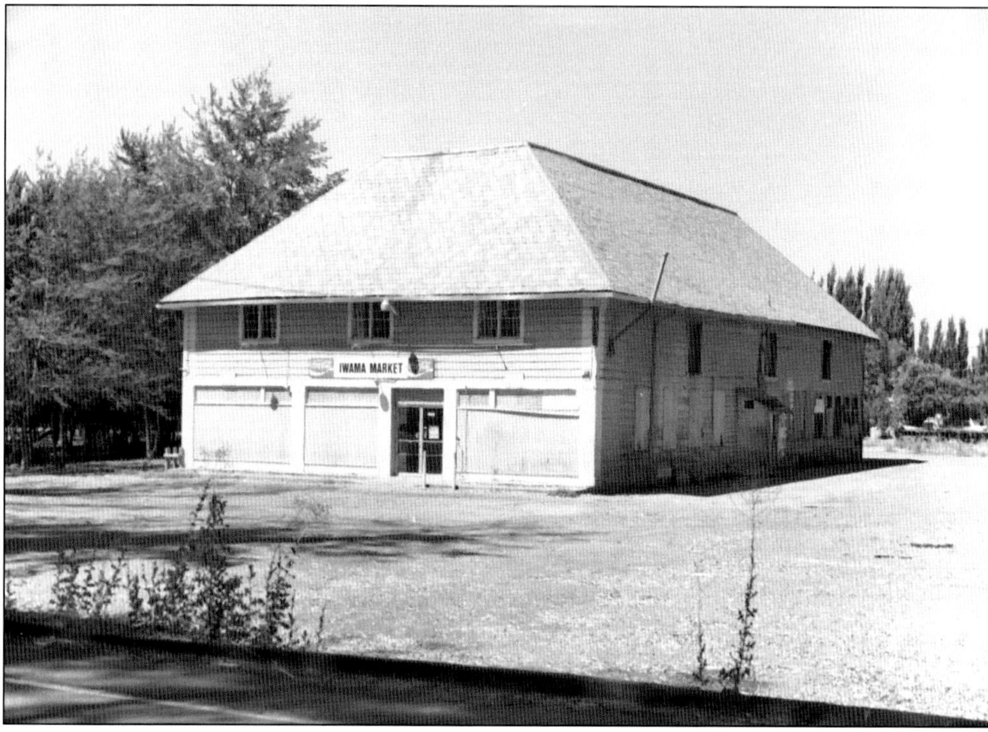

Originally known as Bandana Lou's, a dining and dance hall famous for its fried chicken, this structure was built in 1927 on the site of the Pierce Ranch barn, blacksmith shop, and bunkhouse. After World War II, Frank Iwama opened his market downstairs, as seen in the photograph below. For many years, the top floor remained a popular social center for dances. (Both, VHC.)

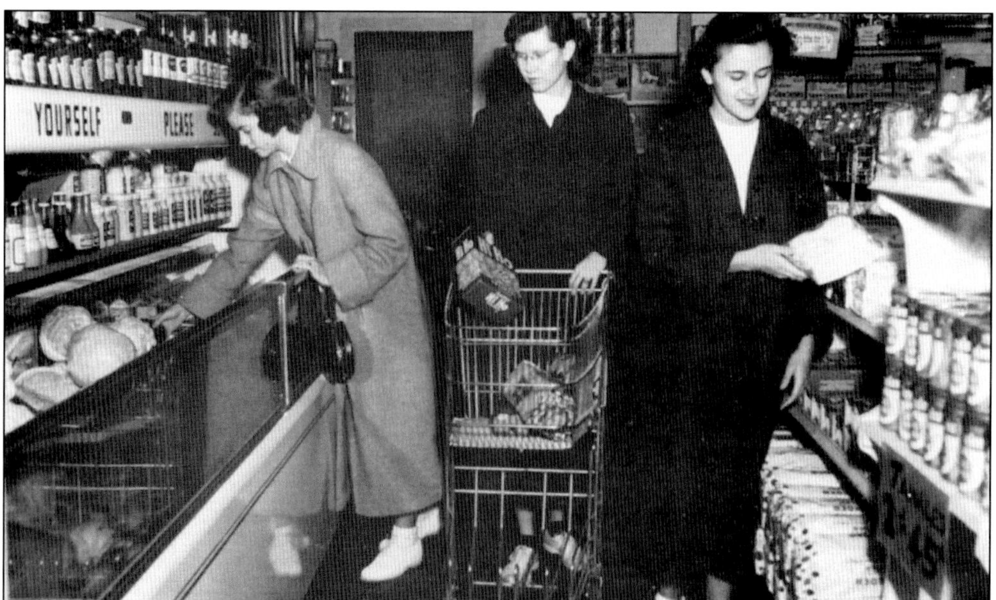

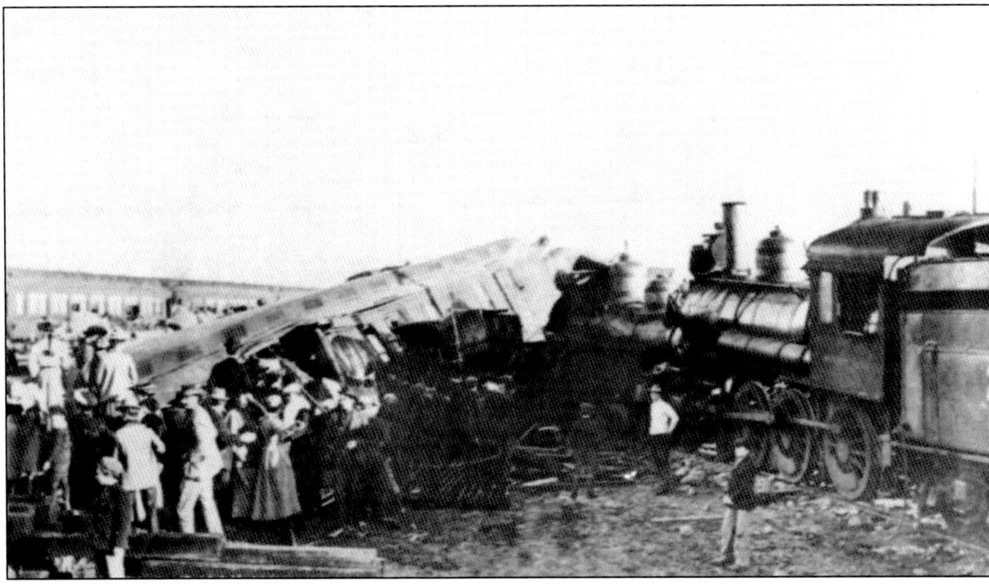

The year 1904 closed out with a tragic bang when, on December 31, Southern Pacific Engines Nos. 2167 and 1269 suffered a head-on collision near the Suisun station that killed one engineer. (VHC.)

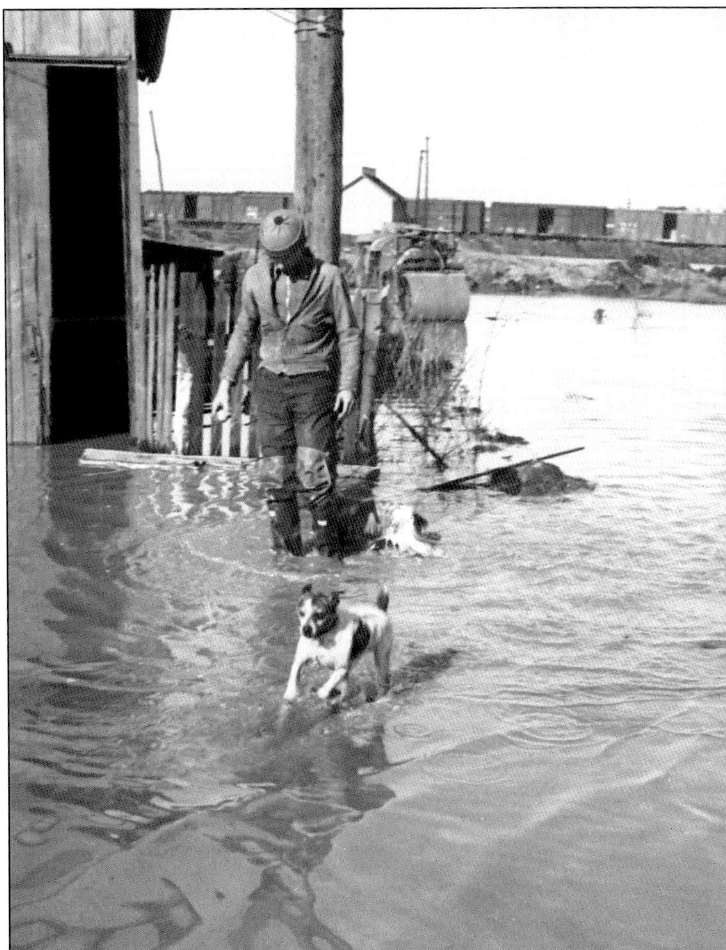

Situated on a tidal marsh, flooding was a constant concern for Suisun City, as seen in this 1910 photograph of Tom Vaughn and his dog. (VHC.)

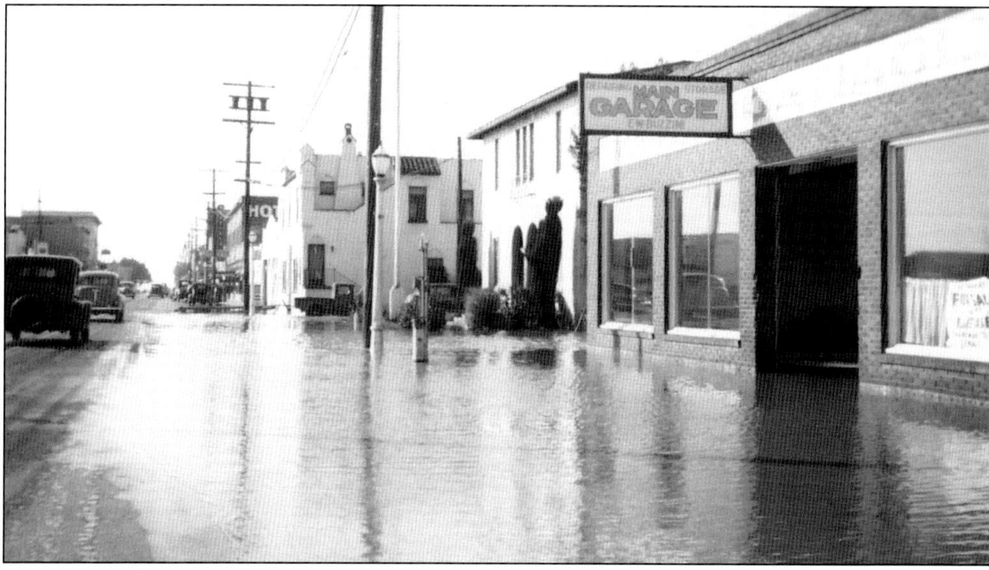

In 1944, Ed Buzzini's garage and the neighboring veterans' hall were flooded in a winter storm. (SHEC.)

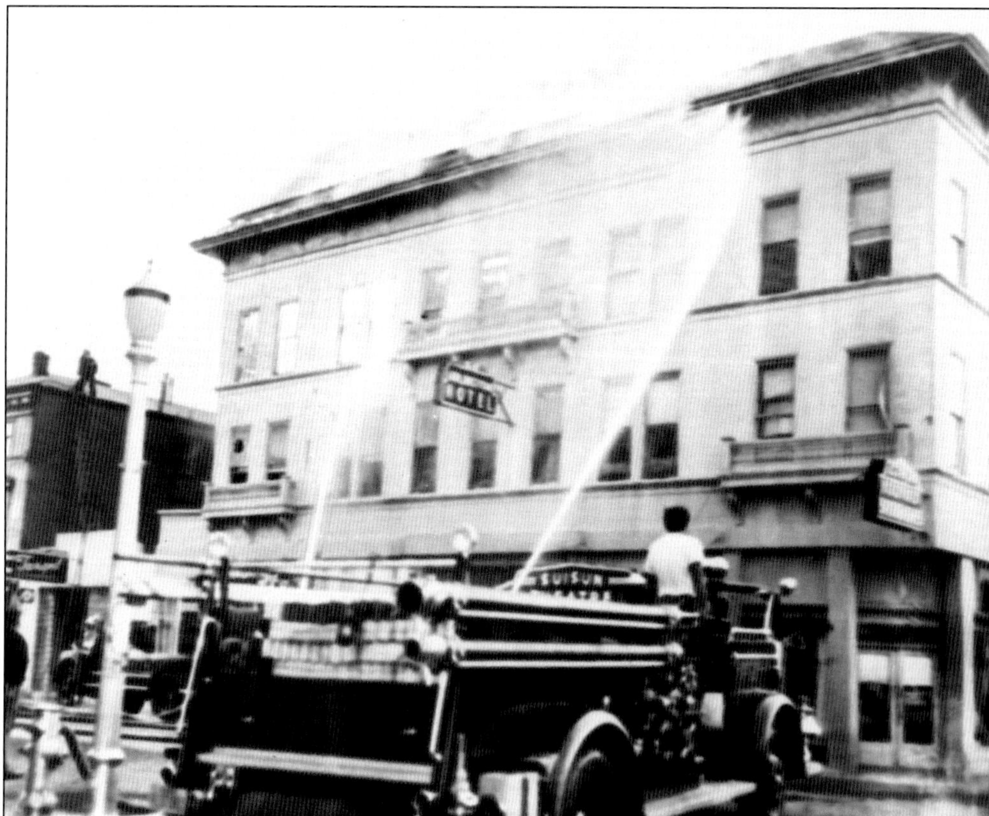

Firefighters battle the 1958 blaze that would destroy the Arlington Hotel, a fixture of the Suisun City Plaza. Luckily, its neighbors fared better than those of its predecessor, the Roberts House; the fire was largely contained to the hotel itself and not the entire city. (VHC.)

Five

Cordelia

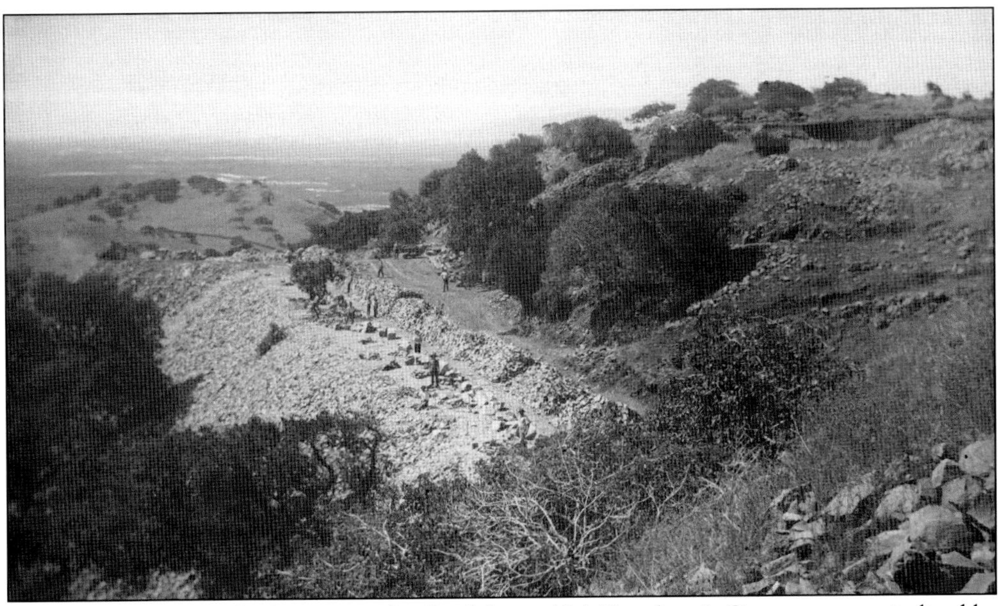

Thomasson Quarry, also known as the Cordelia and McNaughton's Quarry, was capitalized by the aptly named E.B. & A.L. Stone Company. It was located on Nelson's Hill above Cordelia and connected by a spur railroad line to docks at Suisun City for shipment. The quarry opened around 1875 and operated for approximately 20 years. Street paving blocks were the main product and were used extensively to line San Francisco's streets. As road construction methods changed, the quarry transitioned to producing crushed rock. (VHC.)

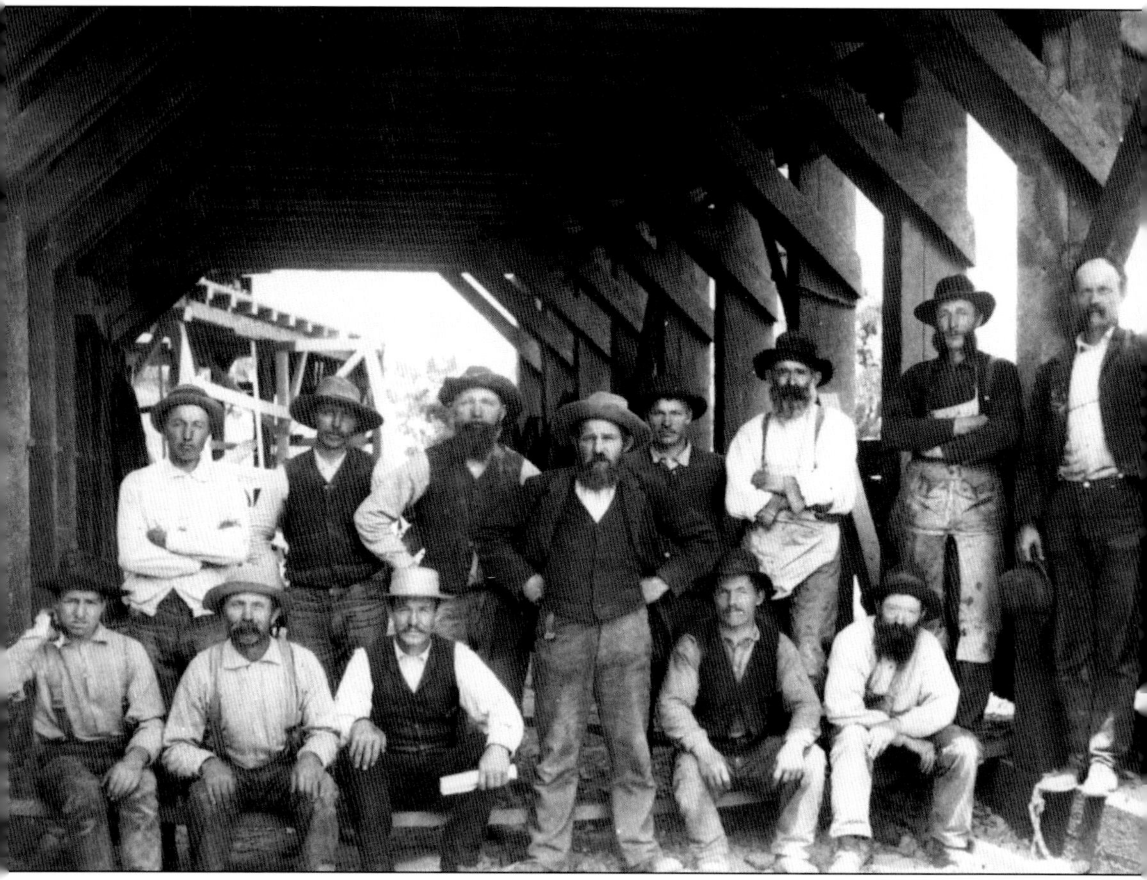

Here is a quarry crew at Nelson's Hill, then known as Bridgeport Hill, in the 1890s. Standing front and center surrounded by his crew is William Nickels. Behind him on the far right, from left to right, are Claus Dittmer, Henry Goosen, and Alex Erickson. (VHC.)

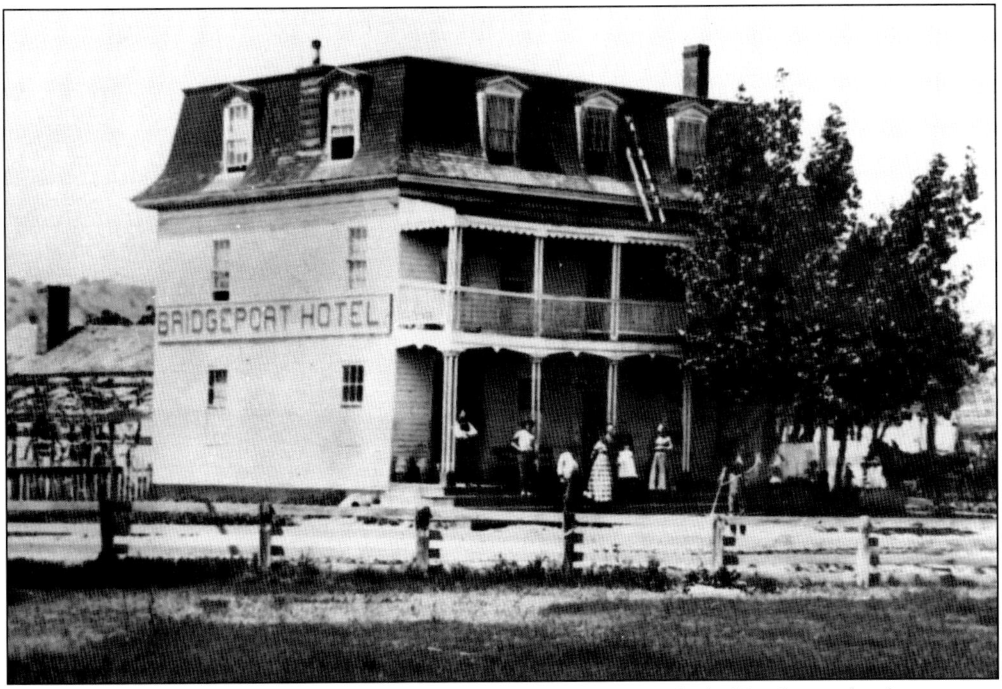

Cordelia, the second oldest town in the county, was once situated a half mile north of its present location. In anticipation of the California Pacific Railroad, the township's businesses relocated nearer the proposed railroad station of Bridgeport. C.J. and Louisa Jane May Pittman, owners of the Pittman Hotel since 1855, were among those who moved. The US Postal Service eventually rejected the name Bridgeport because there was a town of the same identity in Mono County. Thus, Bridgeport was renamed after the last township, Cordelia, and the hotel followed suit, as seen below. C.J. passed away in 1864, before the arrival of the railroad. With many accolades, Louisa continued the operation of the hotel with the help of her daughter and son-in-law Carrie E.J. Pittman Martin and Henry Martin until her death in 1889. (Both, VHC.)

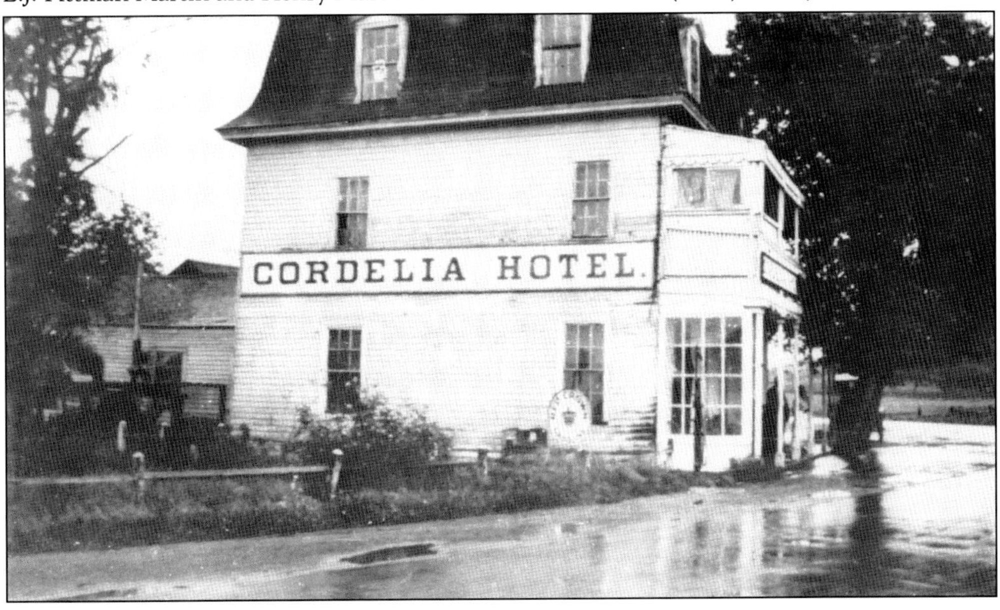

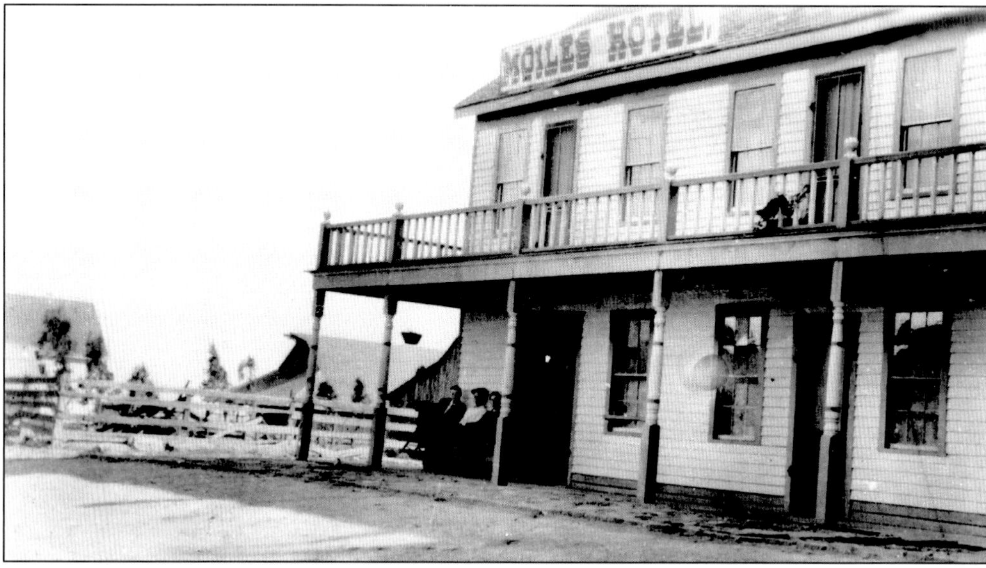

The Moiles Hotel was located south of the railroad tracks across from the P. Siebe & Co. General Merchandise store. A convenient boardinghouse for cowboys and quarrymen, it served as a social center for the wild little town. Eventually, Adeline (Moiles) McNaughton, the sister of William and Henry T. Moiles, would manage the 15-room hotel while raising eight children on her own. She had the assistance of two waitresses and a Chinese cook. She also hosted a Chinese laundry in the back. The Moiles Hotel was torn down in 1950, but its original stone icehouse is still standing and can be seen in the photograph below. (Above, VHC; below, ED.)

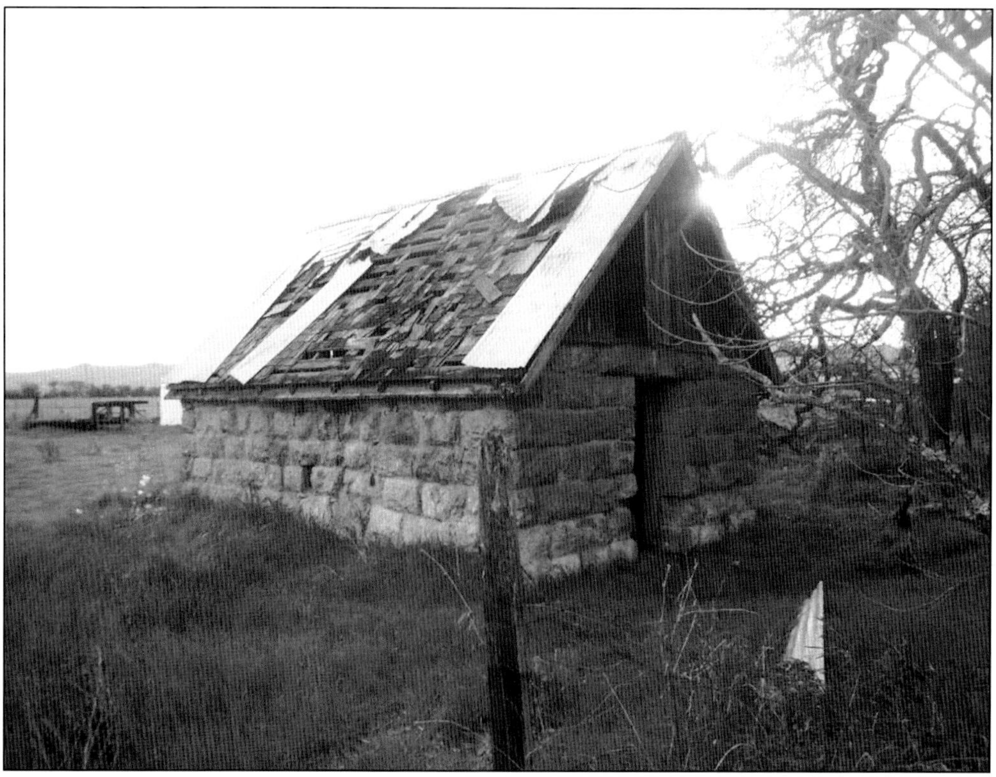

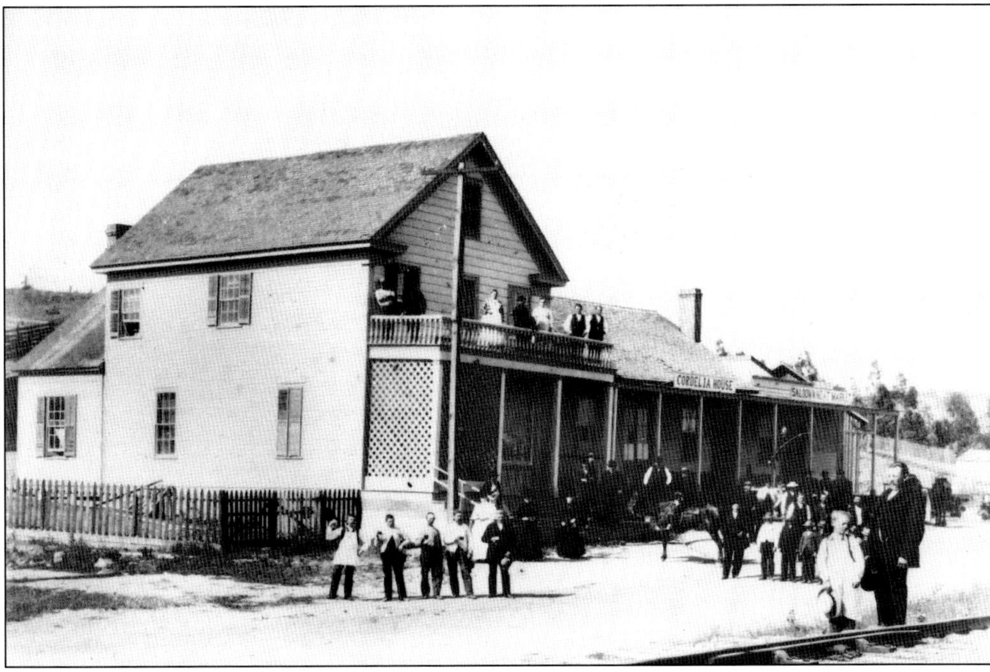

This 1880s photograph is of Dunker's house, saloon, and meat market, also known as the Cordelia House. In later years, a second story was added to the meat market, and the entire operation was taken over by brothers Matthias and Julius Glashoff, as seen here. (Both, VHC.)

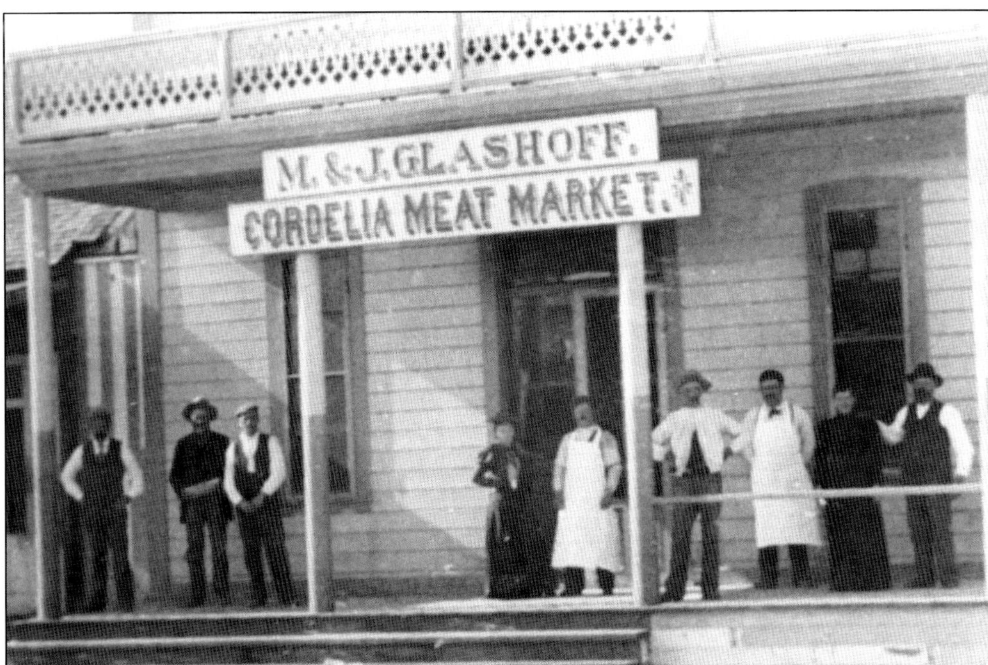

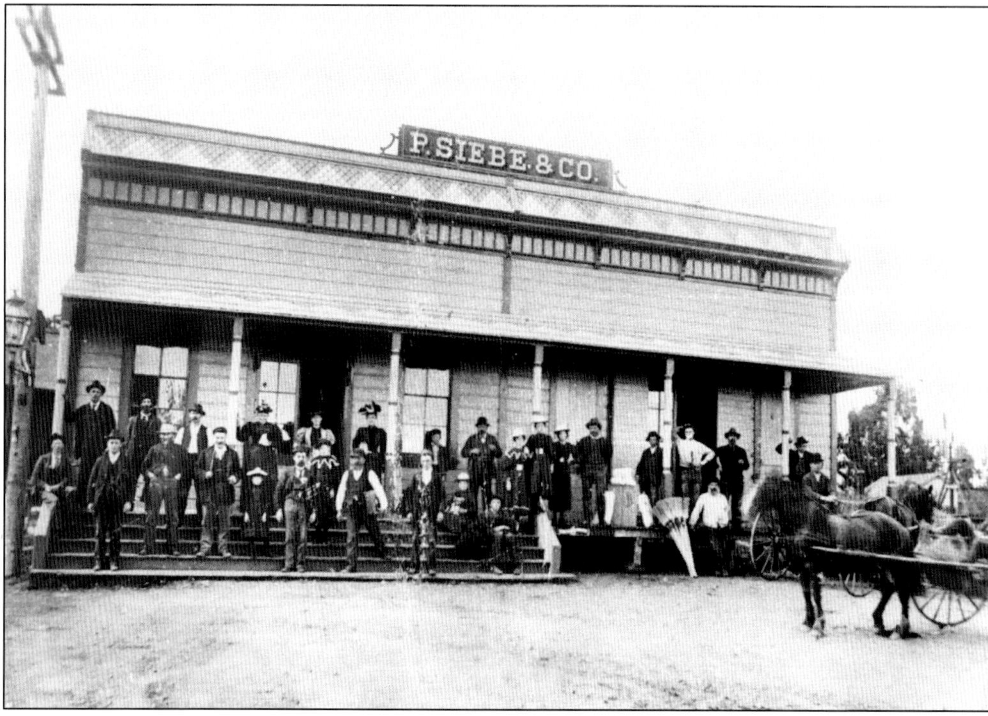

The P. Siebe & Co. General Merchandise store offered everything a person could want, including chocolate, dry goods, clothing, and even a public telephone. It was owned and operated by Peter Siebe Sr. and Otto Glashoff. In this picture are, from left to right, (first row) first, Peter Larson (seated); second, Curtis Siebe (lower step); sixth, Peter Siebe Sr.; and twelfth, Claus Dittmer; (second row) first, Peter Siebe Jr.; fourth, Catherine E. Siebe (Peter Sr.'s wife); and eighth, Otto Glashoff. (Above, VHC; below, SCHS.)

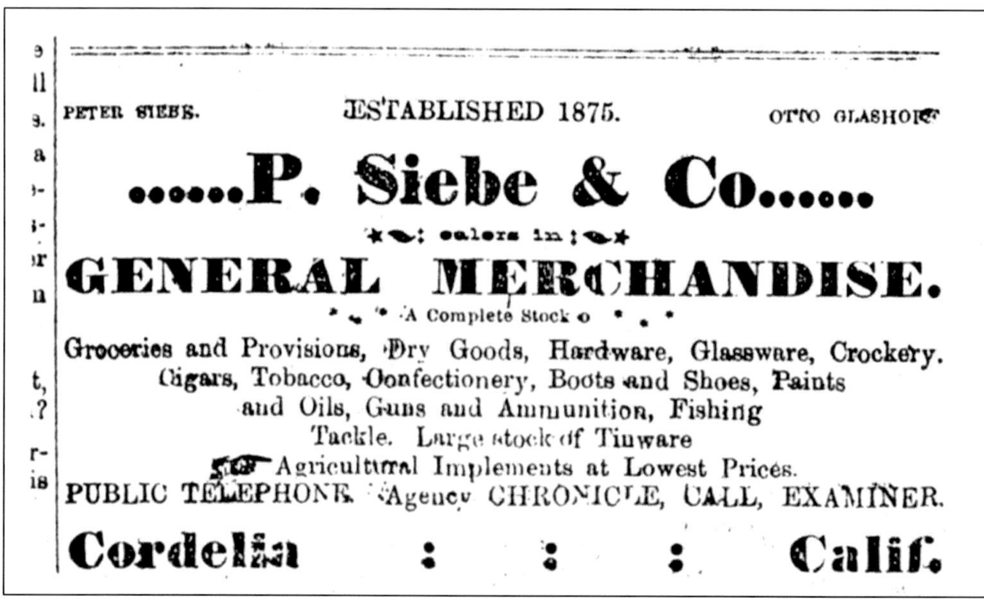

PETER SIEBE. ESTABLISHED 1875. OTTO GLASHOFF

......P. Siebe & Co......

Dealers in:

GENERAL MERCHANDISE.

A Complete Stock o

Groceries and Provisions, Dry Goods, Hardware, Glassware, Crockery. Cigars, Tobacco, Confectionery, Boots and Shoes, Paints and Oils, Guns and Ammunition, Fishing Tackle. Large stock of Tinware

Agricultural Implements at Lowest Prices.

PUBLIC TELEPHONE. Agency CHRONICLE, CALL, EXAMINER.

Cordelia : : : Calif.

Three of Peter Siebe Sr.'s sons, Peter Siebe Jr., J. Henry Siebe, and Claus Siebe, assisted with operations of the P. Siebe & Co. General Merchandise store. In this photograph, Peter Siebe Jr. can be seen standing to the left on the porch in front of store with his cousin Harold Siebe. (VHC.)

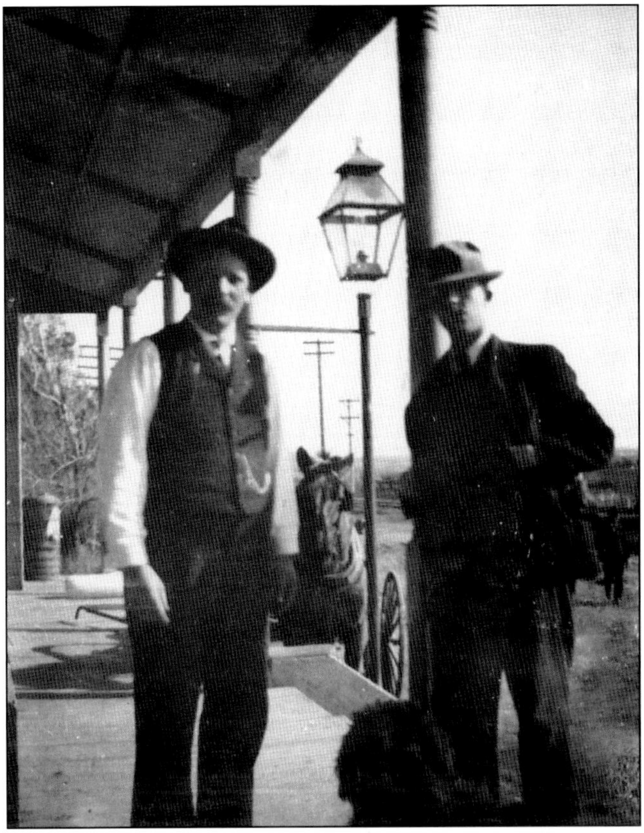

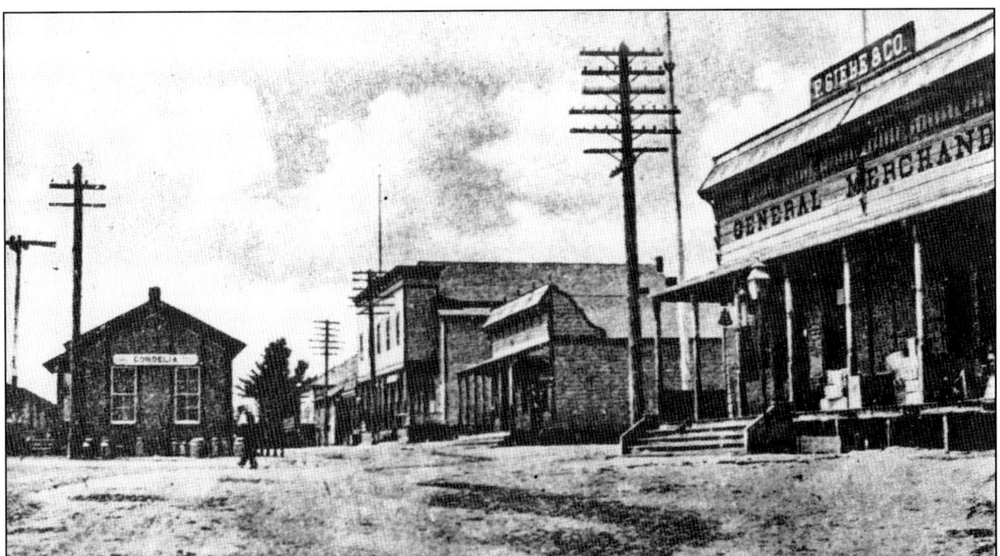

This view of Main Street includes, from left to right, the Cordelia depot, Studer's Bar (later Thompson's Corner), the firehouse, Chris and John Dunker's saloon and meat market, the post office (with a barbershop and X-Ray Publishing Office, the local newspaper), and P. Siebe & Co. General Merchandise store. On June 22, 1939, a fire that started underneath the Dunker's stairwell destroyed all but Studer's Bar. (VHC.)

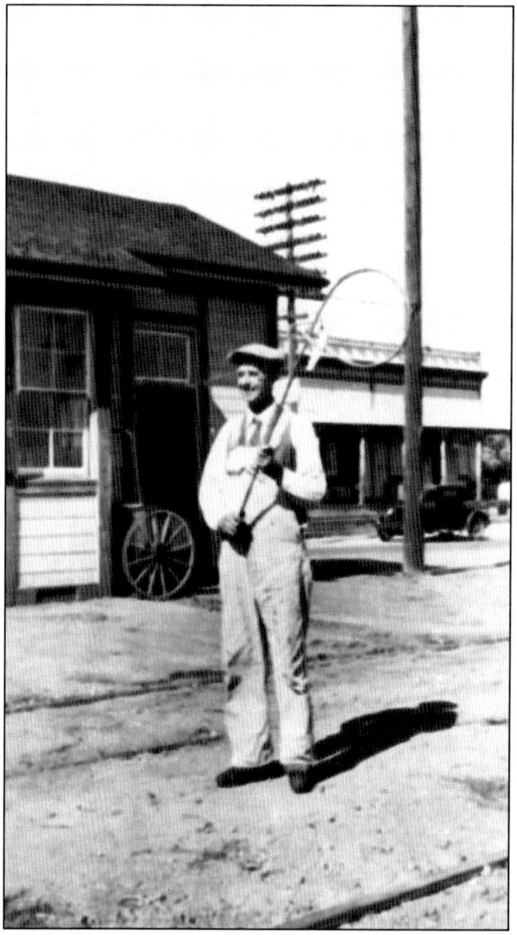

Henry Stoneman Pedrick, Southern Pacific station agent, is delivering a message to a passing train at Cordelia. He was married to Mildred Pedrick and had two sons, Arthur and Wilbur. The Cordelia station is on the left, and the P. Siebe & Co. General Merchandise store is in the background on right. (VHC.)

Here is an image of the Cordelia Episcopal Church, established in 1878 by the Ramsey, Stilts, Martin, and O'Neill families. It later became a Methodist church. The building was torn down around 1910. (VHC.)

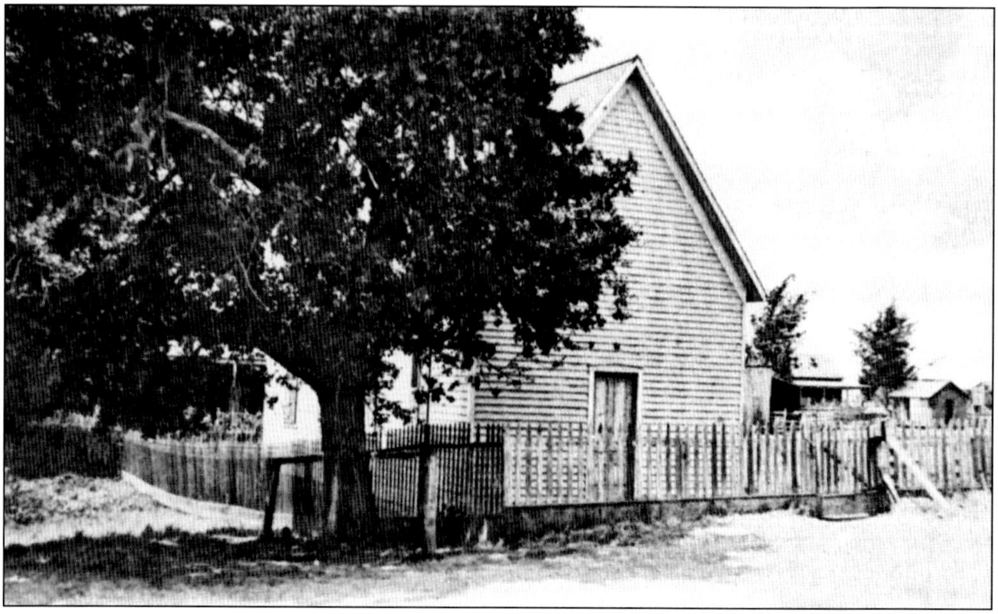

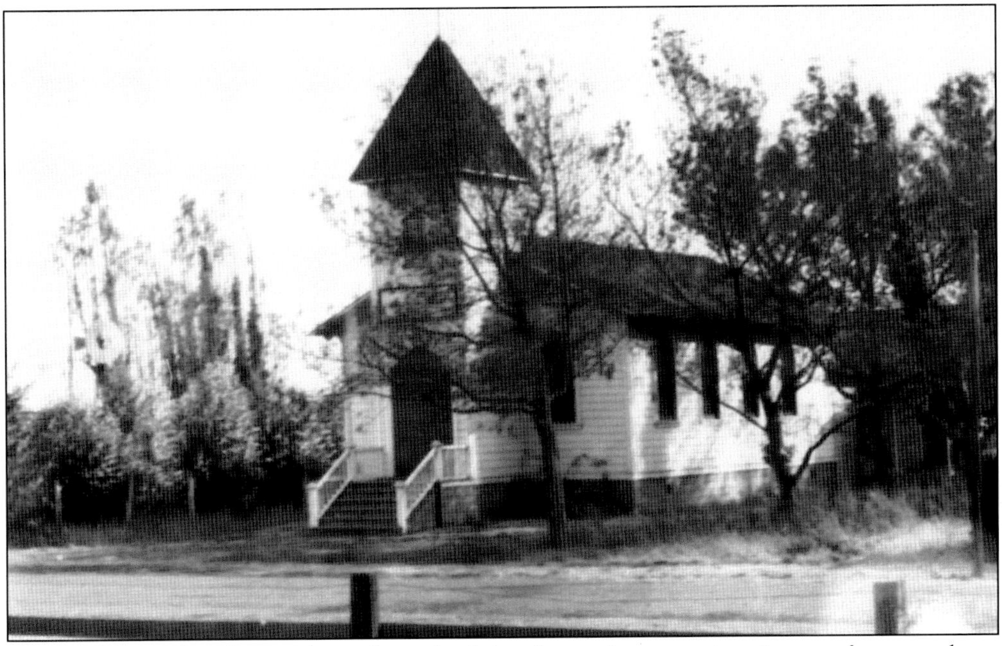

The Lutheran church seen here flourished thanks to the many immigrants from northern Germany and Scandinavia who settled in Cordelia. The building was later moved to Broadway Street in Fairfield. (VHC.)

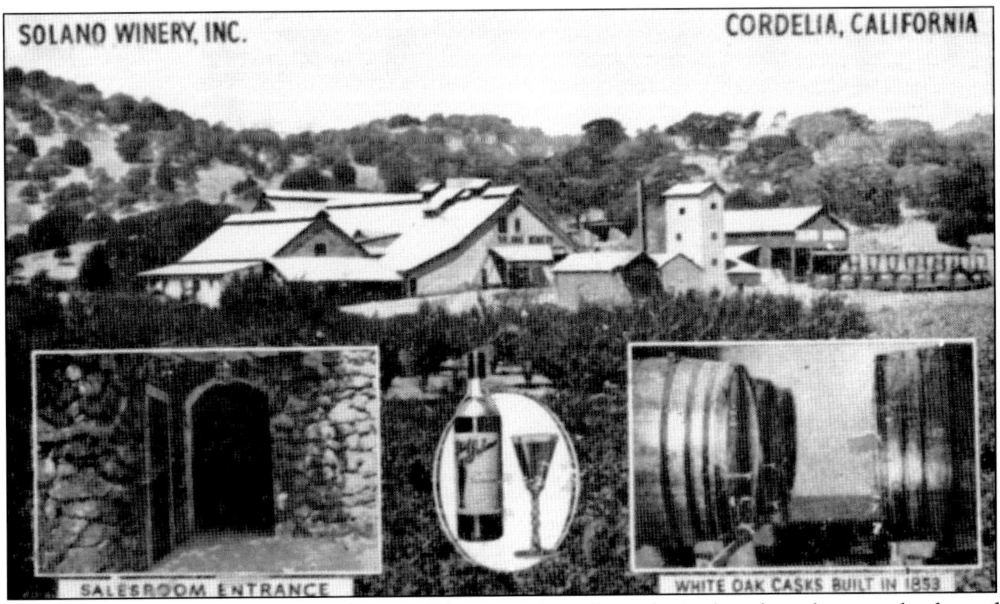

The Cordelia Winery was located east of the township along the railroad tracks near the foot of Nelson's Hill. It was one of the few wineries issued a permit to continue production of wine during Prohibition. Vineyards were one of the first agricultural endeavors in Green Valley, introduced as Italian, Austrian, German, and Portuguese immigrants brought their viticulture know-how to their new home. The area had a wealth of wineries, and a resurgence of family wineries is happening today throughout Suisun and Green Valleys. (VHC.)

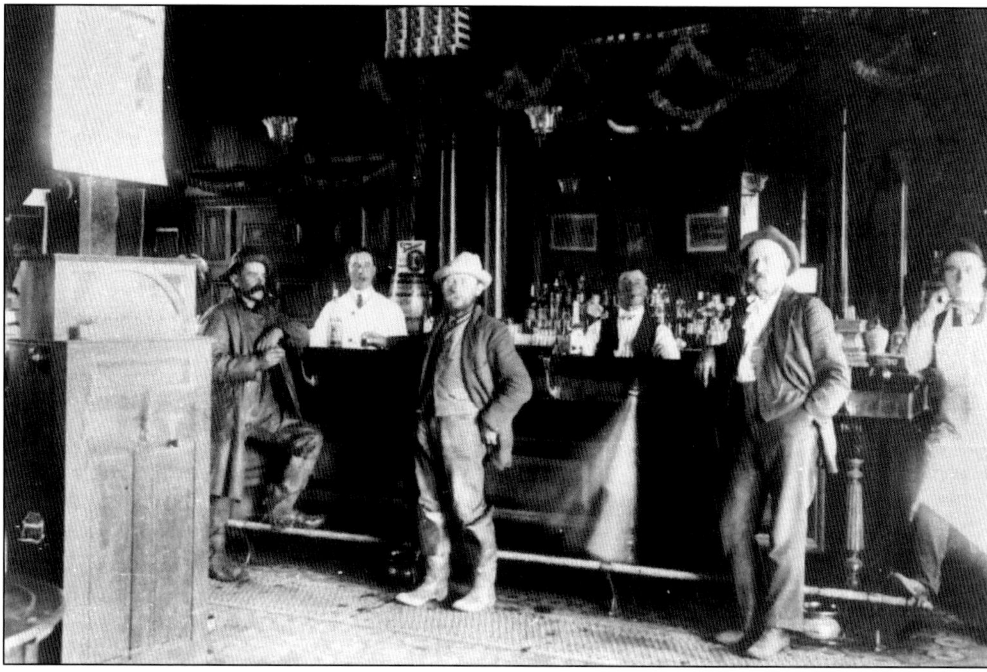

This early-1900s photograph from inside Dunker's saloon includes, from left to right, unidentified, John Dunker (bartender and butcher), Albert Peters (railroad laborer who boarded with the Schmidt family), Chris Dunker (bartender and butcher), Henry T. "Pop" Forse, and Henry Schinkel (butcher). Pop Forse was married to longtime Green Valley schoolteacher Ella Forse. A handwritten poster advertising the Dunkers can be seen in the foreground to the left. (VHC.)

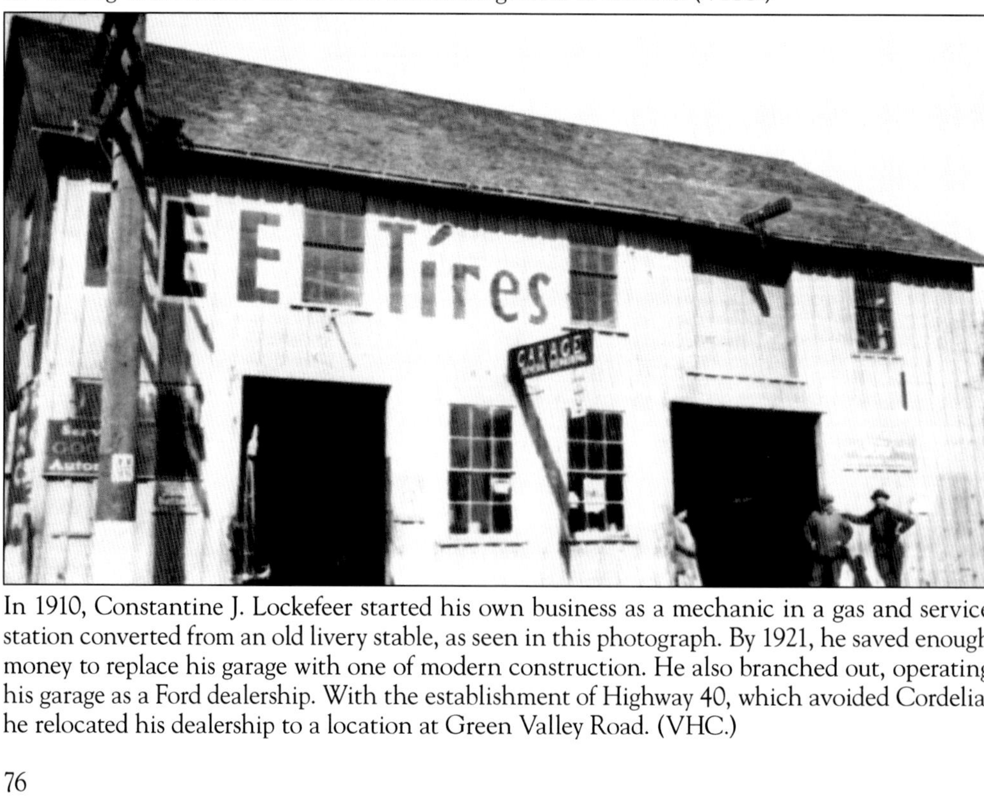

In 1910, Constantine J. Lockefeer started his own business as a mechanic in a gas and service station converted from an old livery stable, as seen in this photograph. By 1921, he saved enough money to replace his garage with one of modern construction. He also branched out, operating his garage as a Ford dealership. With the establishment of Highway 40, which avoided Cordelia, he relocated his dealership to a location at Green Valley Road. (VHC.)

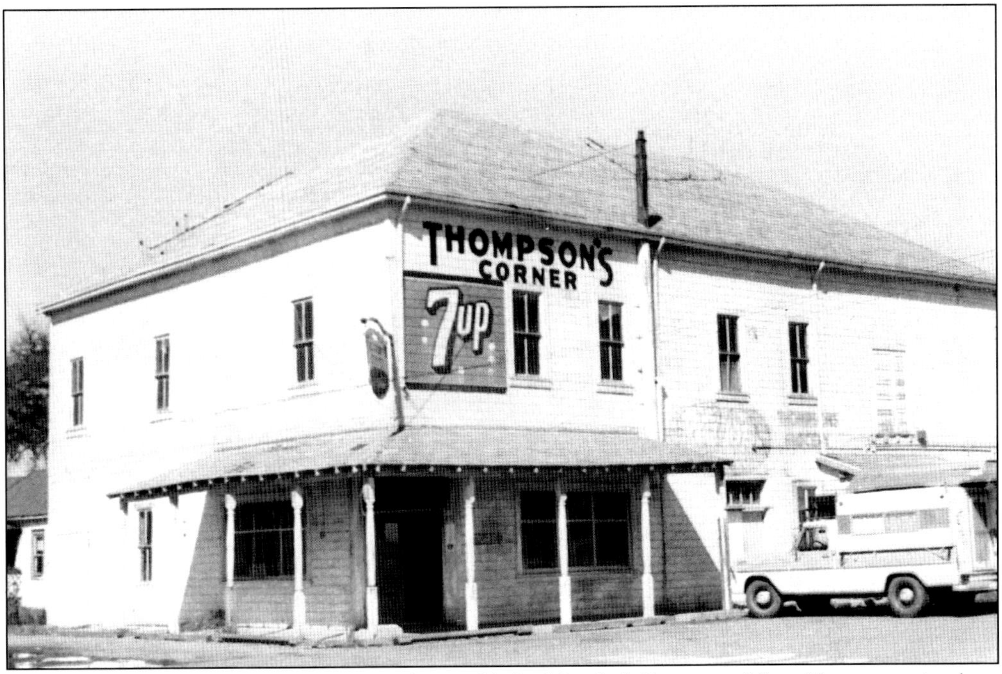

Brothers Jim and Henry "Old Man" Studer established Studer's Bar, one of the oldest operating bars in the county. The saloon was downstairs, and upstairs offered dining, dancing, entertainment, and, according to local lore, a brothel. After 1940, Charles Thompson purchased the bar, and it became known as Thompson's Corner. It is the only business still operating in old town Cordelia and remains the social center of the community. Anyone who is anyone has been to Thompson's Corner! (VHC.)

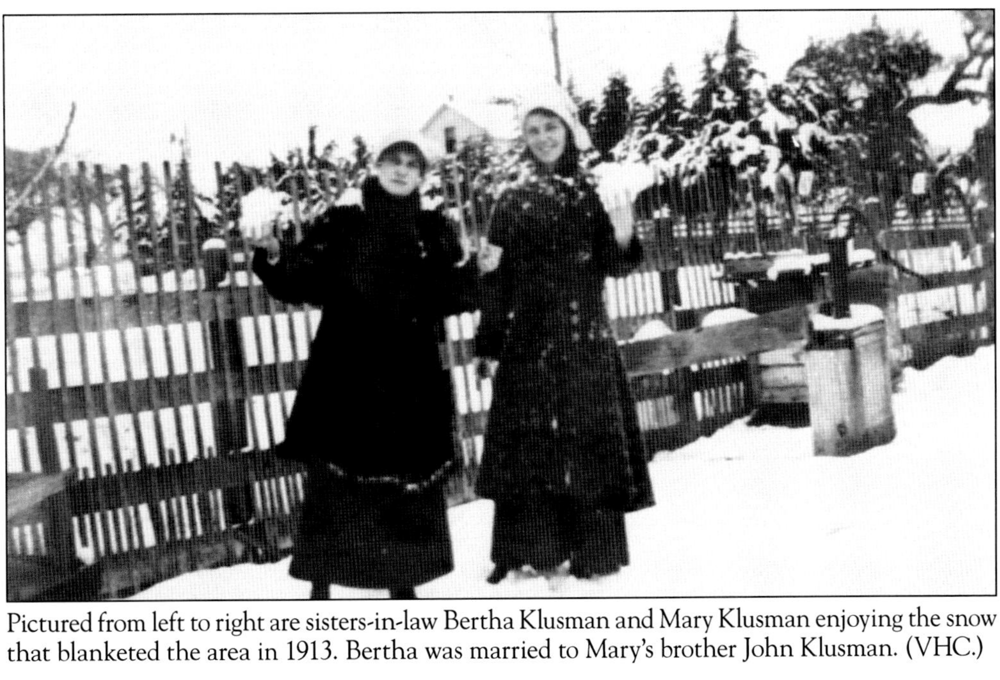

Pictured from left to right are sisters-in-law Bertha Klusman and Mary Klusman enjoying the snow that blanketed the area in 1913. Bertha was married to Mary's brother John Klusman. (VHC.)

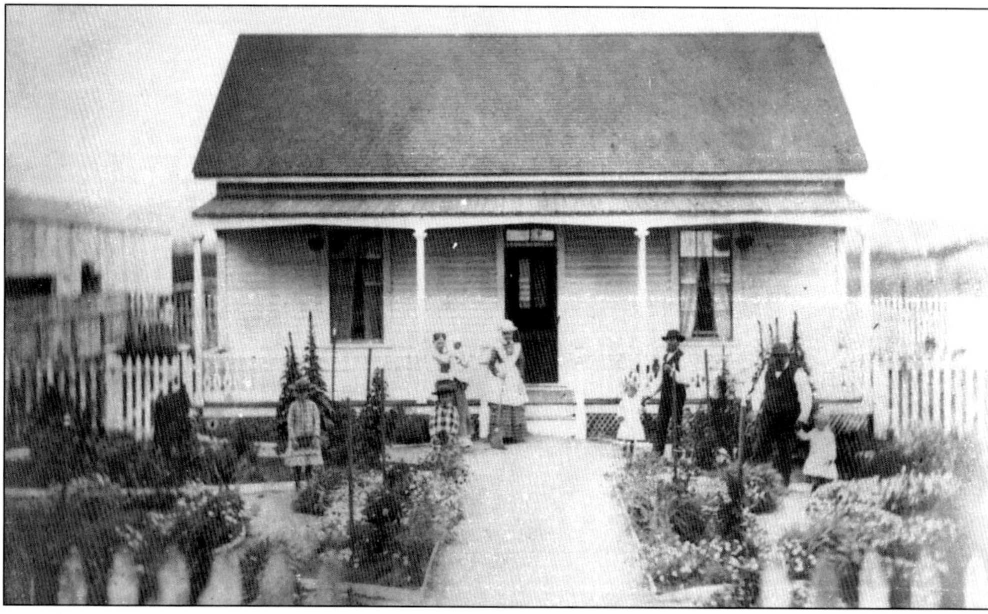

Members of the Otto Glashoff family are, from left to right, (first row) Katie Glashoff (daughter) and Tillie Glashoff (daughter); (second row) Marie Glashoff (wife) holding Tillie Glashoff (daughter), Anna Dunker Glashoff (sister-in-law), Clara Glashoff (daughter) holding hands with her uncle Matthias Glashoff (Otto's brother), Otto Glashoff, and Sadie Glashoff (daughter). They are pictured around 1887 in front of their quaint saltbox home. Otto Glashoff was a prominent businessman in Cordelia. (VHC.)

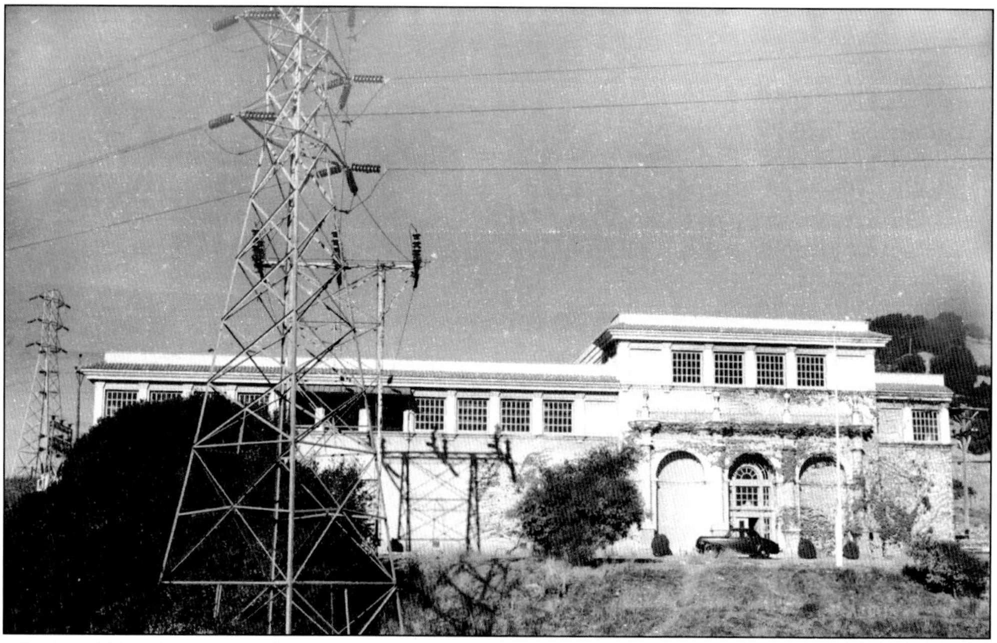

The 1915 Pacific Gas & Electric Company Cordelia substation was famed for being the world's largest electrical distribution station at the time it was constructed. The labor required for its construction provided many opportunities for local businesses. It is a reinforced-concrete building made from materials produced from the neighboring town of Cement. (VHC.)

Six

Stone Buildings of Rockville and Green Valley

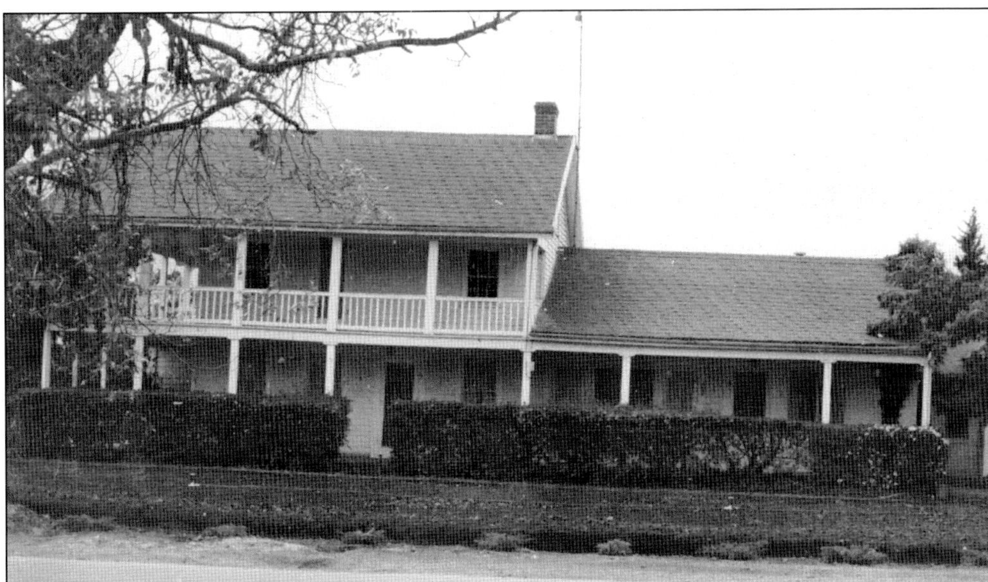

The Stilts house, pictured above, was constructed around an older rubble-stone adobe built in the late 1830s by Gen. M.G. Vallejo's vaqueros. John Stilts purchased the property from Vallejo and enclosed the home with shiplap brought around the Horn. William Pierce completed the final additions to the home in 1890. Frederick S. Jones, famed for establishing the world's largest cherry orchard, later acquired the property. Jones was married to Mary Jones, the sister of Granville P. Swift and niece of famed frontiersman Daniel Boone. (VHC.)

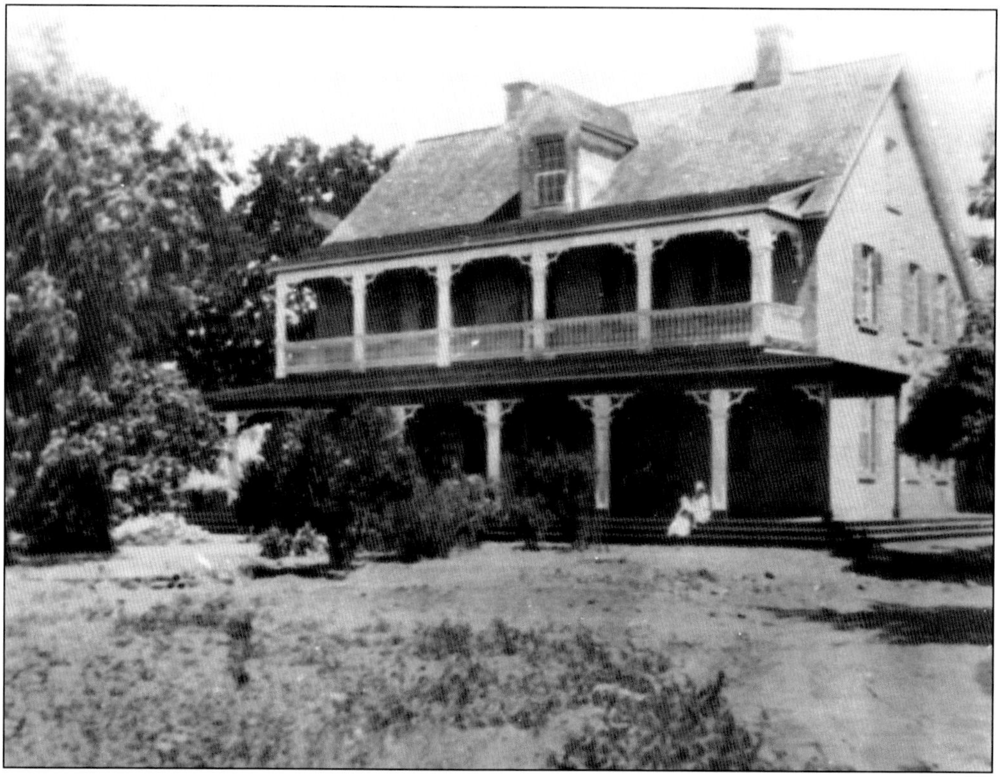

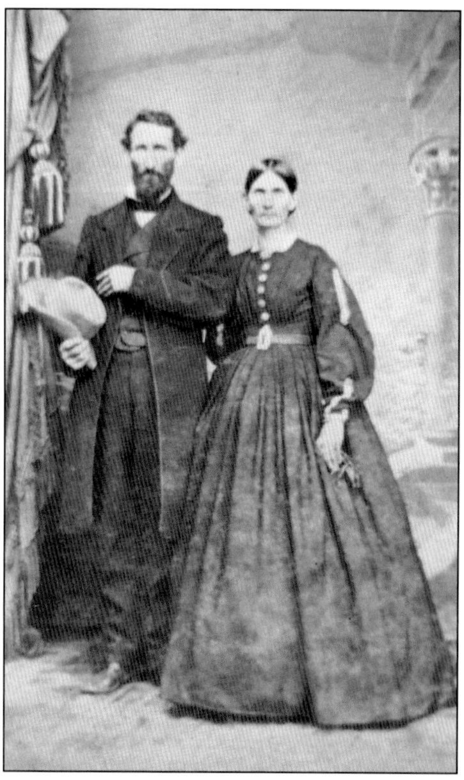

The stately home pictured here was built in 1860 by Charles and Dorothy Ramsay, pictured at left, with stone from his brother William Ramsey's quarry. (For unknown reasons, the Ramsay family, and a couple of other valley families, alternated between two spellings of their last name.) In 1862, the Ramsays, among the Southern sympathizers living in Solano, raised a Confederate flag above the house. An Army detachment from Benicia was sent to quell any potential insurrections and persuaded Charles, with several shots fired into the air, to lower the flag. The house became known as the Nightingale House after it was purchased by Dr. John Nightingale as a ranch for his son Joseph and family. (Both, VHC.)

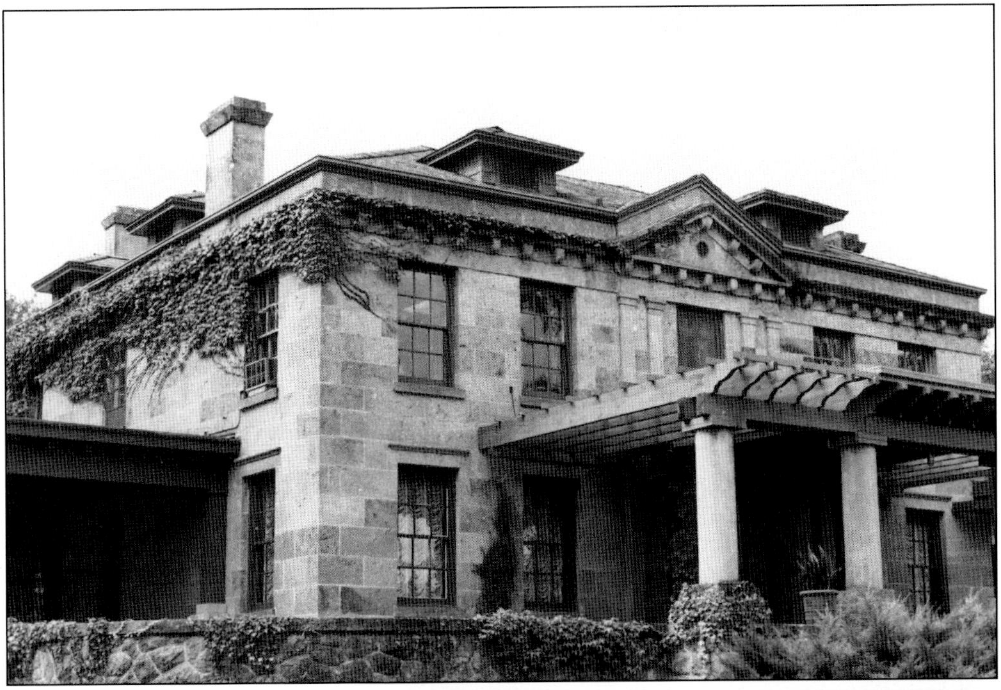

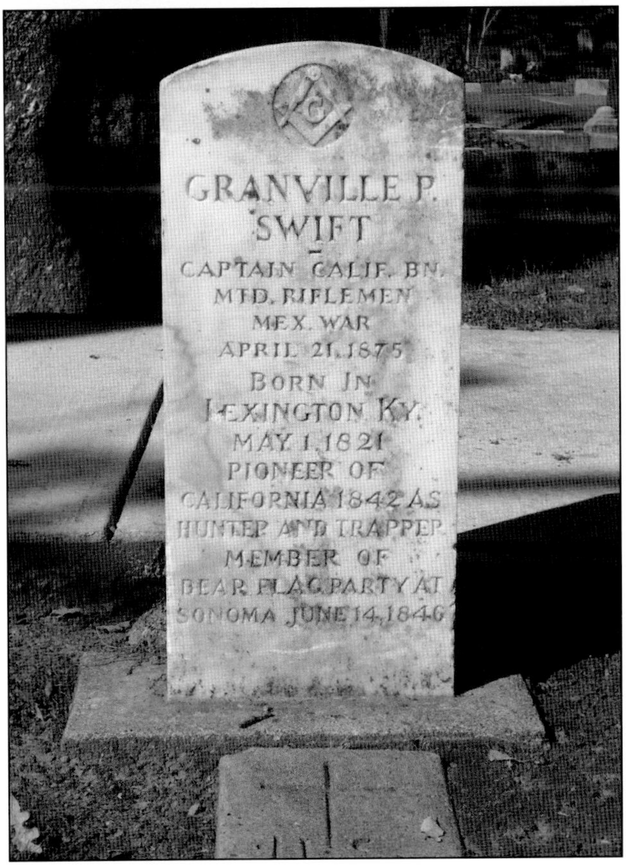

Granville P. Swift, of Bear Flag Revolt fame, acquired this home from James Harbin in 1864 as payment for a debt. Otherwise, Swift was penniless after losing his fortune in Comstock Lode speculation and went back to prospecting, though for quicksilver. Swift had a nasty habit of burying his gold and forgetting where he put it, despite notes to himself such as "1 tin box & 1 Little Bottle Boath in the saim hoal." It is estimated he secreted over $100,000. By 1868, to avoid losing his property in a divorce, he deeded the home to his sister Mary "Polly" Boone Jones. In 1875, Swift was buried at Rockville Cemetery after he suffered a lethal injury from a fall when his mule stumbled on a mountain trail. Green Valley Country Club now owns the home. (Above, VHC; right, ED.)

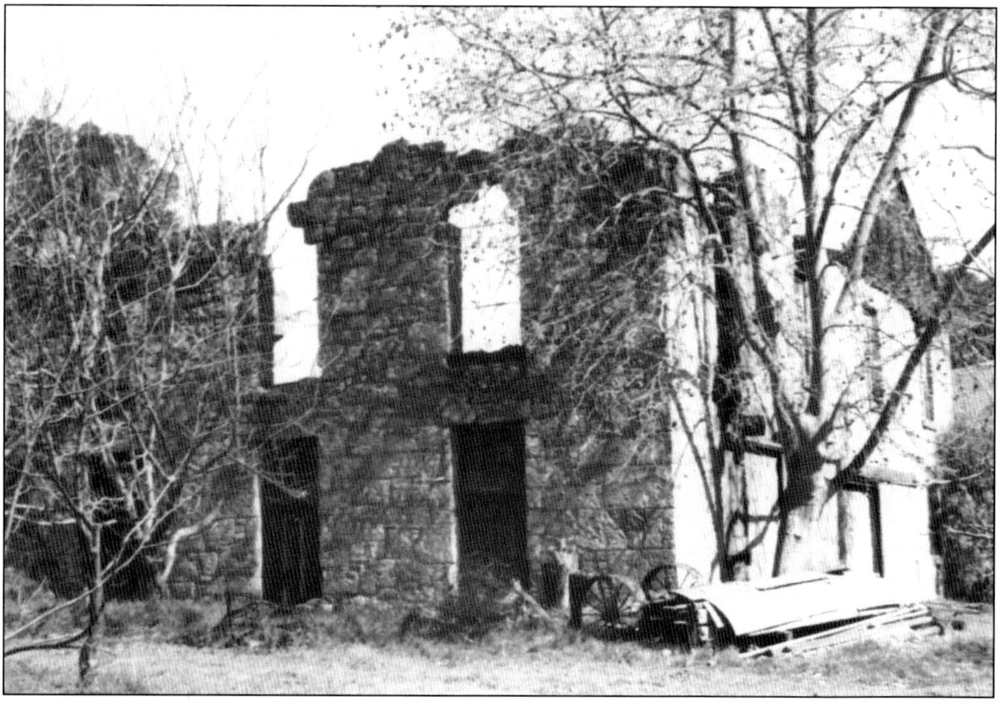

George Dingley built the Dingley Flour Mill, pictured here, in 1859. The mill ruins are said to be haunted by the ghost of Mary Eliza Parker, who was hurled to an untimely death after her dress became caught in a revolving shaft. Mary's fiancé, Eugene Lehe, did not learn of her death until his arrival at Green Valley. The funeral was held at Rockville Chapel. On moonlit nights, it is said one can hear Mary's cries and see flickers of light through the windows. (VHC.)

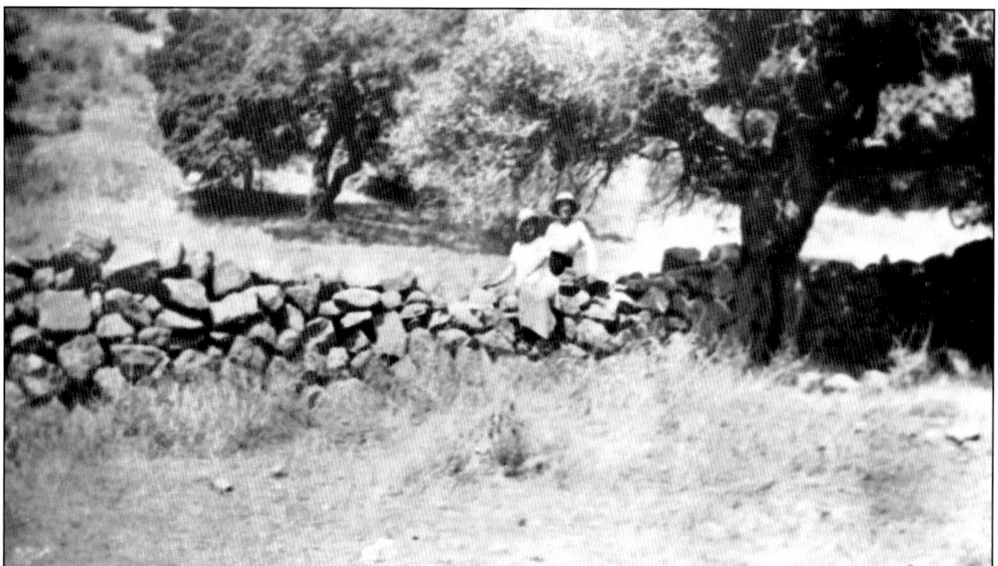

Lulu and Ada Bransombe are posed behind one of the many rock walls that cross Rockville and the surrounding countryside. Construction of the walls is attributed to Chinese laborers who settled in the area after work had been completed on the Transcontinental Railroad in the 1870s and 1880s. (VHC.)

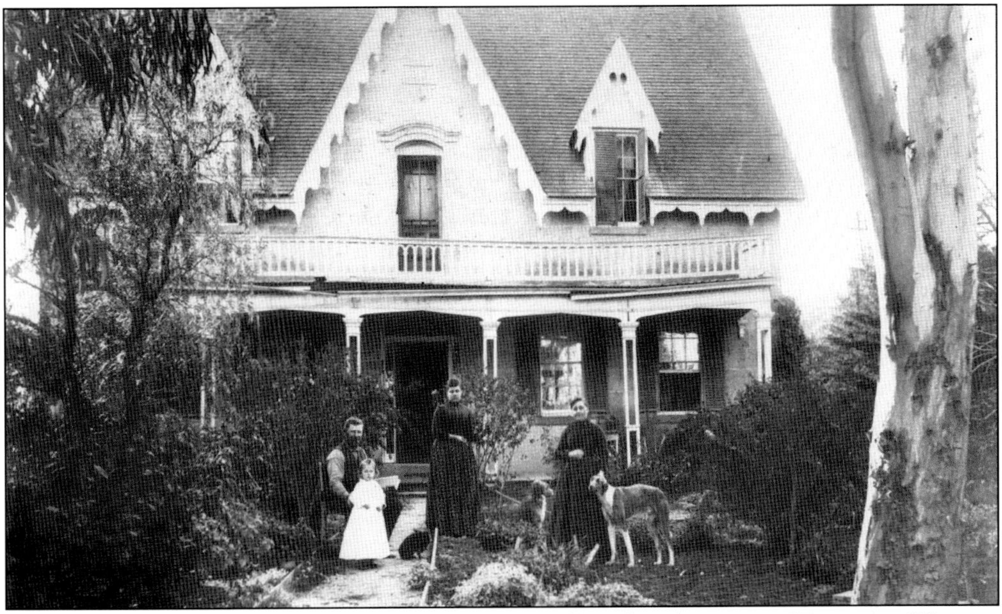

One of the most significant sites in Solano County and listed in the National Register of Historic Places, the Samuel Martin estate represents a layered and complex history. As the ancestral home of the Suisunes, the site has archeological features dating back thousands of years. Samuel Martin had the home built in 1861 from local tufa stone. After Martin's death, his son Henry Martin, pictured here at the far left with, from left to right, daughter May, wife Carrie, and mother-in-law Louisa Jane May Pittman, inherited the estate. Carrie bestowed the estate with the name Stonedene. (SCHS.)

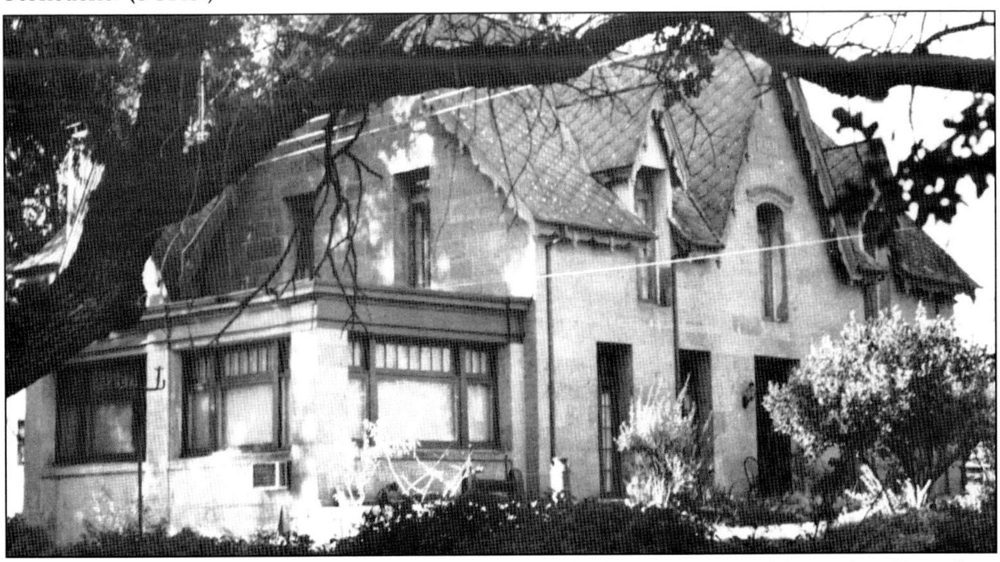

Samuel H.P. Martin, son of Henry Martin, commissioned Julia Morgan in 1926 to update Stonedene after it had fallen into disrepair and to provide separate accommodations for both his and his sister May Smith's families. This view from the south end shows the solarium and french windows added by Morgan. Morgan was also known for her use of solid beams, coffered ceilings, large stone hearths, and Mediterranean details, such as coved ceilings, all of which were design elements utilized throughout the remodel. (SCHS.)

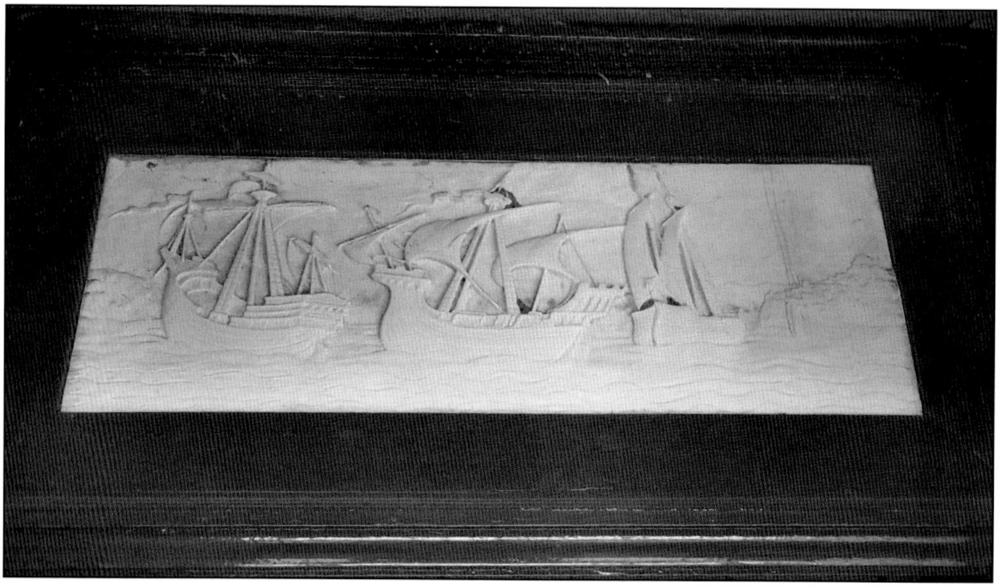

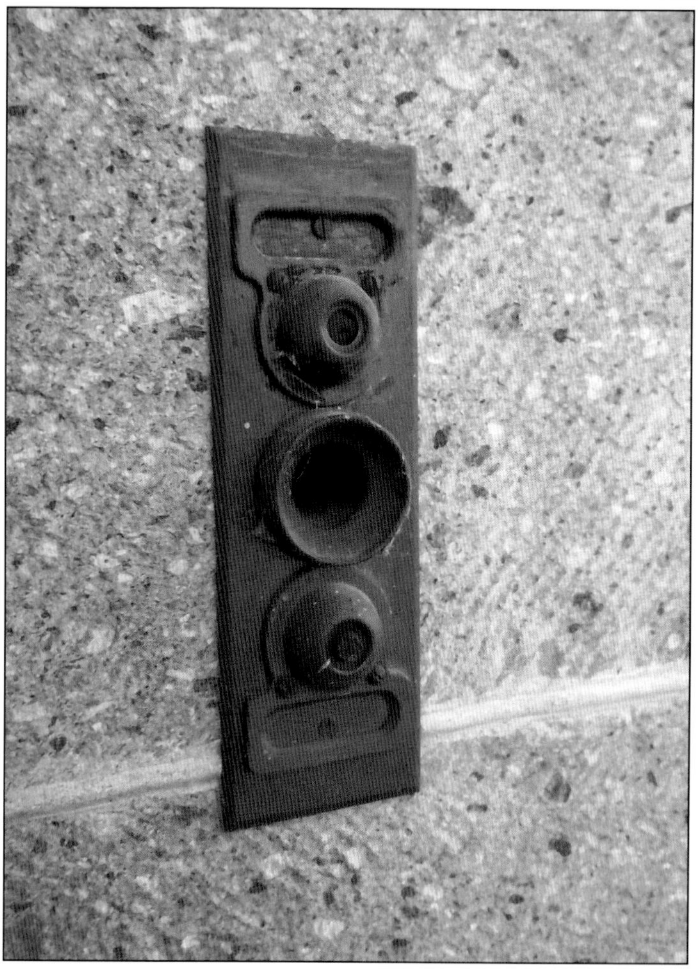

Morgan incorporated many elements of the Arts and Crafts movement in her designs, such as this bas-relief that graces the entryway to Stonedene. Her fine attention to detail extended to even the smallest element, such as this double doorbell that gave visitors the discretion to announce their arrival to the desired family's quarters. In addition to the updates made to the home itself, Morgan designed a matching carriage house that still stands today. (Both, ED.)

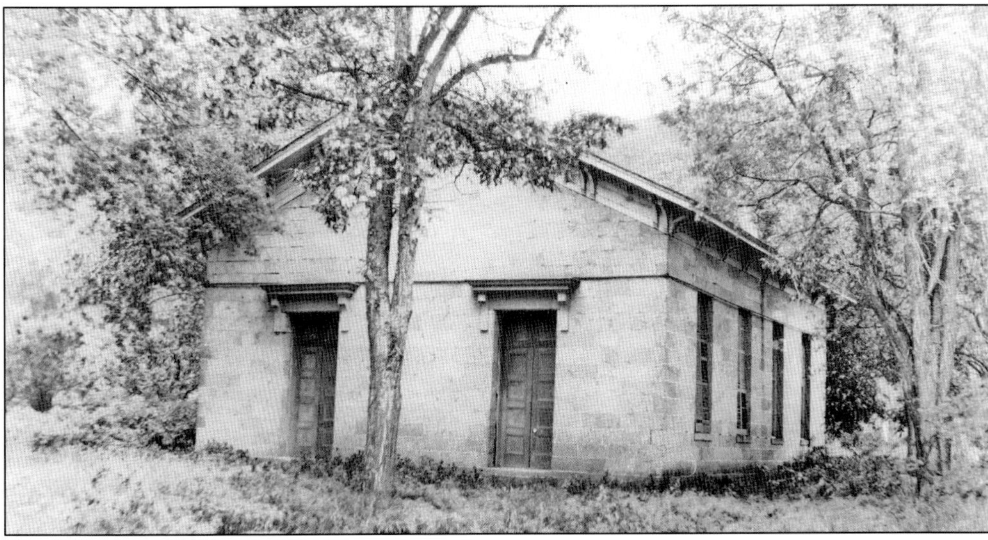

The Rockville Chapel traces its roots to early revival camps held for Southern Methodists along the Suisun Creek, where followers would camp out for a couple of weeks with provisions brought by wagon. The chapel was built in 1856 with funds raised at the revivals on land donated by Landy and Sarah Alford. Nationwide, the Southern Methodists split from the Methodist Episcopal Church over the issue of slavery in 1845. The Methodist Episcopalians met nearby at the "Valley Church," a building later converted into the first Gomer School. (VHC)

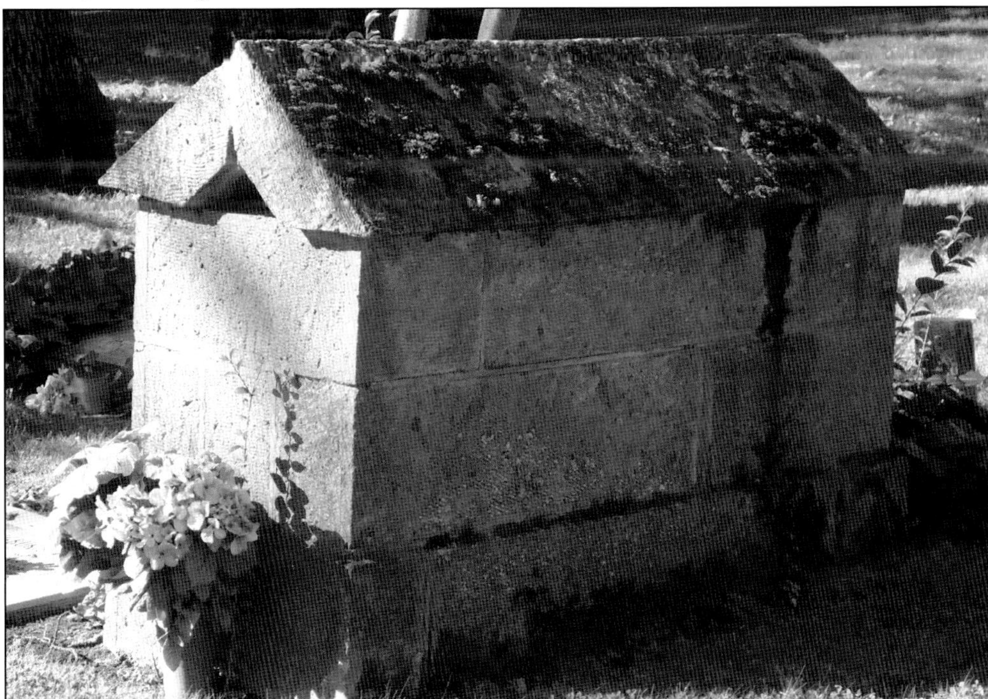

Sadly, the first occupant of the Rockville cemetery was little Sarah Alford, daughter of Landy and Sarah Alford, who had earlier donated the land on which the chapel and cemetery were established. Sarah's death in December 1856 coincided with the first services held at the chapel. Her grave has been affectionately dubbed the "Dollhouse." (VHC.)

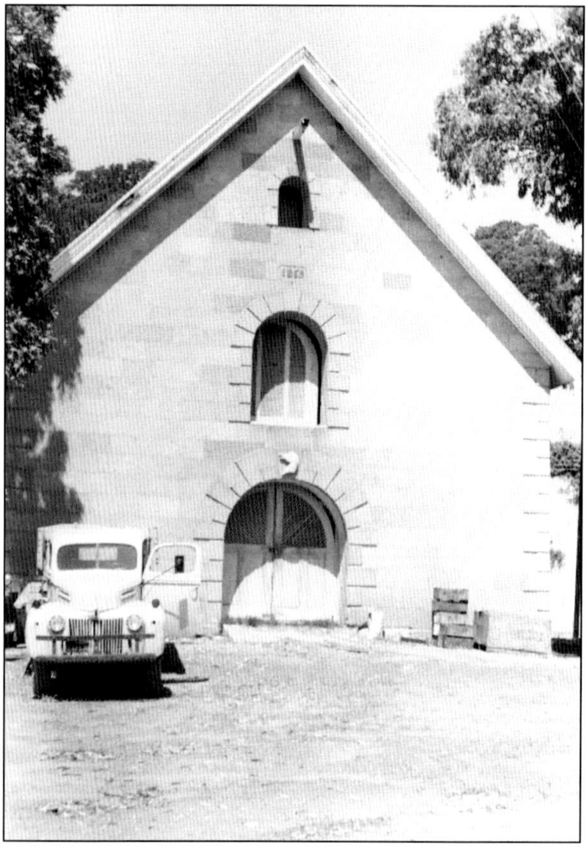

The Baldwin Stone Barn was built in 1865 for Jabez M. Baldwin after he purchased the property from Landy Alford. Construction included the laying of a secret cornerstone that contained an infant photograph of his daughter Katie Baldwin, 1865 gold coins in various denominations, paper currency, and newspapers from the day. There was only one person, William Higgins, a ranch hand, who knew the exact location of the cornerstone, but he took the secret to his grave. (VHC.)

When he was a small boy, John Abernathie, son of L.B. Abernathie, found this bowie knife on the bank of Suisun Creek, two miles north of the Rockville Stone Chapel near the J.B. Baldwin ranch. It may have been dropped in the creek during one of the previous revival meetings. (VHC.)

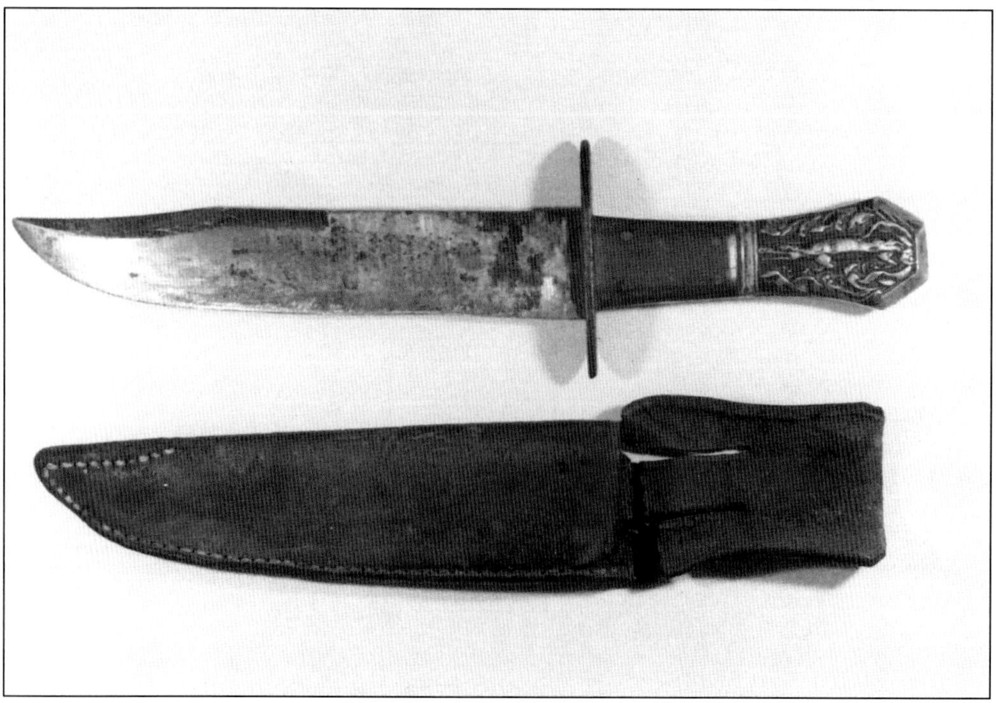

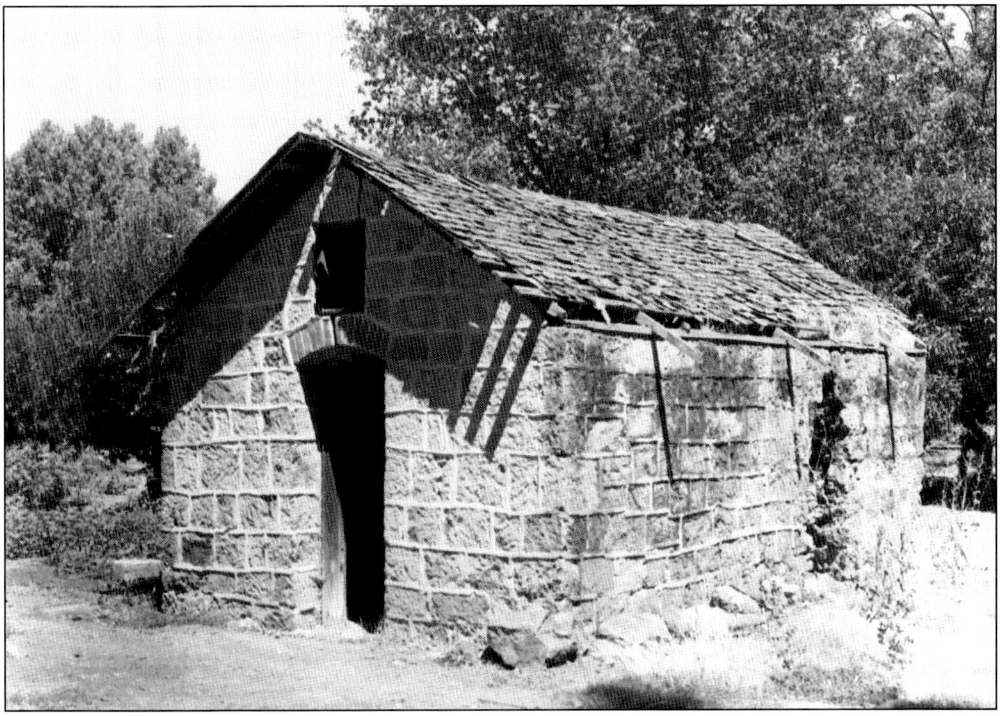

Prior to modern refrigeration, area ranches used stone structures to keep perishables cool in the summer heat. This milk house was built behind the foreman's house at the Pierce Ranch. (VHC.)

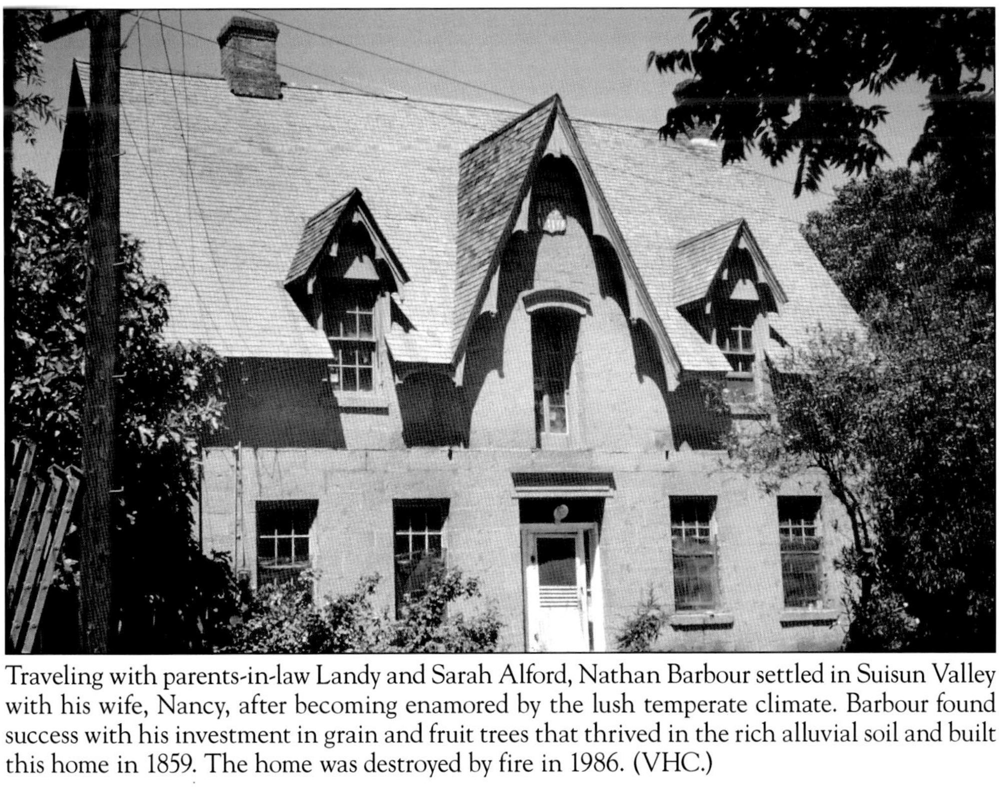

Traveling with parents-in-law Landy and Sarah Alford, Nathan Barbour settled in Suisun Valley with his wife, Nancy, after becoming enamored by the lush temperate climate. Barbour found success with his investment in grain and fruit trees that thrived in the rich alluvial soil and built this home in 1859. The home was destroyed by fire in 1986. (VHC.)

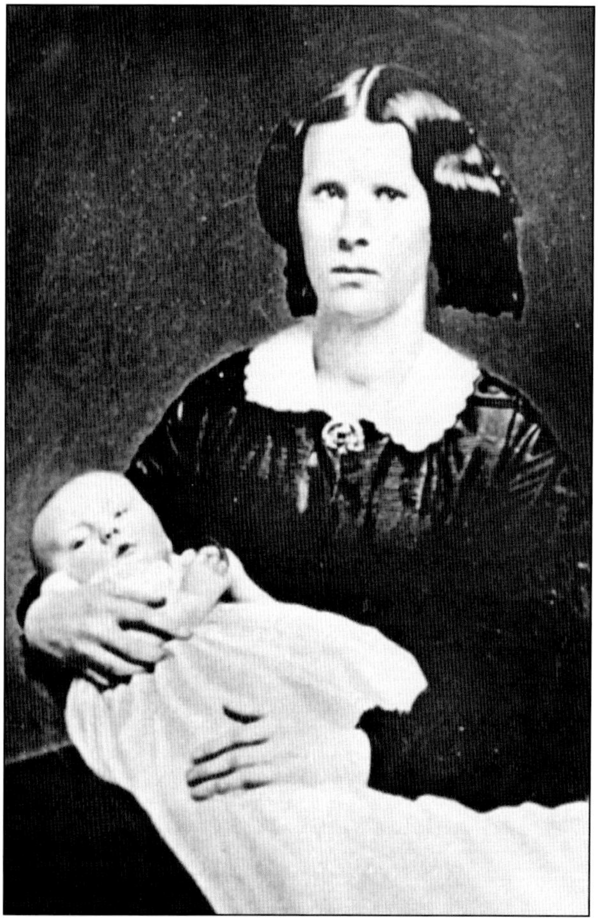

This is a portrait of Nancy Barbour and child. Nancy Barbour was the daughter of Landy and Sarah Alford. A matriarch of the valley, she had 10 children—Willie (died in infancy), Armelia (first American child born in Benicia), Eli, Nancy, Nathan, Julia, Nellie, May, Florence, and Kate. Her daughter Nancy would later make a name for herself by managing a successful fruit orchard. Nancy died of tuberculosis on October 15, 1869. (VHC.)

L.B. Abernathie followed his business partner Jabez Baldwin to California, first settling in Napa then in Suisun Valley. The partners had each amassed great fortunes only to lose a substantial amount in speculation. These are the ruins of the stone house L.B. and his wife, Eunice Park Abernathie, built in 1865. Construction included the laying of a cornerstone with family photographs and documents wrapped in an American flag secreted within. The home burned in 1921. (VHC.)

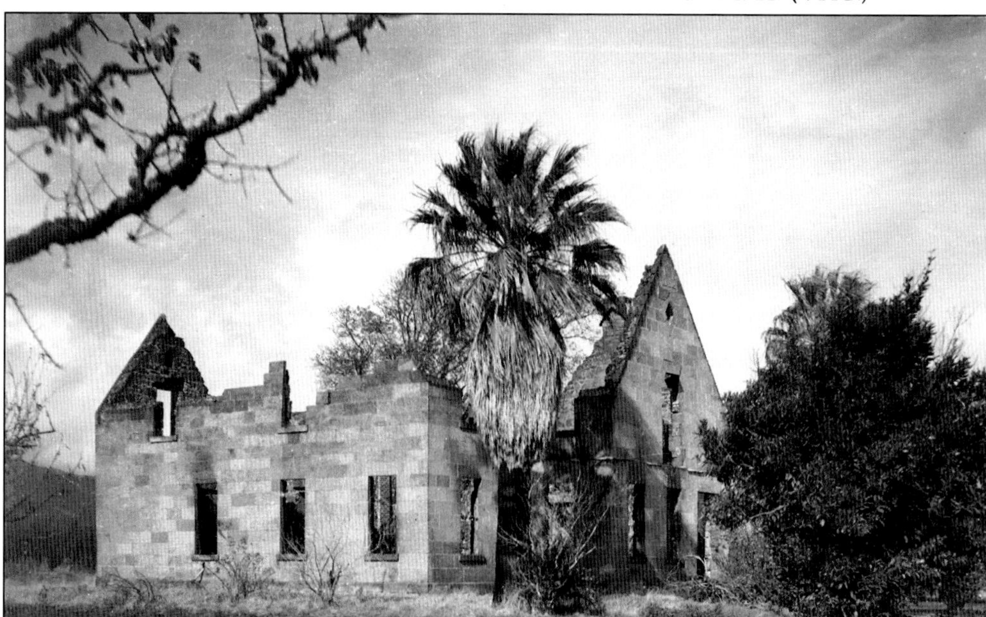

Seven

MANKA'S CORNER

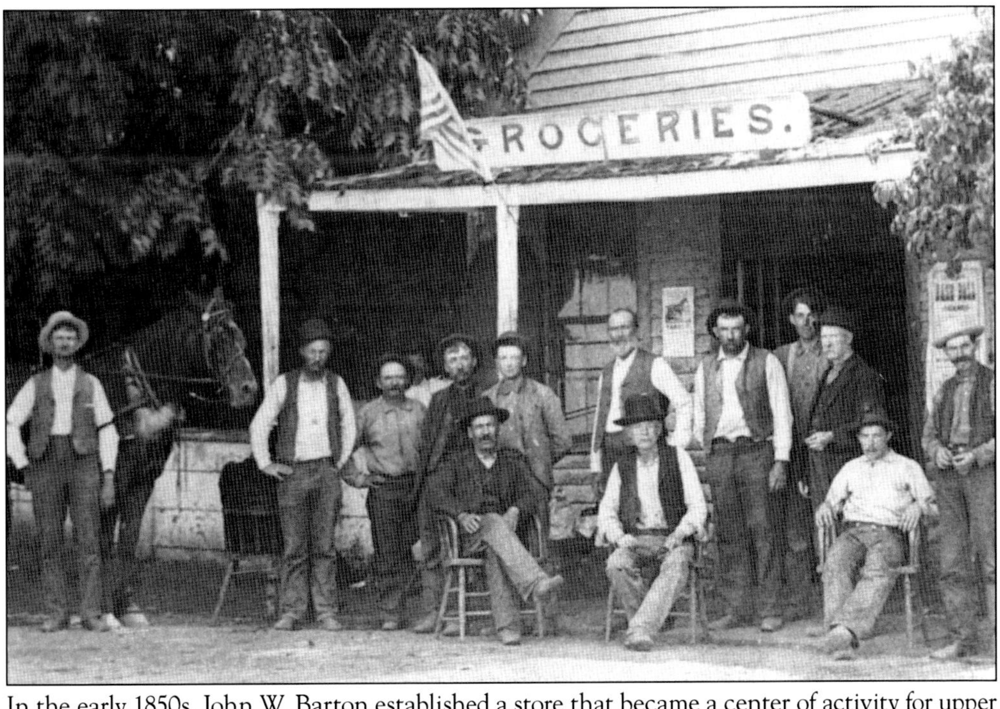

In the early 1850s, John W. Barton established a store that became a center of activity for upper Suisun Valley. He partnered with Christley Manka from 1859 until Barton moved to Fairfield. Manka remained, and thereafter, the area was known as Manka's Corner. Manka offered a store, bar, dance hall, and accommodations with featherbeds for weary travelers. John Wagner, the bare-headed man seen in this photograph, continued operations after Manka's death. (VHC.)

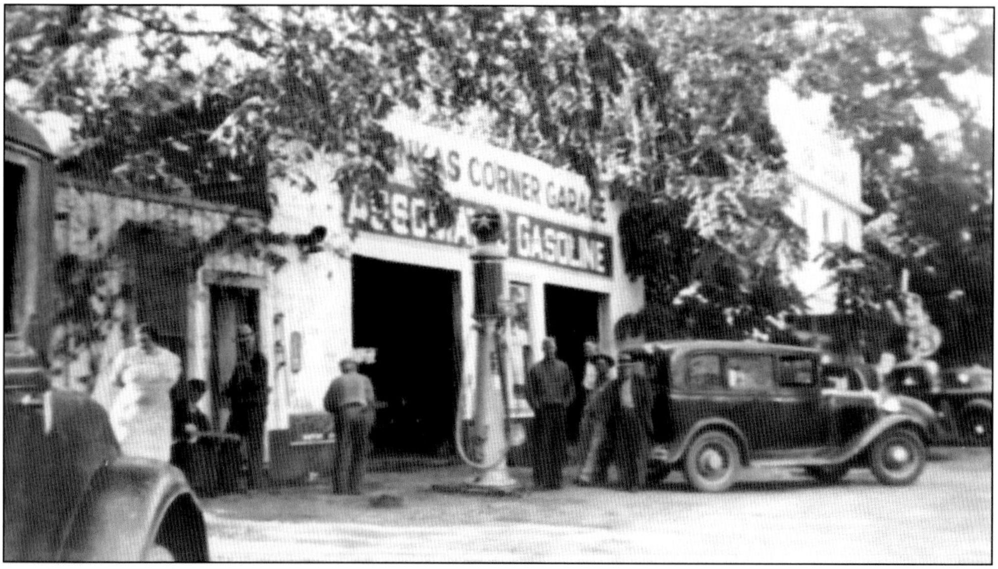

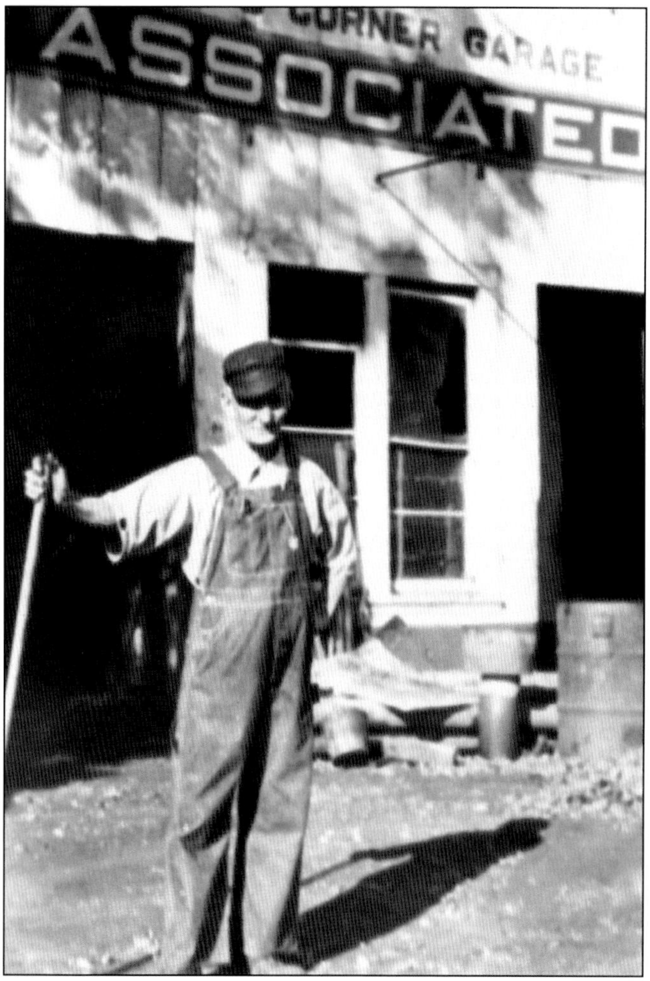

From left to right are Junia E. Reams, Calvin "Bainey" Reams (her husband) playing guitar, Fred Thedens, Ted Reams (Bainey's brother), William Reams (Bainey's brother), and three unidentified men by a car. This photograph was taken in front of the Manka's Corner Garage in November 1940. (VHC.)

Calvin "Bainey" Reams is seen standing in front of the service station at Manka's Corner Garage, where he worked as a mechanic. He was born in 1873 and was married to Junia E. Moody Reams, with whom he had four children, Dorothy, Glenn, Elsie, and Jane. (VHC.)

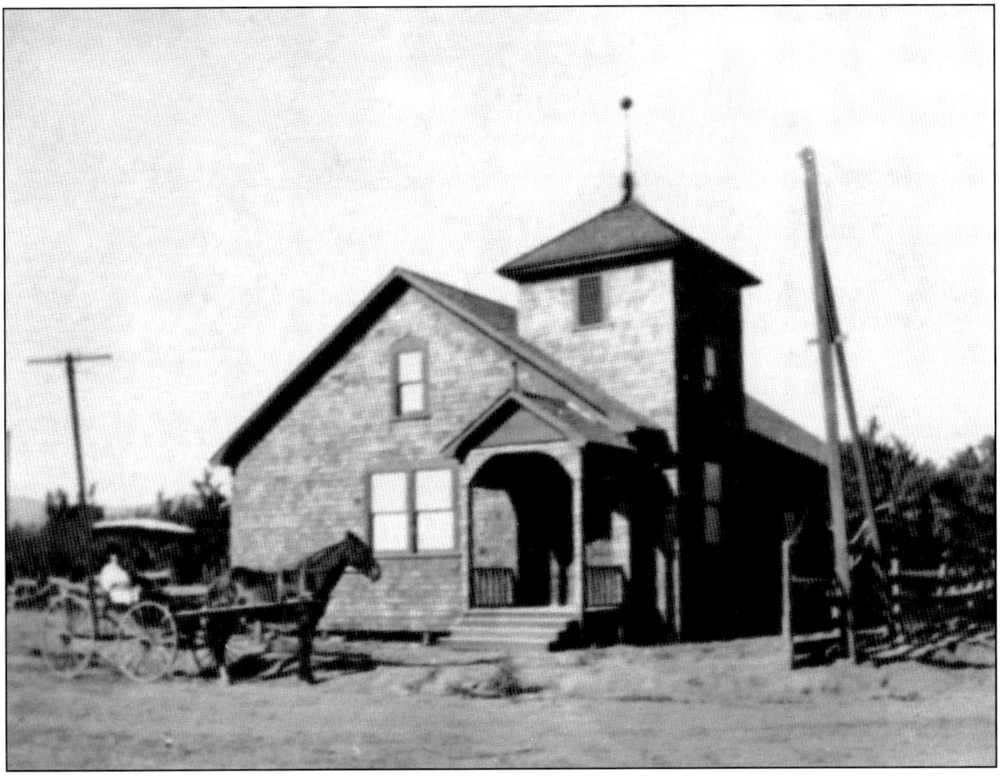

A Baptist congregation built this church at Manka's Corner. It was conveniently located near Ledgewood Creek, the site for the congregation's baptisms. (VHC.)

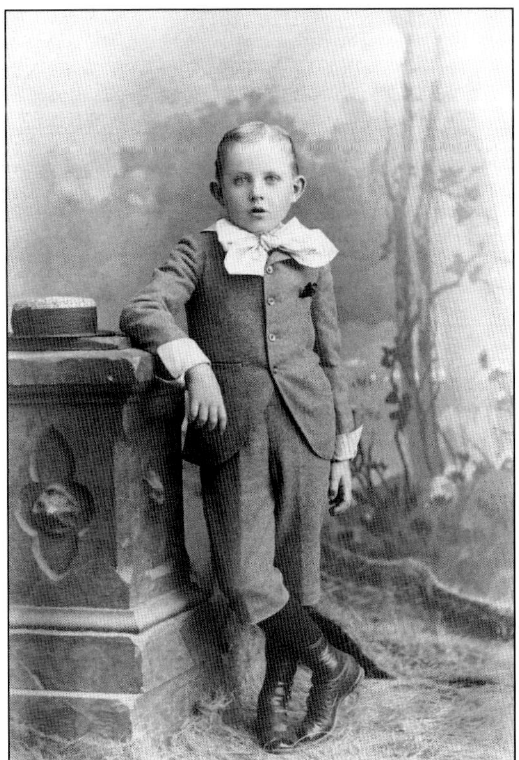

George C. Wagner, whose father, John, owned Manka's Corner after Christley Manka passed away, followed in his father's footsteps by becoming a salesman when he grew up. (VHC.)

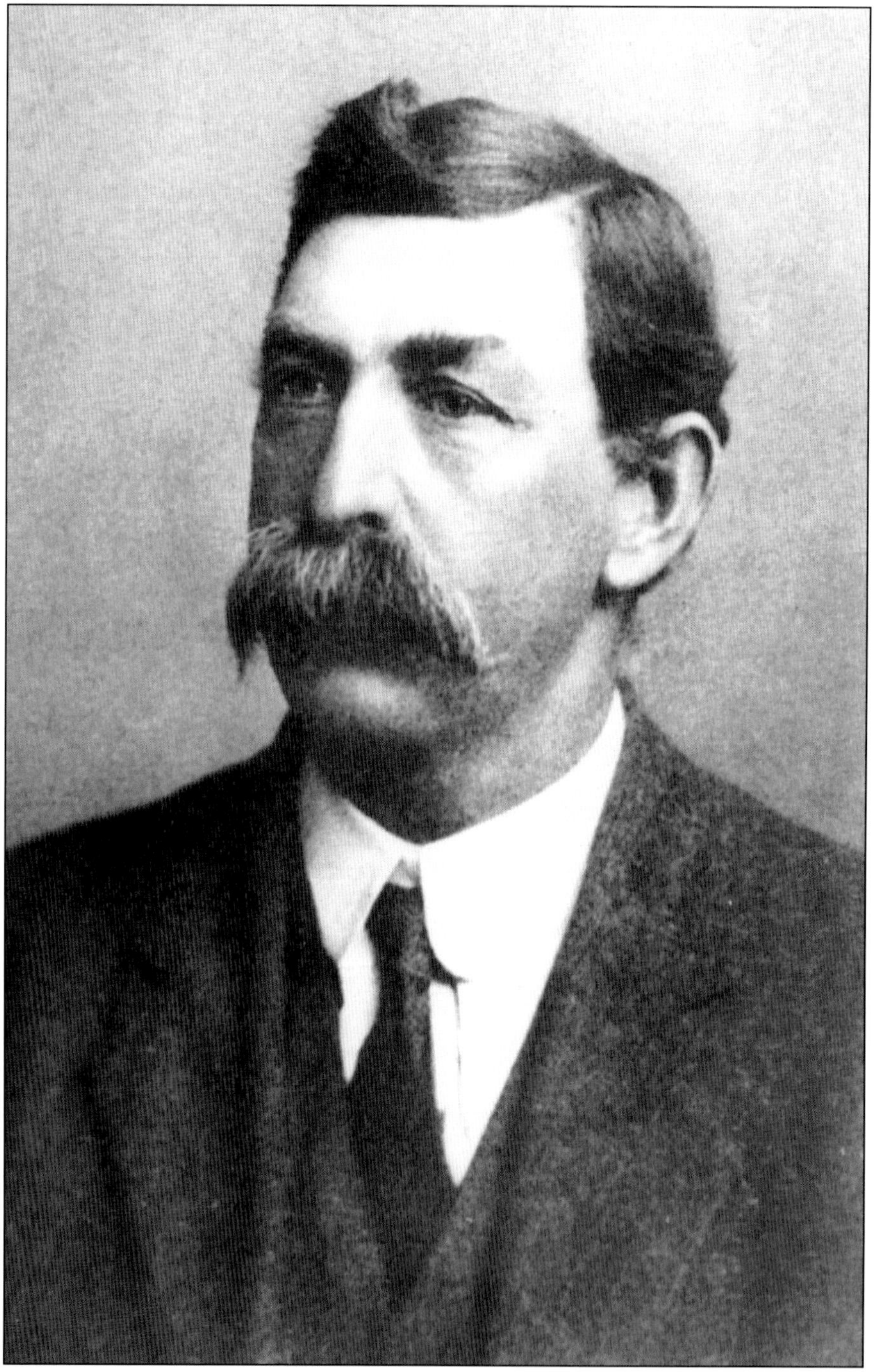

Franklin Oscar Scarlett settled adjacent to Manka's Corner and established a prosperous orchard and livestock ranch with the early assistance of R.D. Robbins, founder of the Bank of Suisun. Robbins promised Scarlett that if he would manage the former Brown Ranch on the bank's books, then for $100,000 payable at Scarlett's convenience, he could have the title. Scarlett and his son Walter worked hard and paid the loan off within 20 years. At one point, the ranch employed 135 people. (VHC.)

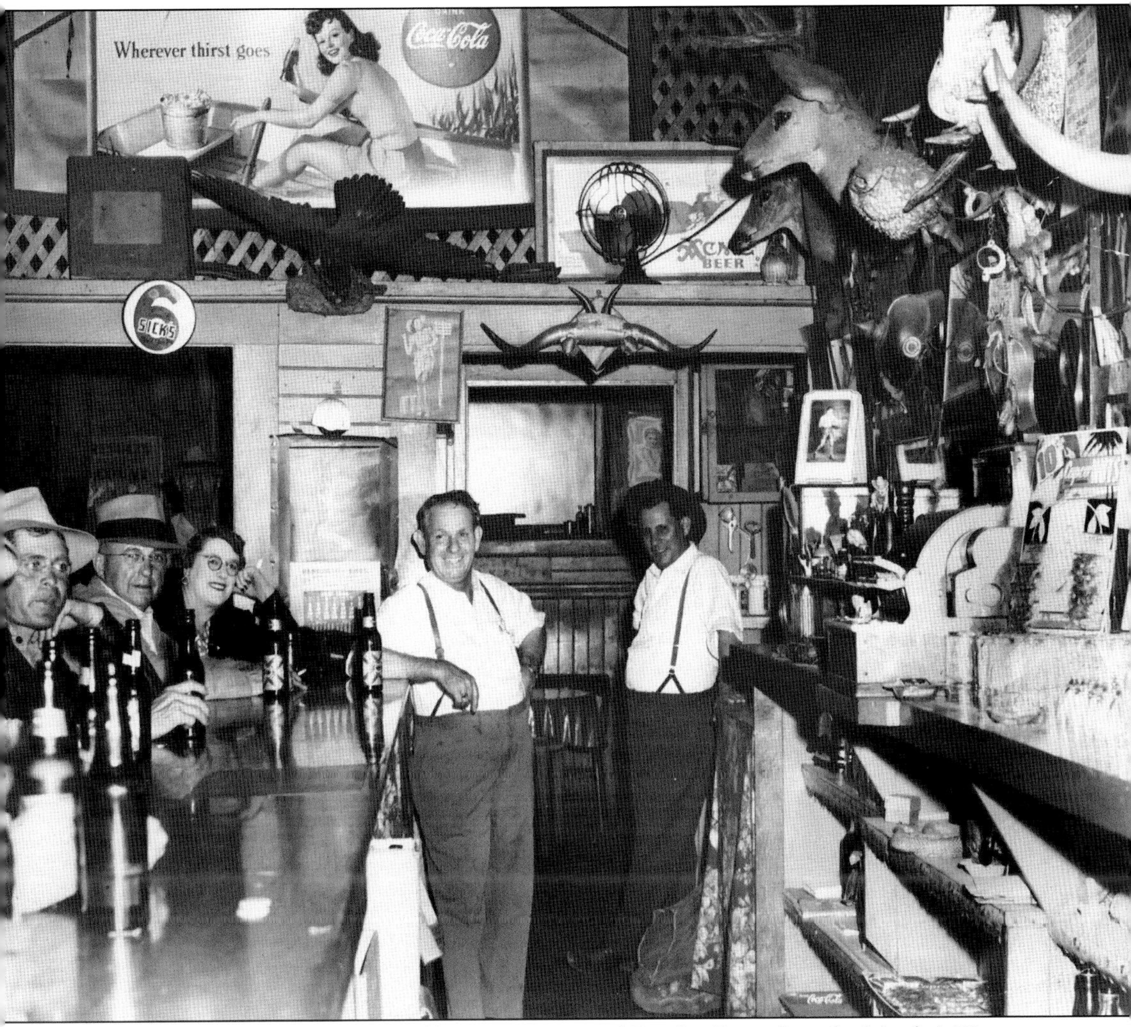

Following Prohibition, brothers William, George, and Presley Jones bought Manka's Corner. They removed the top floor and added a barbershop for Presley to operate. This photograph from summer of 1944 shows Billy (left) and George (right) manning the bar with a bevy of happy patrons. (VHC.)

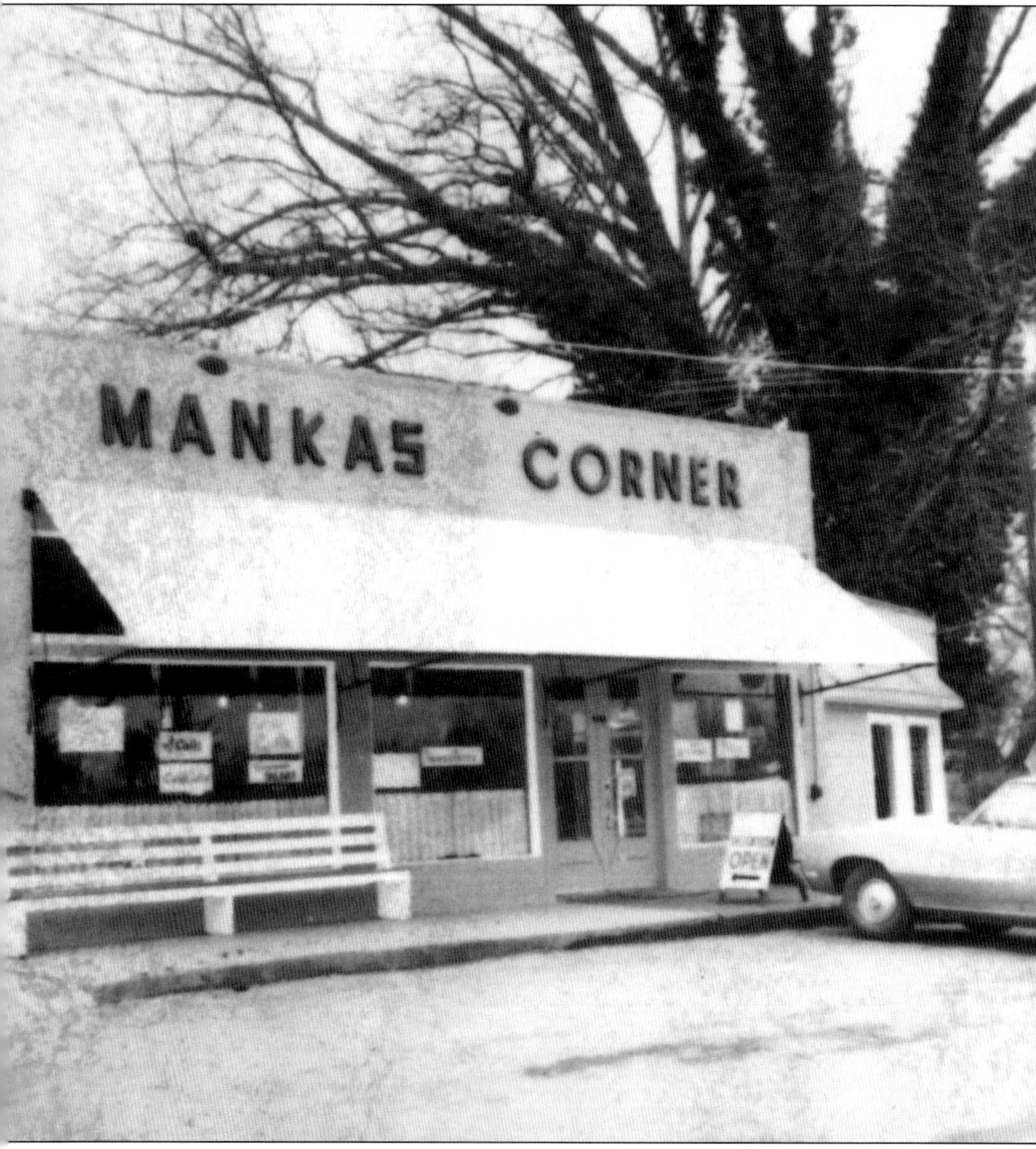

Up to the present day, Manka's Corner has continued to be a one-stop destination for tourists and locals alike. It has housed a tavern, a post office, a barbershop, a stage stop, and a myriad of other services. This photograph shows its incarnation as a delicatessen. It is now a stopping point for local art and farm tours. (VHC.)

Eight

School Days

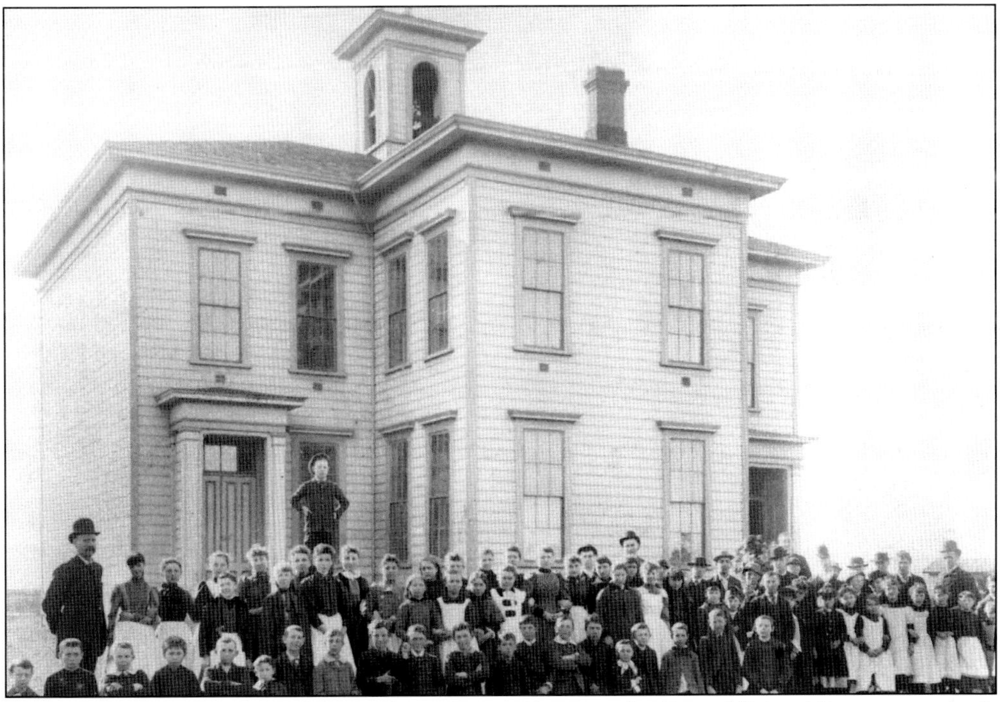

The Suisun Grammar School, located on Morgan Street in the Crystal School District, was built for $5,000 during the tenure of C.W. Childs. C.W. Childs, who later taught at the State Normal School in San Jose, was principal from 1868 to 1877. Construction of the two-story structure that had four departments was funded through a tax. The older students were taught on the top floor. (VHC.)

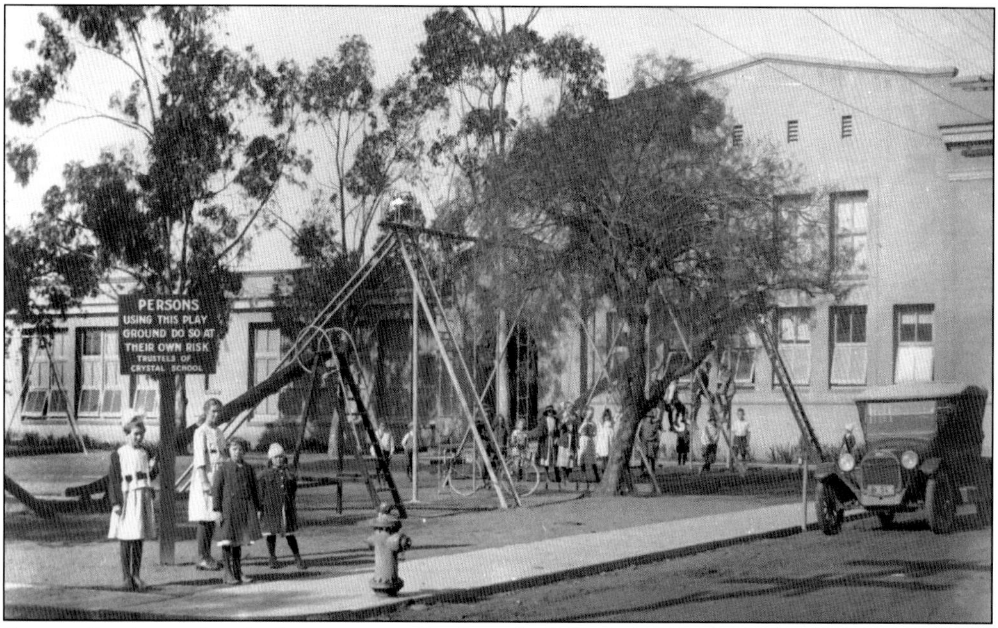

Eventually, the student body outgrew its facility, which had also become outmoded by changing educational methods. Edwin J. Symmes and William H. Crim Jr. were hired to design a new grammar school. In 1916, the Mission Revival–style new school was completed. In addition to the four classrooms, there was a domestic science room, manual training room, teachers' lounge, principal's office, and neighborhood club hall, which doubled as an extra classroom. (VHC.)

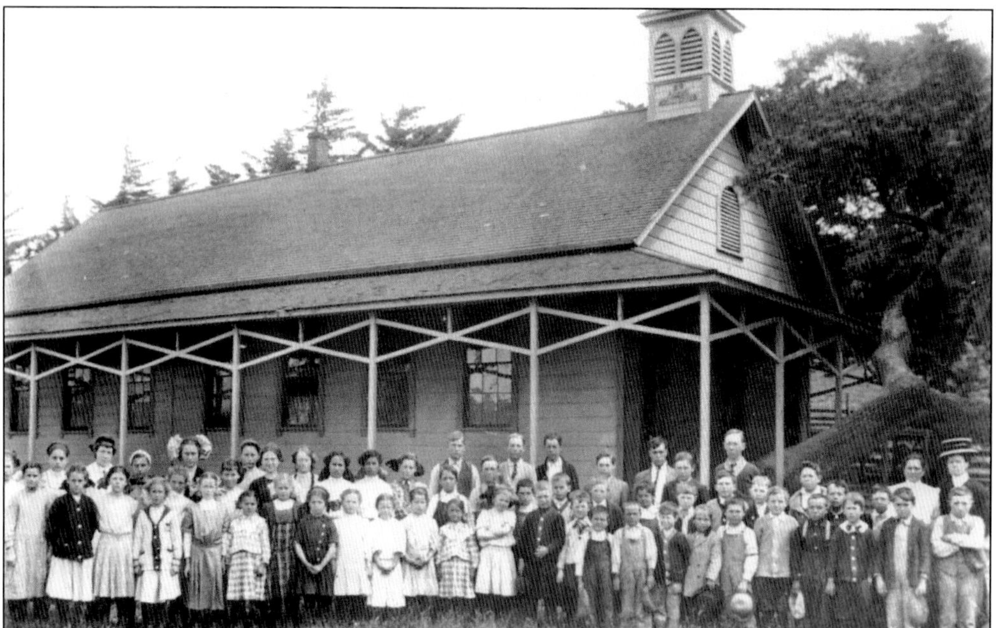

Here are students of Green Valley School around 1907. Green Valley School District was established in 1854. This school was built in 1883 and commenced use in August of that year. Ella Forse, the woman in the hat on the far right, taught grades one through four there nearly 40 years. Also pictured is Mary B. Hardin, who taught grades five through eight. (SCHS.)

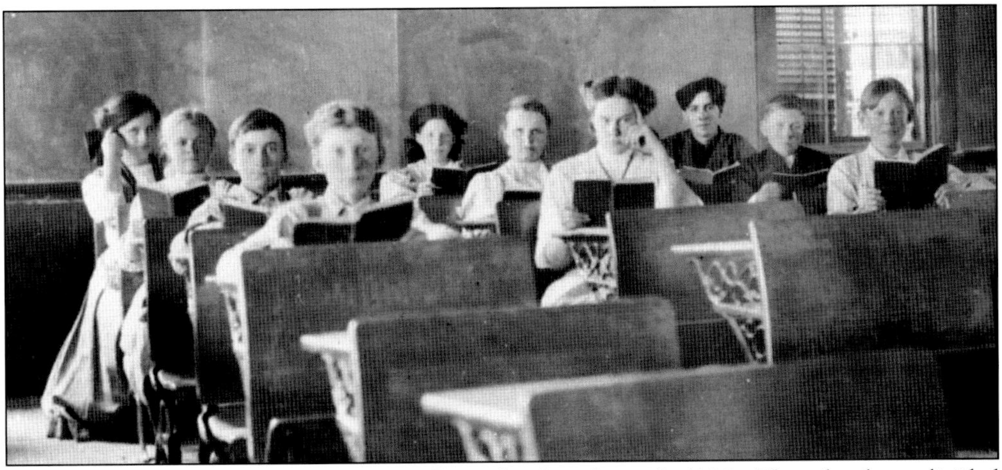

Pictured here is the interior of Green Valley School in the early 1900s. The school was divided into two rooms. Grades one through four were taught in one room, and grades five through eight were taught in the other. The girl on the far left is Hazel McNaughton, who became Cordelia's postmistress at age 17. Her mother managed the Moile Hotel, across from the Cordelia Hotel. Samuel H.P. Martin is third from the left. Clarence Glashoff is sitting in front of Martin. (SCHS.)

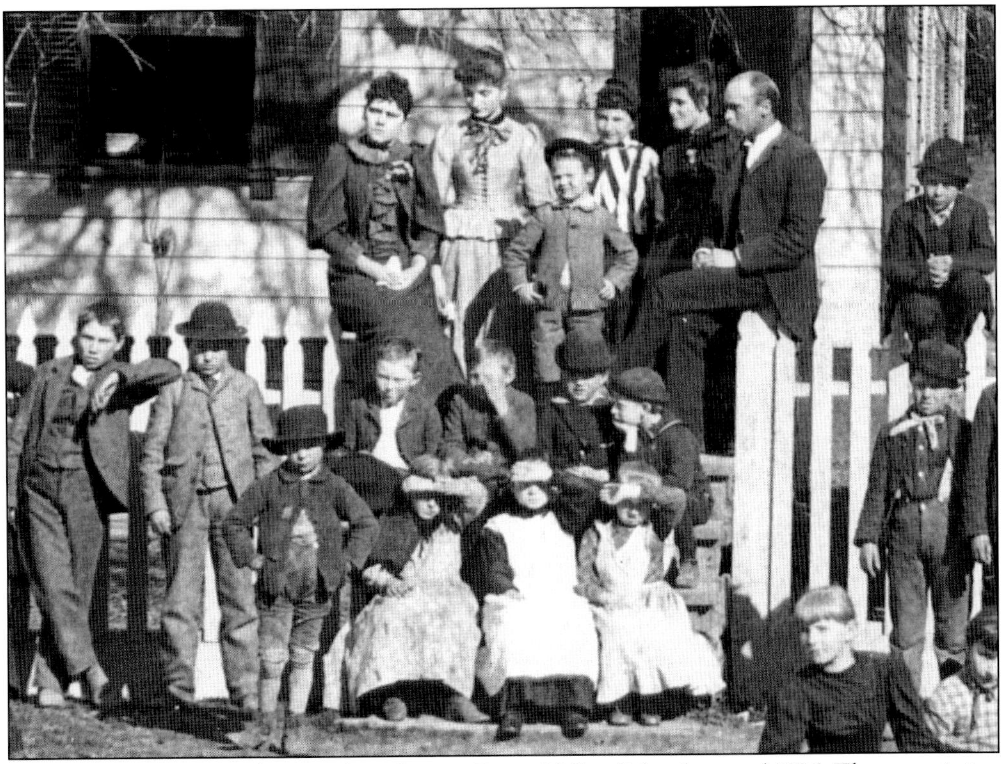

This close-up shows students and teachers at Green Valley School around 1896. The man sitting on the railing is Dan H. White. White was teacher and later principal at Green Valley School from 1889 to 1898. Born in Petaluma, White was also editor of the *Cordelia Star* and *X-Ray*, Cordelia's local papers. His wife, teacher Sara E. Higgins, is wearing a black-and-white striped dress in the center of this photograph. White ran for and won the office of Solano County superintendent of schools, serving from 1898 and continually reelected until retiring in 1938. (VHC.)

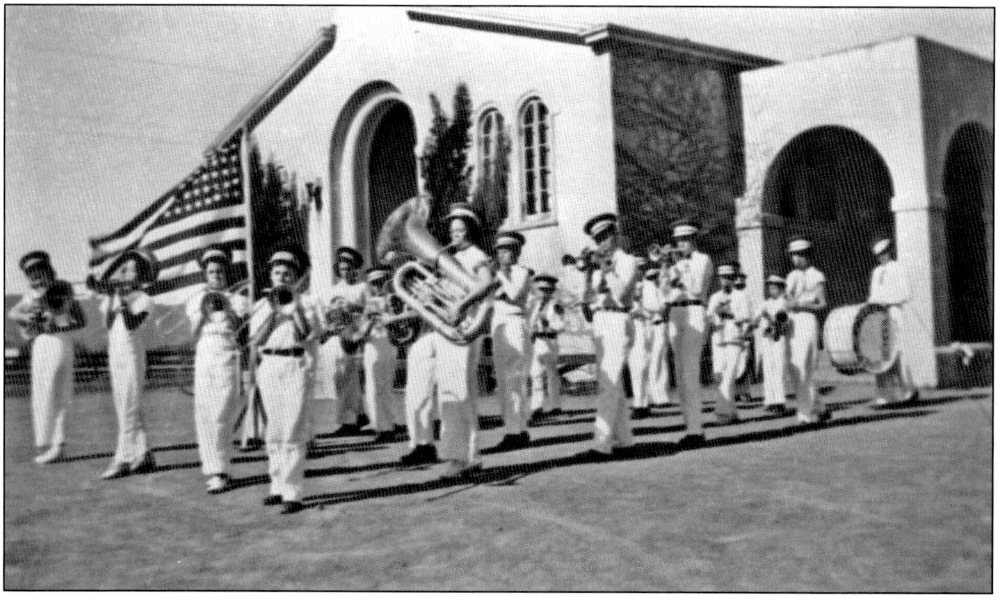

The Green Valley marching band is pictured in front of the school. This structure was built to the west of the original schoolhouse in 1926. Here, it is pictured before the many additions built over the years to accommodate Cordelia and Green Valley's growing population. (VHC.)

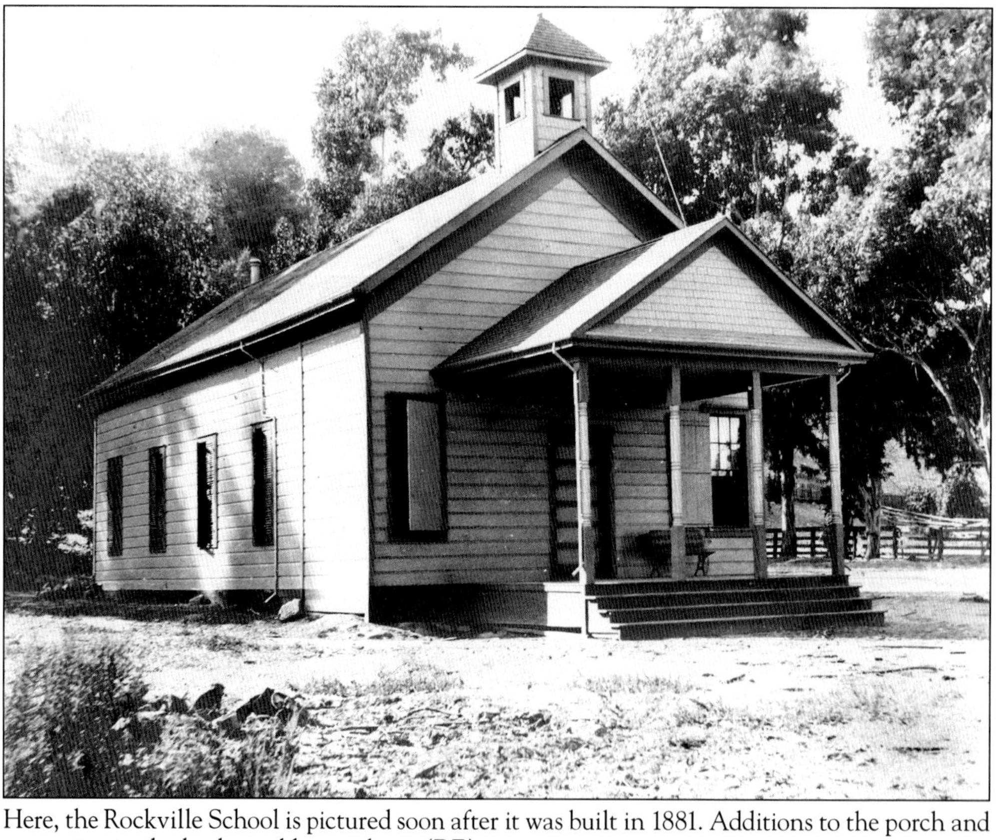

Here, the Rockville School is pictured soon after it was built in 1881. Additions to the porch and expansion in the back would come later. (DF.)

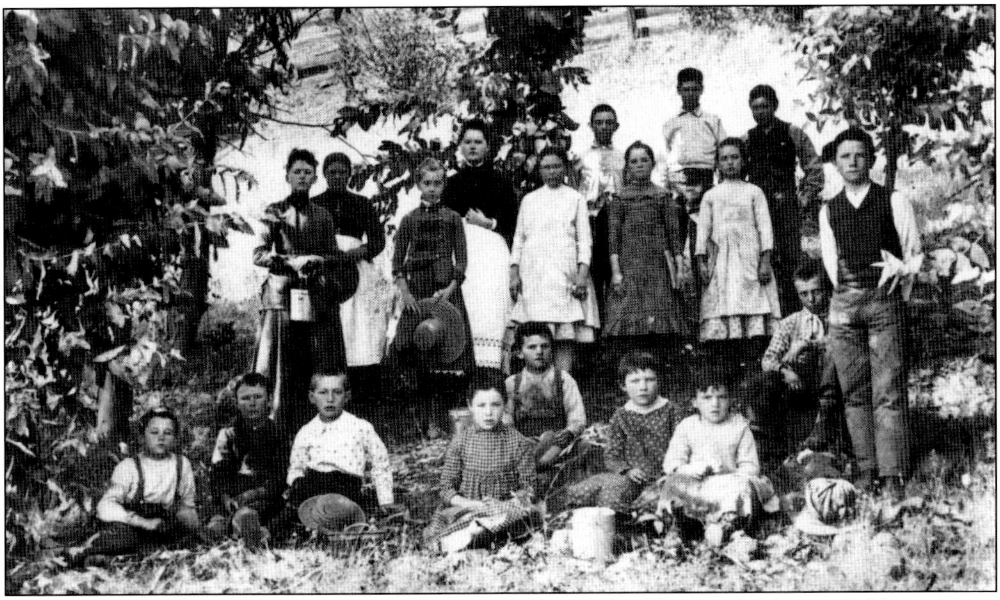

The 1889 students of Rockville School are, from left to right, (first row) Johnnie Baldwin, James M. Davisson, Walter H. Rich, Minnie McDonald, Charley Eberle, Marjorie "Margie" Davisson, and Nettie Eberle; (second row) Carrie "Dollie" Baldwin, Julia Belle Pangburn, Eula Sarah Rich, Bertha E. Baldwin (teacher), Maude Pangburn, Mabel McDonald, Mary Eberle, Frank Neat (the minister's son), and Eddie Gardner; (third row) Fred McDonald, Will Marvin Bronson, and Jack McDonald. This photograph was taken on school grounds. (VHC.)

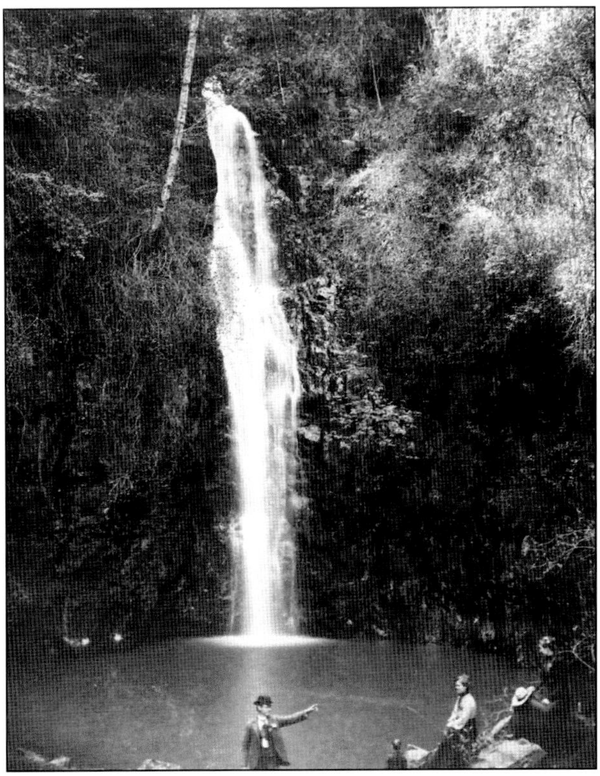

One of the most beautiful views in the state and said to rival Bridalveil Falls at Yosemite, Green Valley Falls was a popular recreational destination for city and valley alike. In the spring, when the lilies and irises were in bloom and the ferns were lush, the passing of each school year was regularly marked with large class picnics attended by all of the local schools. Closed to the public after World War II, the falls now serve as a watershed for the city of Vallejo. (VHC.)

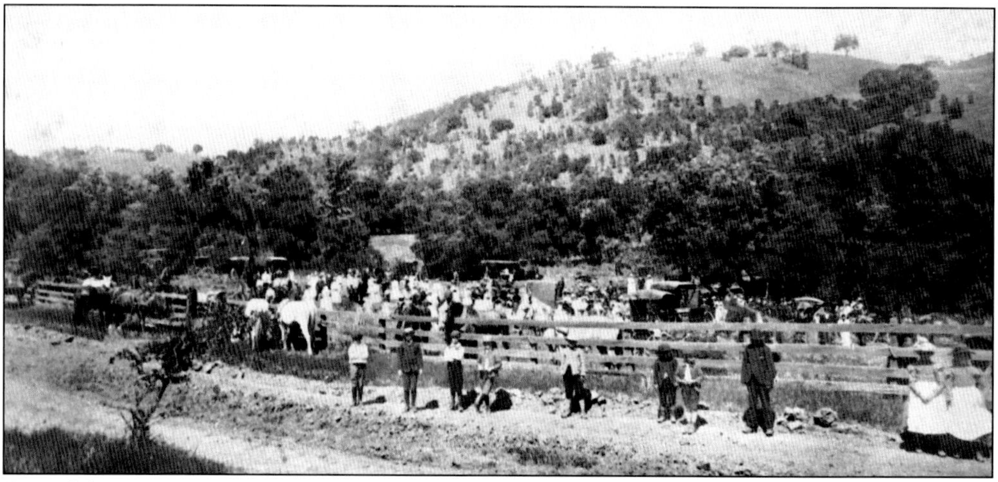

One of the most anticipated days in the school year was the school picnic held every year. Students and their families would pack up lunches and amusements and proceed to a chosen spot. Teachers considered it important socialization. In this photograph, a picnic is being enjoyed off Rockville Road between Green Valley and Rockville Corners. (VHC.)

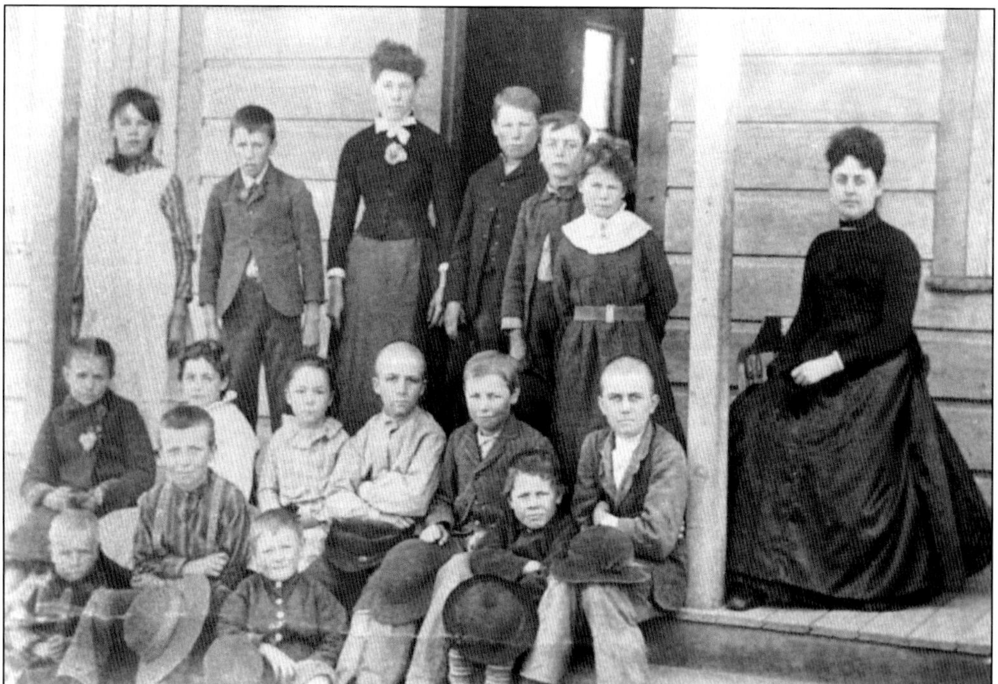

Students of the old Gomer School are, from left to right, (first row) Maynard O. Bailard, Ed Gardner, Winfield S. Bailard, and Delbert H. Bailard; (second row) Ella Mae "Grace" Sheldon, Nell A. Davisson, Harriet "Hattie" Sheldon, Harry Sheldon, Gilbert Bailard, and Winfred C. Sheldon; (third row) Mae Dellita Davisson, Charles C. Bailard, Emma Bailard, Frank Bailard, John R. Davisson Jr., Sadie May Bailard, and teacher Luella Gillespie. This original structure had been built in 1857 as a church. It was named for William Gomer, who, with his wife Jane, had settled the land surrounding the schoolhouse and who had provided the parcel on which the school was relocated. (VHC.)

After a vote on April 28, 1900, Gomer School, or Suisun No. 2, was built later that year to replace the schoolhouse that had burned earlier in 1900. In an early county superintendent of education's annual report, the original school was deemed "a disgrace to the state." In this photograph, Mary Bauman is the teacher, second from the right in the back. Her father-in-law, Jacob H. Bauman, owned the old Gomer property surrounding the school. (SCHS.)

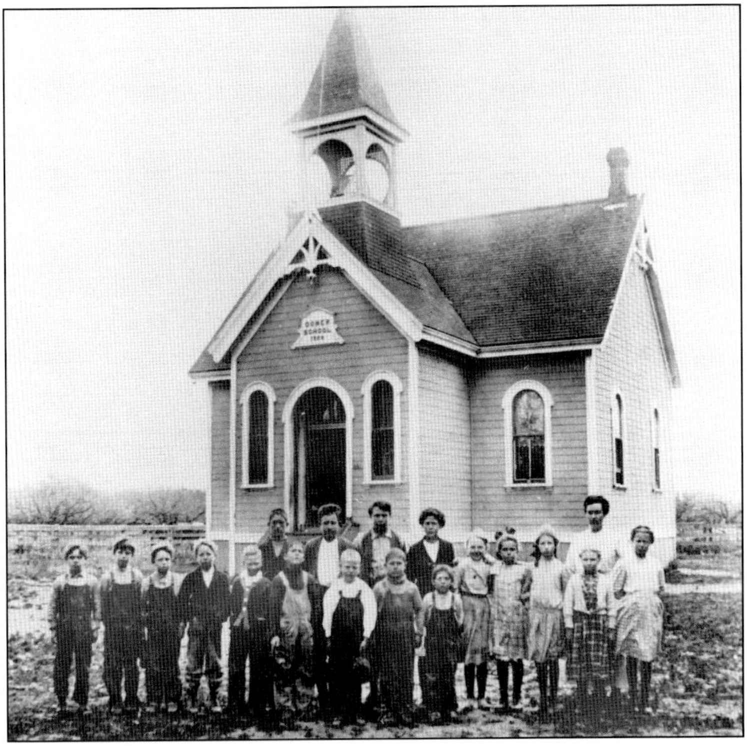

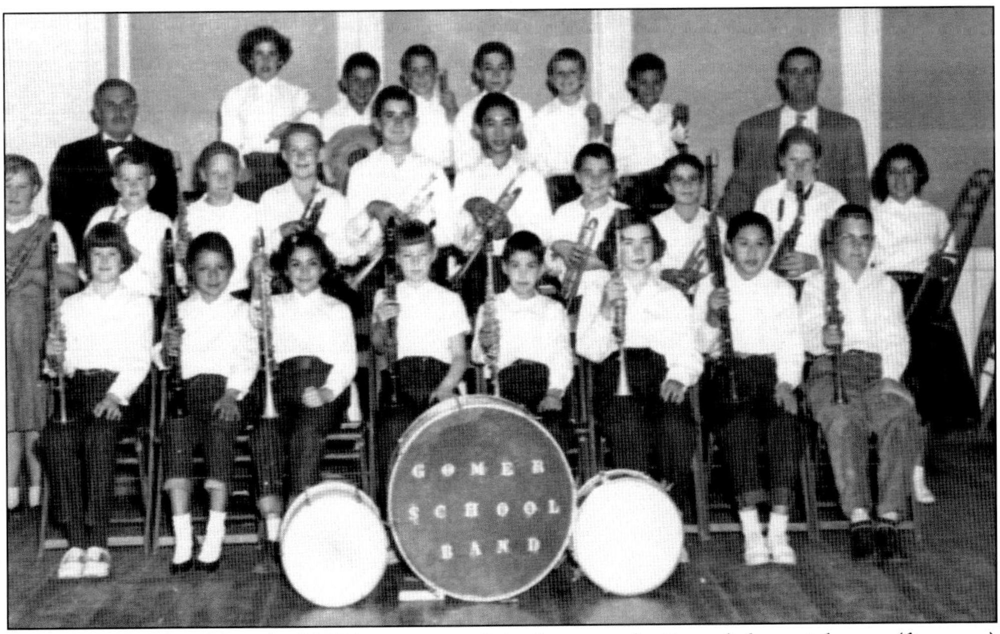

The Gomer School band of 1956 is seen in this photograph. From left to right are (first row) Susan ?, Toni Rodriguez, Mary Solorzano, Darlene ?, Ronald Darville, Carole Lewis, Elsie Low, and Randall Allen; (second row) Annita Torrence, Robert Johnson, Larry Sumner, James Shephard, Jim Tipton, Robert Low, Robert Moy, Bernard Tornay, Gary Sumner, and Louise Rodriguez; (third row) music teacher George F. Neill, Kay Binstock, Vernon ?, David Bowland, Joe Solorzano, Tim Tipton, Lonnie ?, and unidentified. (VHC.)

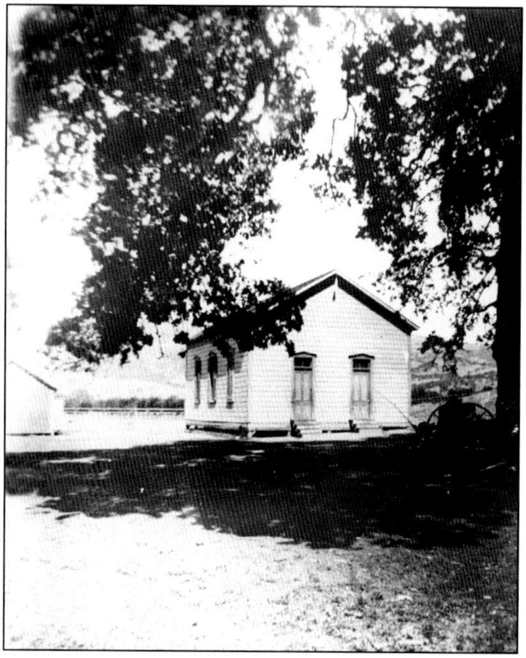

Suisun Valley School was built in the 1880s to serve children from the Upper Suisun Valley. The first school in the area was at John W. Barton's store at Manka's Corner and was taught by Barton's daughter, Isabella. Classes began in his storeroom but eventually were taught in a later structure at Manka's Corner shared with the Masonic lodge. The school's identification with Barton ended when he sold out to Christley Manka and the Barton family moved to Fairfield in 1859. These series of schools were known as Suisun District No. 1. (VHC.)

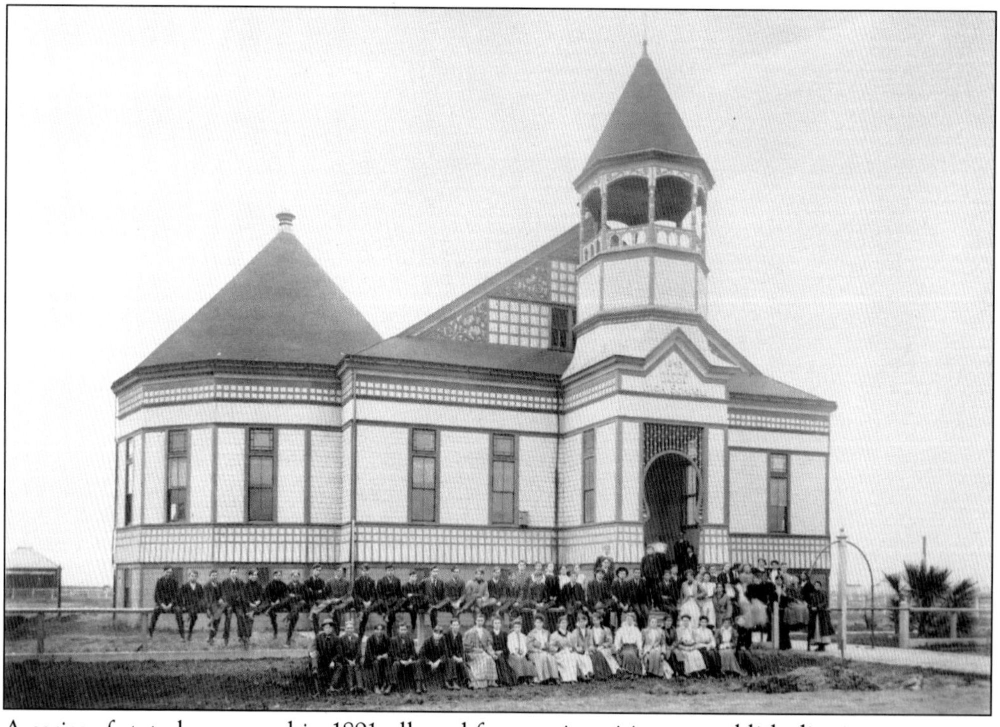

A series of state laws passed in 1891 allowed for growing cities to establish districts to support high schools. To replace an earlier one-room schoolhouse, construction of the Armijo Union High School, pictured here, commenced in 1893. Armijo Union High School was attended by students who had completed their primary education throughout Green Valley, Fairfield, and Suisun City and Valley. This structure was replaced in 1914 by a new Armijo High School, and this Queen Anne–style structure was demolished. (SCHS.)

Nine

Outdoor Pursuits

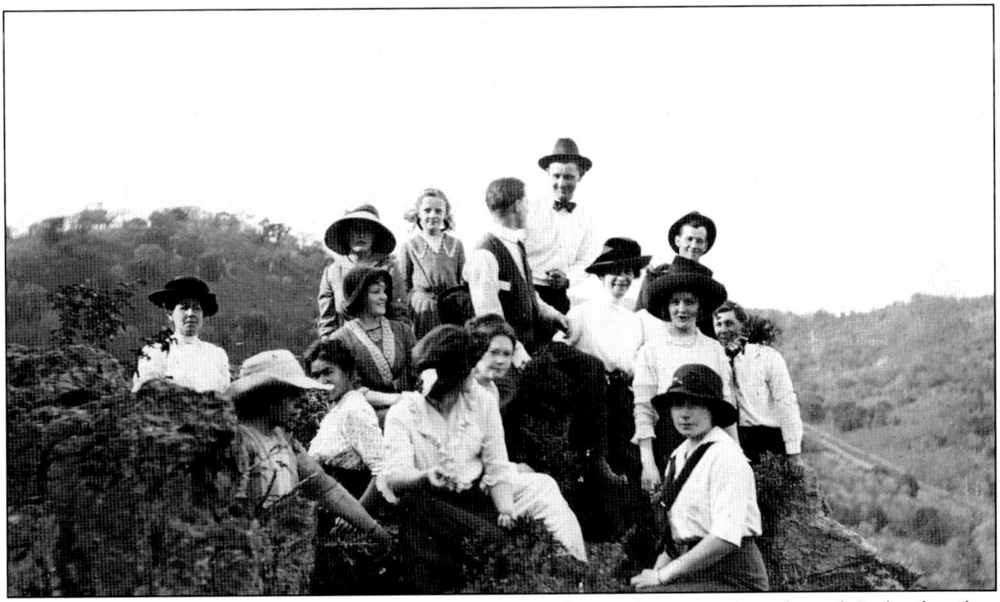

In this photograph from the early 1910s, members of the Morrison, Vogel, and Siebe families and guests enjoy the view from a peak overlooking Suisun Valley. It is in an area now known as Rockville Park, which to this day entices visitors with its lofty vistas, ancient woodlands, and verdant meadows. (DF.)

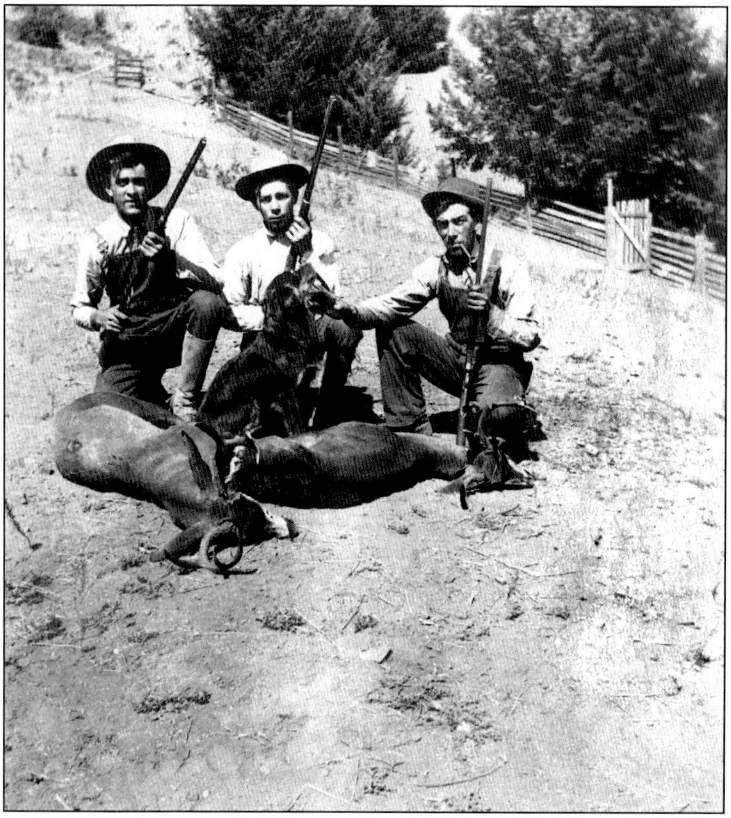

Game was abundant throughout the marshes and hills of Suisun. Hunters had their pick of rabbit, deer, elk, and even bear. Here, Harry Siebe (center) and his companions have bagged two deer. (DF.)

The grass and woodlands of the Suisun Valley offered ample points of interest for, from left to right, cousins Willie Griffiths, Ellard Williams, and Carmen Williams to explore. (DGS.)

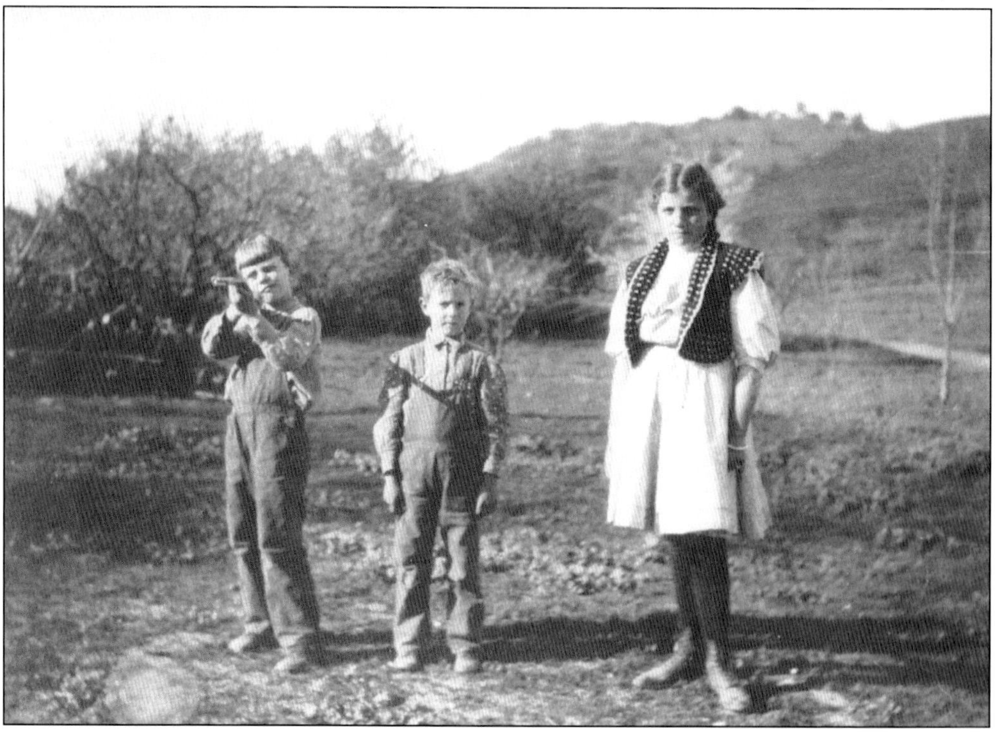

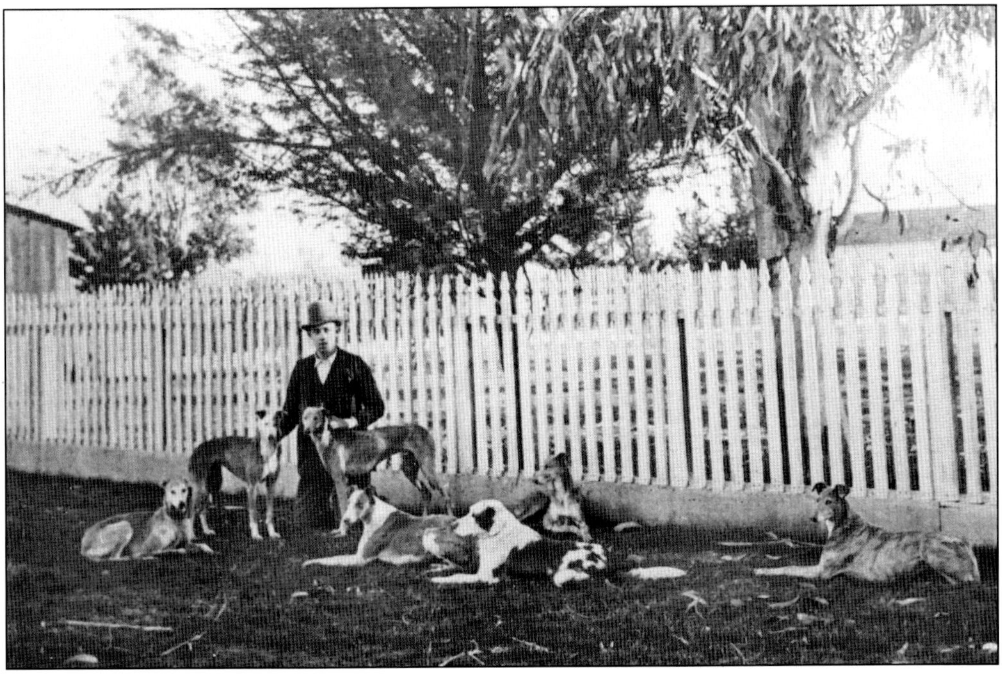

Located on the edge of the marsh at Cordelia, the California Kennels were nationally renowned breeders of award-winning hunting dogs. Successful hunting depended on the well-trained dogs, as seen in these photographs from the 1890s. California Kennels supplied hundreds of dogs to gun clubs and individual hunters throughout the Western United States. (Both, VHC.)

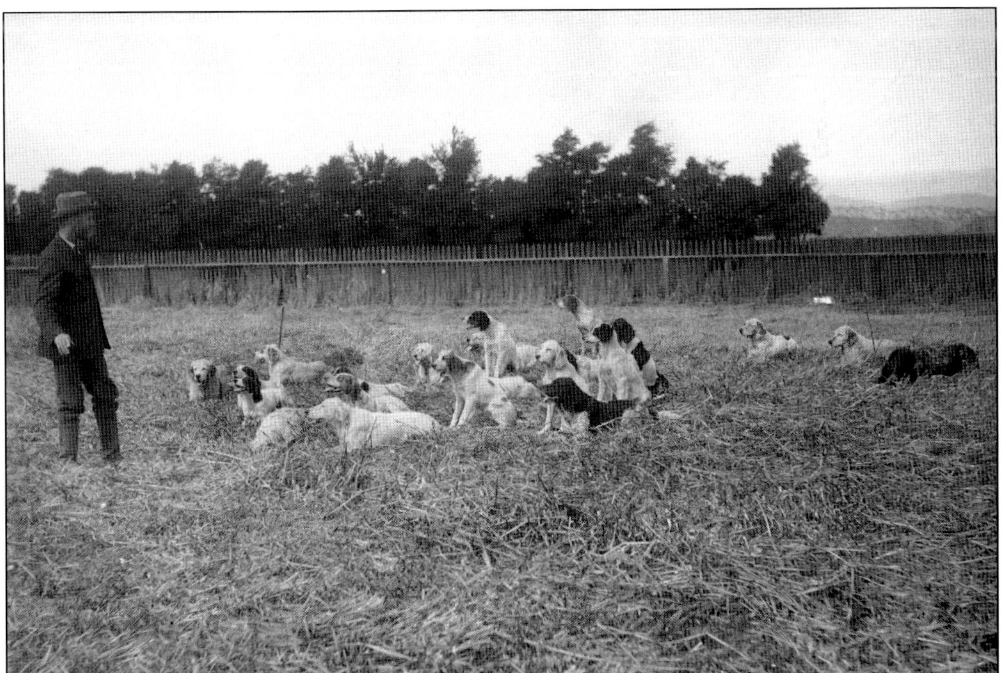

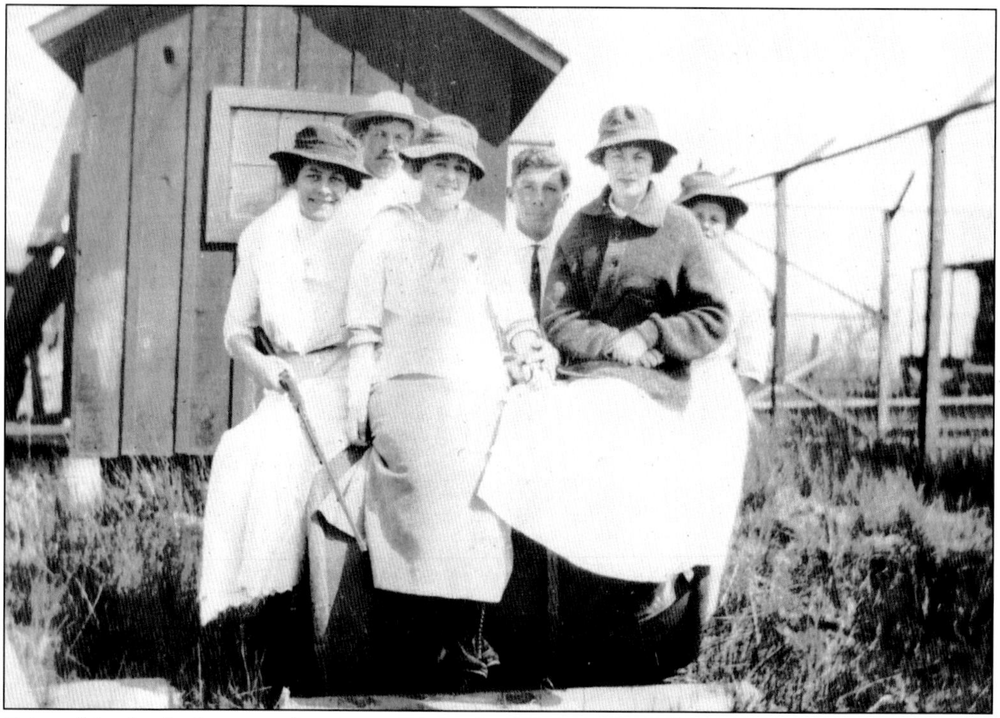

Suisun Marsh, the largest saltwater marsh in the Western United States, is a crucial stop on the Pacific Flyway for millions of migratory birds. The earliest hunters in the area were market hunters who culled massive amounts of fowl on an industrial scale to supply markets in San Francisco. By the late 1870s, they had been supplanted by sportsmen. So popular was the sport that the Central Pacific Railroad established four special stops in Suisun Marsh, called Goodyear, Cygnus, Teal, and Jacksnipe, between Cordelia and Benicia to transport sportsmen from all over California. (DF.)

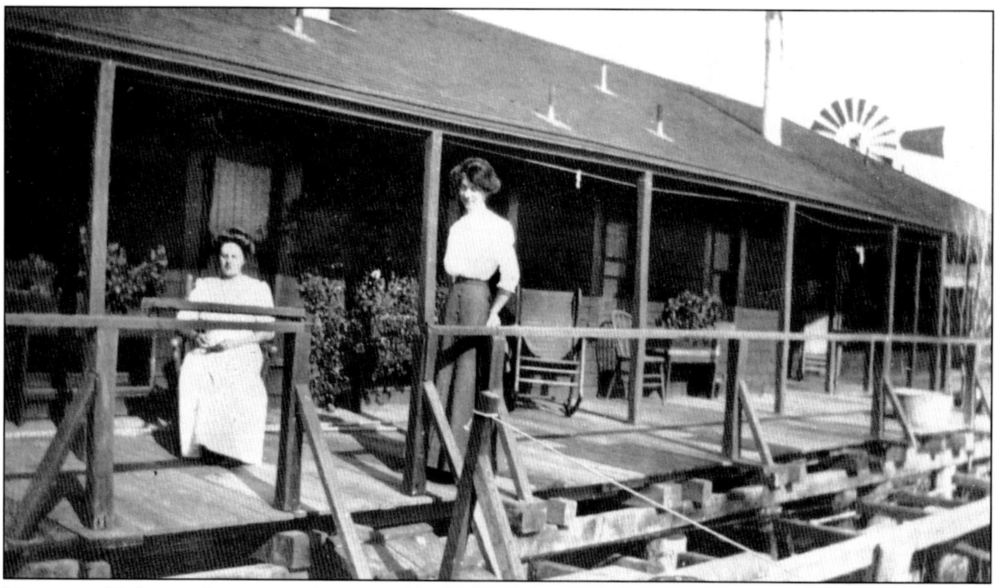

Margaret Siebe, right, is standing on the deck of the Family Gun Club at Pierce Harbor. Her cousin Fred Siebe was the club gamekeeper for 10 years. (DF.)

Suisun Marsh is critical habitat for the fisheries of the central West Coast. It offers the perfect environment for the countless numbers of fish, such as salmon, bass, sturgeon, and the endangered delta smelt, that sustained native populations in early times and draws novice fishermen today. Peter L. Siebe is holding the catch of the day—a lovely salmon. (DF.)

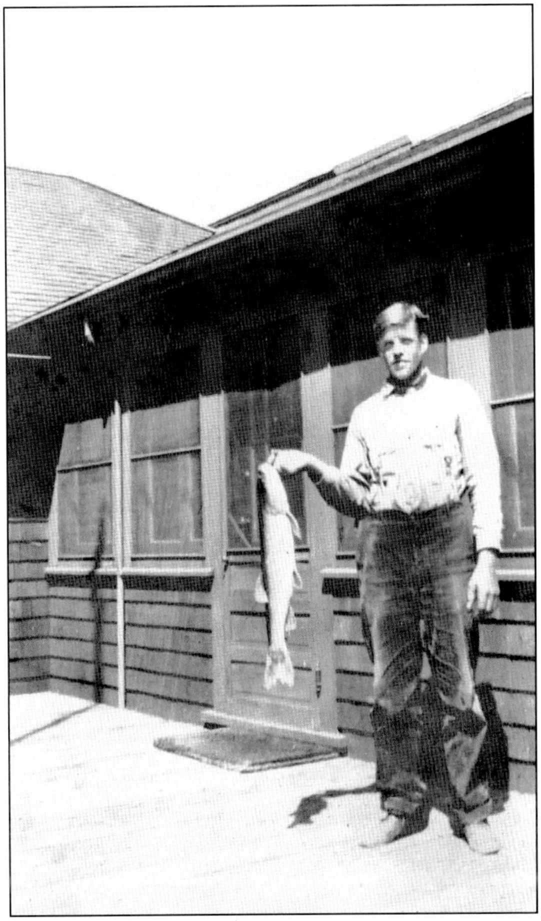

To seek health and relaxation, Suisun families would often travel during the summer to camp or stay at the surrounding natural spring resorts such as Adams, Bartlett, Boyes, and Vichy Springs. (DF.)

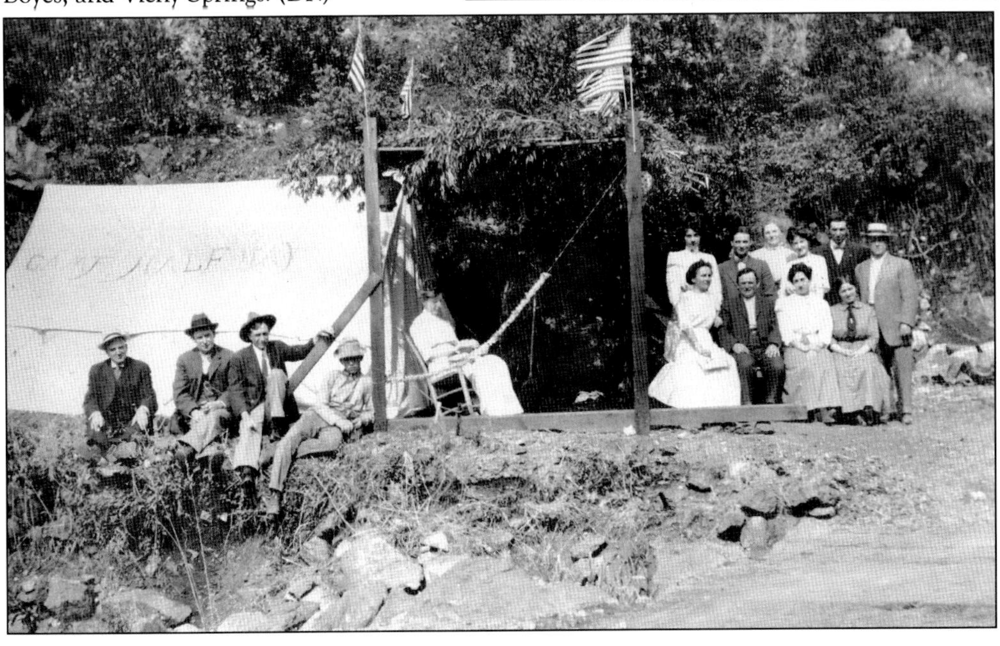

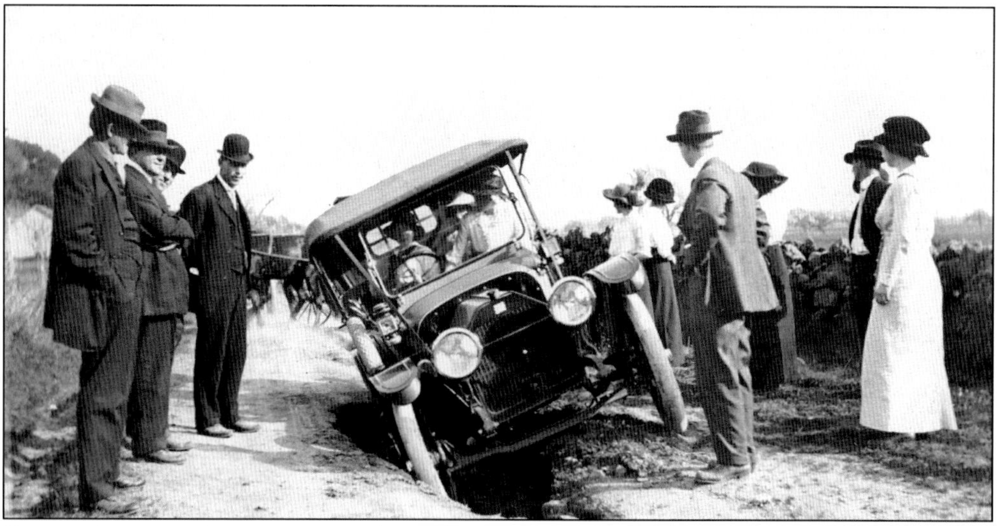

Solano County roads were notoriously rough, but this 1910s Cadillac has hit more than a pothole on Rockville Road. The "country drive" became a fun thing to do as automobiles became popular and accessible. However, earlier automobile drivers had to contend with roads better suited to their four-legged predecessors. Rockville Road followed the earlier stage route that linked Sonoma with Sacramento. Charles Vogel is standing at the far left, and daughter Emma Vogel is sixth from right. (DF.)

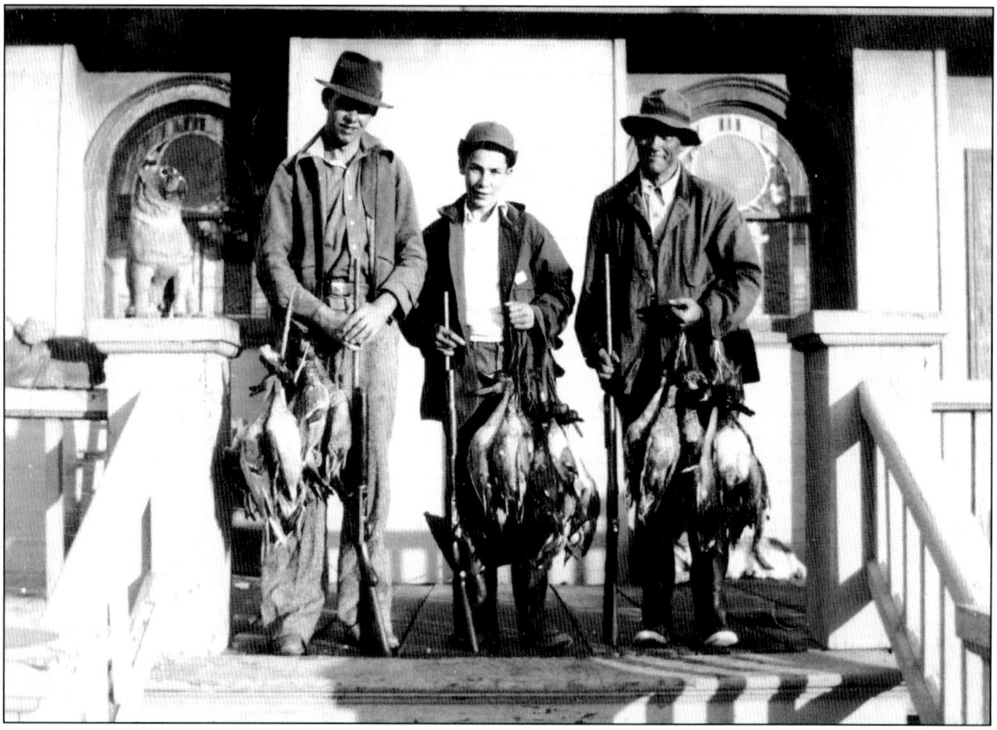

Roos Club was an elite duck-hunting club famed for its stained-glass windows and elegant interior. It was founded by San Francisco clothier Achille Roos and assumed by his nephew Col. Robert A. Roos. From left to right in this photograph are cousins Harold Siebe, Lester Siebe, and Peter L. Siebe, Harold's father and the trusted club manager for Colonel Roos. (DF.)

Ten

A Thriving Community

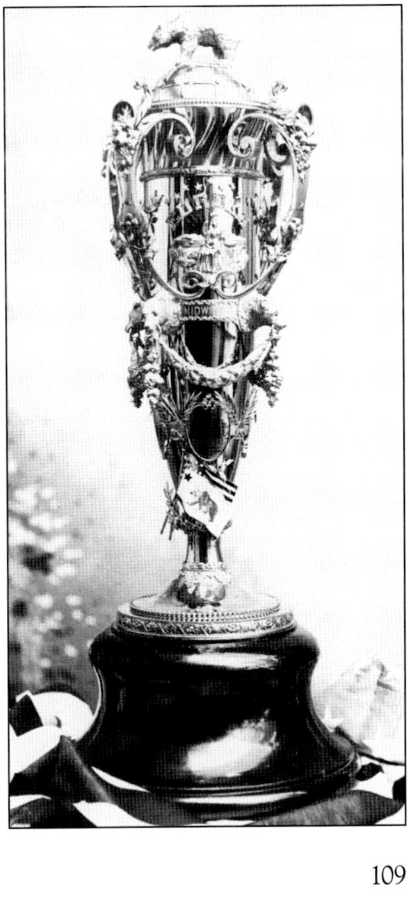

Among Solano County's lost treasures is the 1894 California Midwinter International Exposition Trophy, manufactured by famed Shreve & Co. at a cost of $5,000. The trophy, made of solid gold and encrusted with precious stones, was presented at a grand ceremony to Solano County for its exquisite display of produce at the California Midwinter International Exposition at San Francisco. Bands played, poems were read, and a procession went through town. The trophy was eventually placed on display at the Ferry Building in San Francisco but was stolen in February 1910 and never found again. (SCHS.)

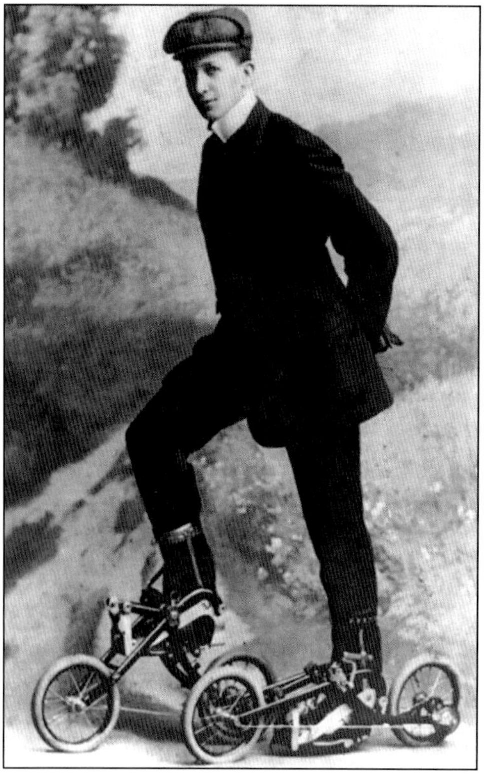

Inventor extraordinaire Charles A. Nordling devised this interesting mode of transportation and patented the invention in 1913. Suisun City would be home to several inventors who made everything from expandable pantaloons to dish-washing machines, sewing needles, and a plethora of farm equipment improvements, but the pedal skate by far was the most unique invention. (Left, courtesy George Grantham Bain Collection, Library of Congress; below, courtesy US Patent and Trademark Office.)

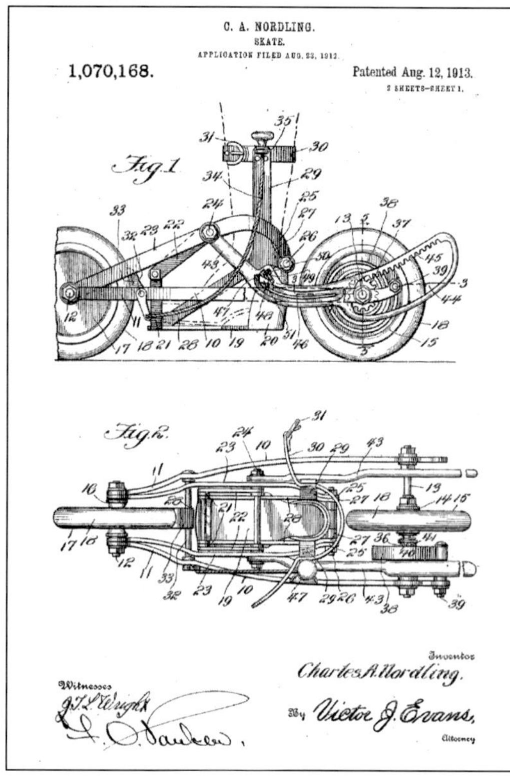

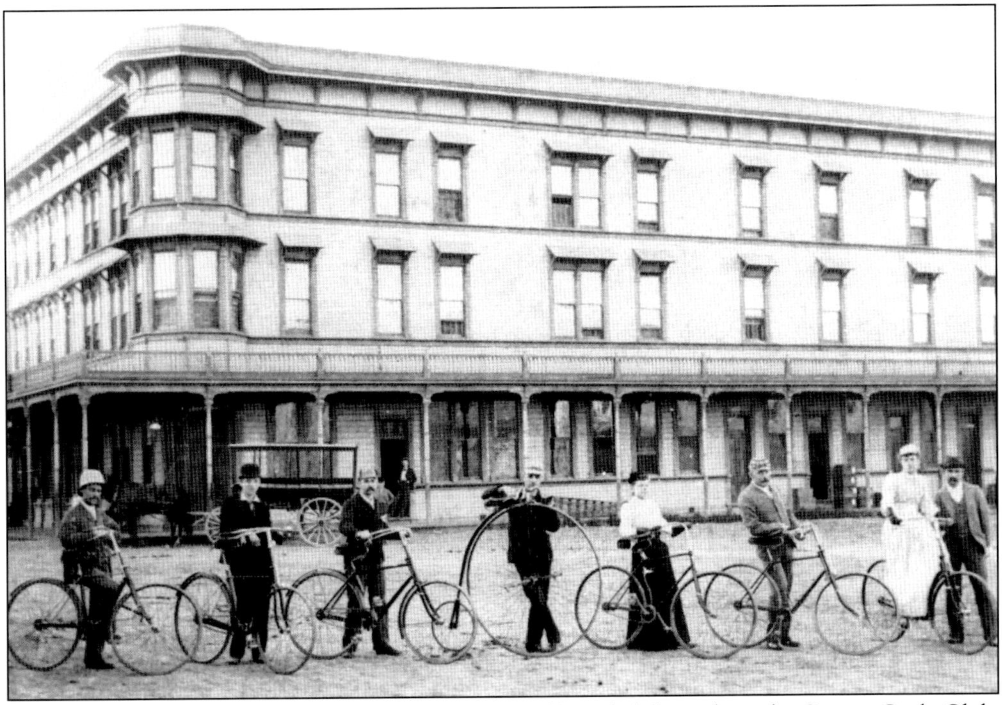

The affluence that came from a thriving economy allowed clubs such as the Suisun Cycle Club, pictured here around 1880, to prosper. A bicycle at the time was extremely expensive at an average cost of $150 ($3,400 in 2012). The fellow at the far left wearing a topee is druggist Edgar Reed Whitby. The second couple from the right is William and Georgia Bryan, owners of the Arlington Hotel, seen in the background. (VHC.)

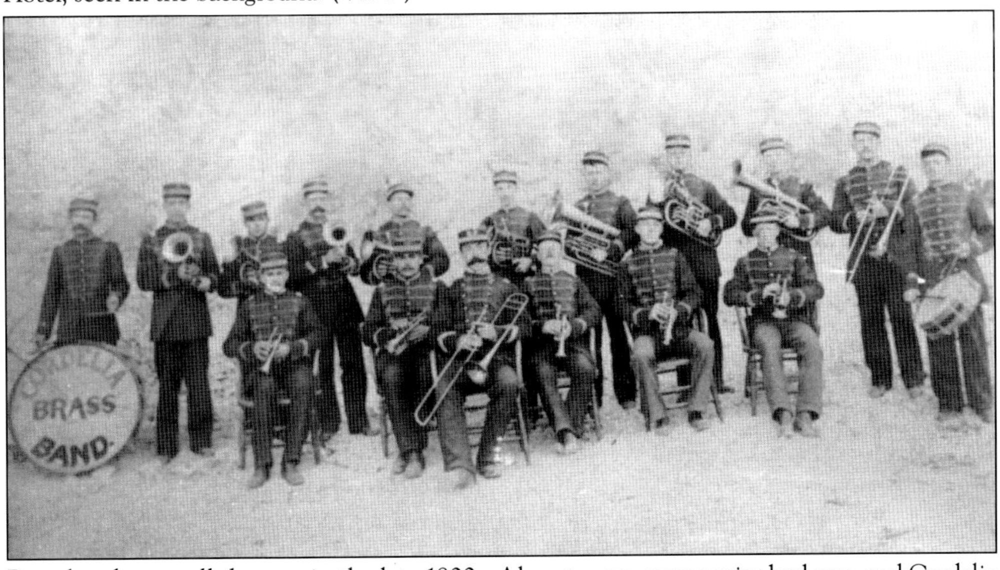

Brass bands were all the rage in the late 1800s. Almost every community had one, and Cordelia was no exception. The Cordelia Brass Band members are, from left to right, (first row) two unidentified, bandleader Julius Glashoff, Chris Dunker, Henry Meyer, and unidentified; (second row) Billy Capell, three unidentified, Larry Higinson, two unidentified, Curtis Siebe, Henry Siebe, Peter Siebe Jr., and Frenchie Collins (snare drum). (VHC.)

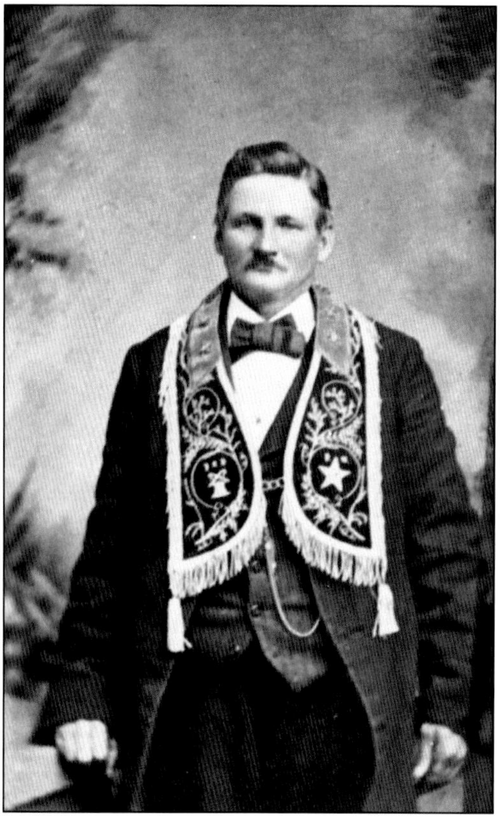

The International Order of Odd Fellows (IOOF) Suisun Lodge No. 78, a fraternal mutual aid organization dedicated to helping those in need, was organized in Suisun on September 13, 1858. Among the prominent members of the lodge was Garret Henry Pangburn, seen here in his IOOF ceremonial collar. The 1872 Suisun IOOF Building, which still stands today, was one of the few buildings spared from the devastating fire of 1888—when the flames were quelled with bottles of beer. (VHC.)

Chartered as Lodge No. 55, Free and Accepted Masons, Suisun's Masons first met at the Armijo Adobe in 1855. Later that same year, they built a lodge shared with the local school district at what is today Manka's Corner. In 1856, they secured a deal with Hiram Rush to add a third floor for the lodge's exclusive use to a commercial building he was constructing in Suisun City, provided they cover its cost. The 1888 fire interrupted construction of a subsequent hall. The Masons continued building with salvaged brick, and the Masonic Hall in this photograph still stands today. (VHC.)

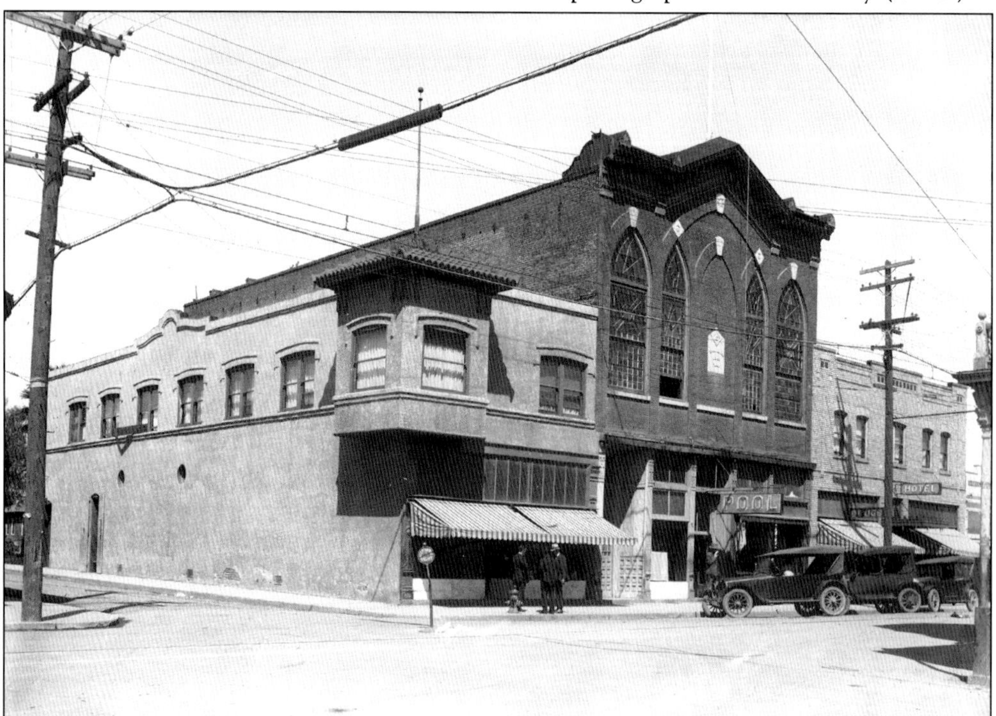

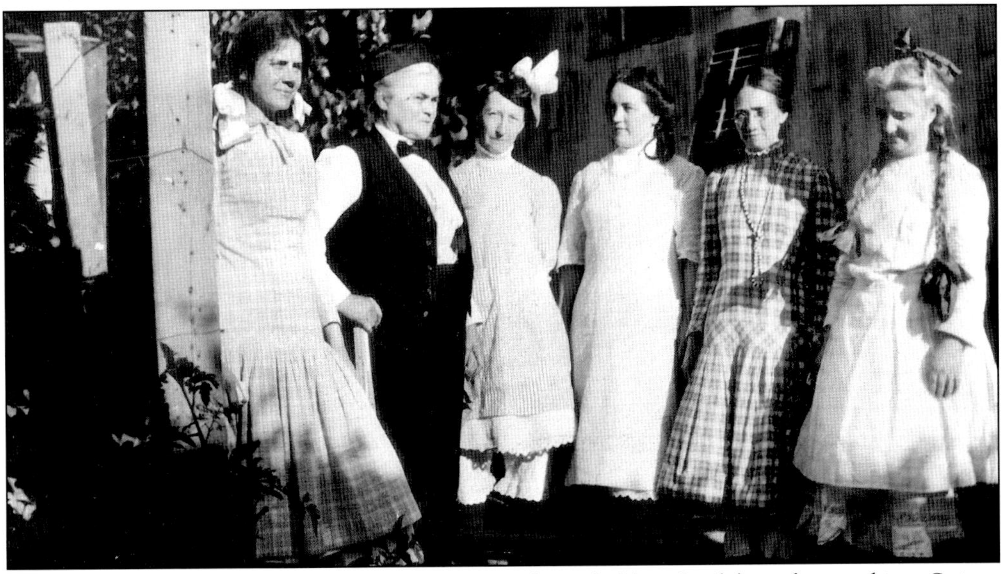

These "youthful" ladies may be on their way to a dance held at Cordelia referenced in a Suisun Valley letter written in 1901. The guests attending the dance had to dress as schoolchildren. Themed parties, dances, pageants, and clubs were always popular amusements. (DGS.)

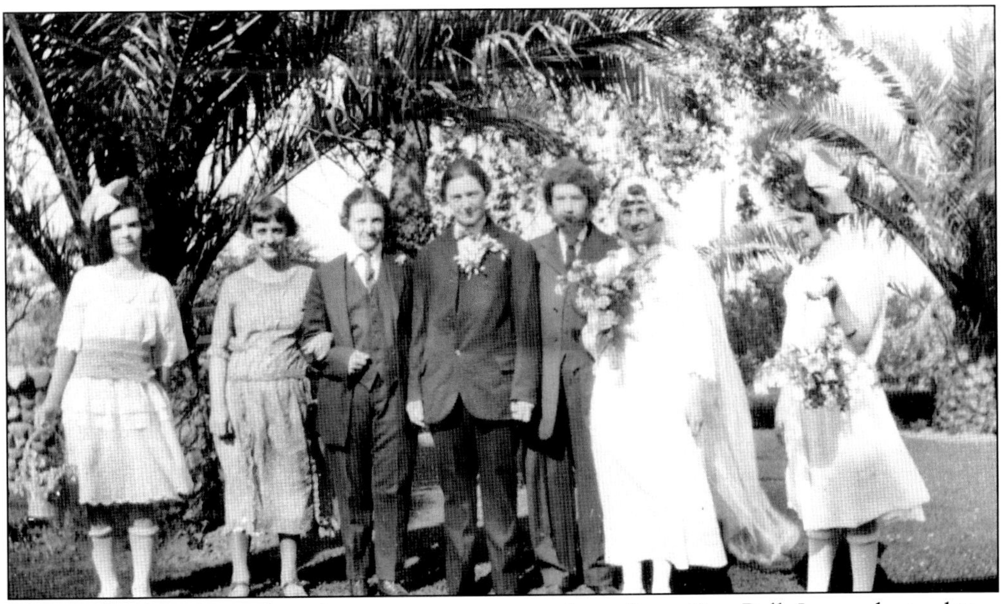

He must have said yes when the question was popped at a Leap Year Ball. It was the tradition to hold fanciful balls for leap year, where a lady could do the asking for her intended's hand in marriage. If by chance the answer had been no when the lady asked the sir to marry her, then he would have owed her a kiss and a silk dress. In this case, "bride" John Schmidt (second from right) and "groom" Elizabeth Schmidt (center) were married in real life on November 4, 1911. (DF.)

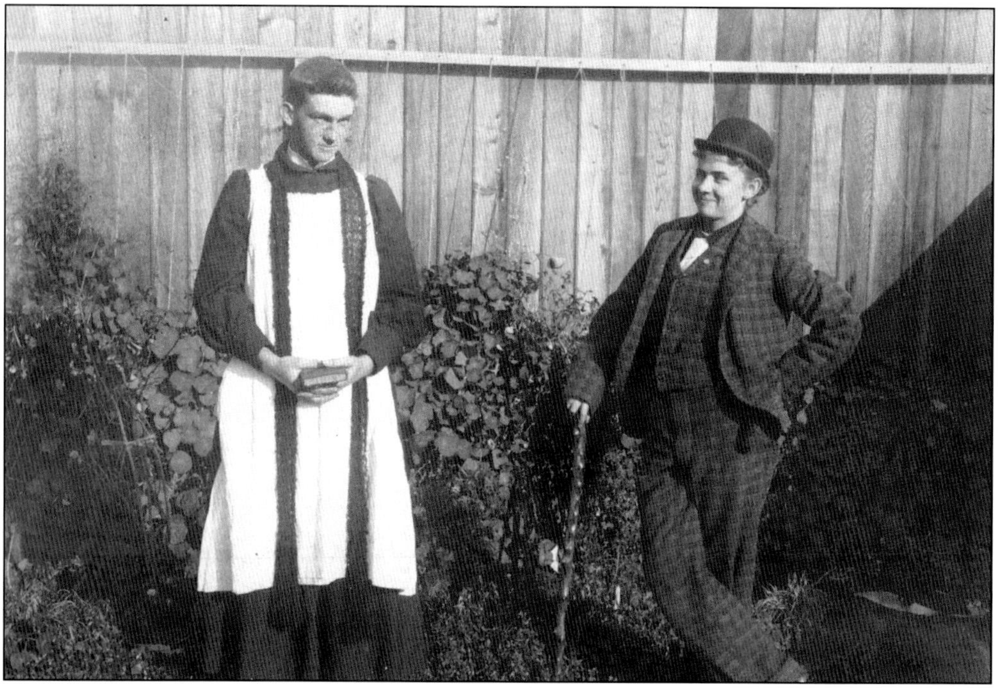

Reminiscent of a popular vaudeville act of the day, siblings Robert Francis Williams (left) and Mary Winifred Williams (right) are sporting quite a look. (DGS.)

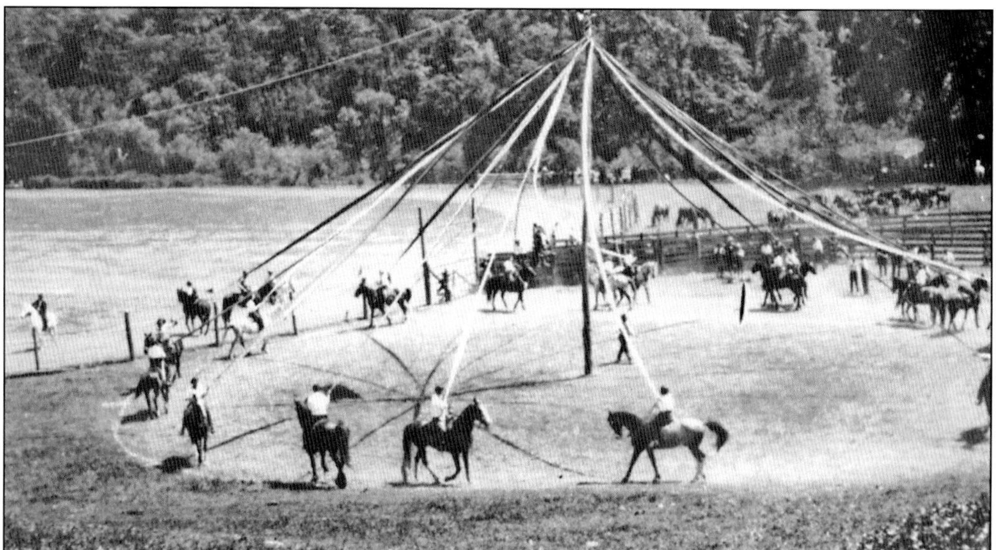

During the early 1920s, the Scally brothers would hold an annual rodeo complete with May Pole. The winding of the May Pole included 20 girls, foregoing the customary side saddles for standard saddles and riding in a choreographed and perfectly synchronized performance. A truly popular event, the rodeo was attended by as many as 2,000 people. (VHC.)

Taken in 1914, these fine young Suisun "gentlemen" are, from left to right, Mildred Wilson, Helen LaShelle, Lucille Lenahan, and Clare Newman. Clare, who later married Ray McFall (bookkeeper for the Pierce Ranch), was a founding member of the Wednesday Club and became the first woman mayor of Suisun City. (VHC.)

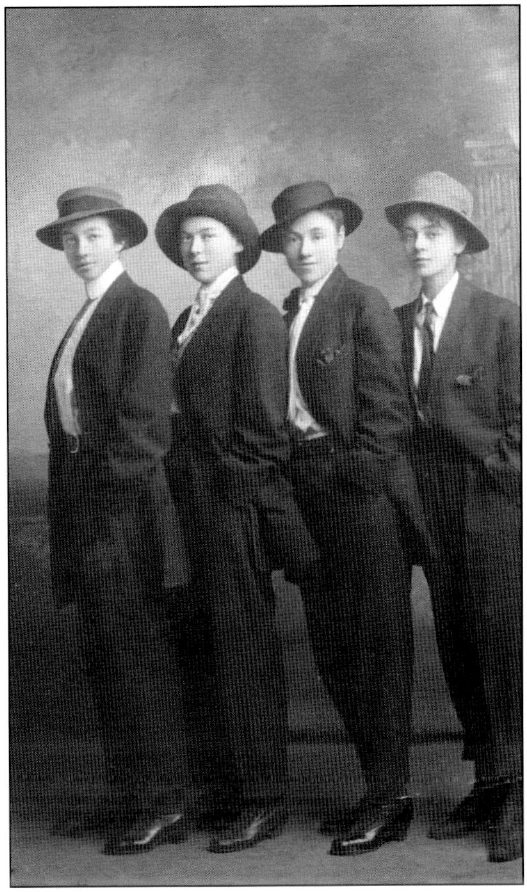

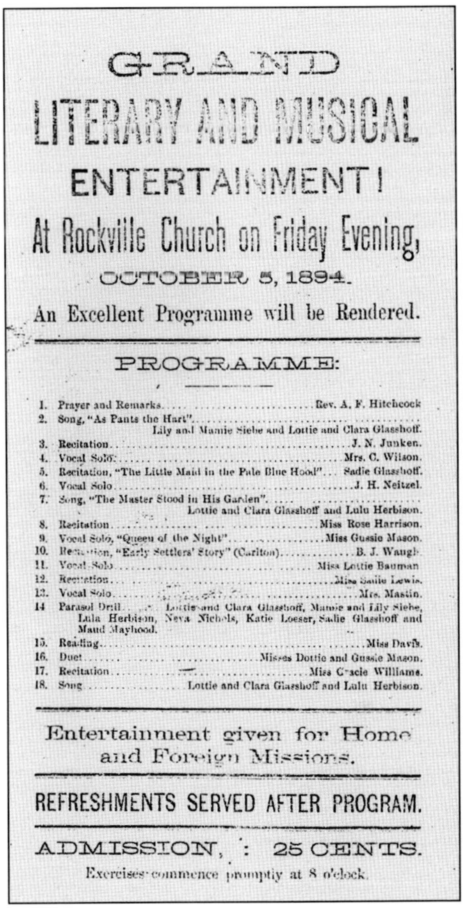

GRAND

LITERARY AND MUSICAL

ENTERTAINMENT!

At Rockville Church on Friday Evening,

OCTOBER 5, 1894.

An Excellent Programme will be Rendered.

PROGRAMME:

1. Prayer and Remarks.......Rev. A. F. Hitchcock
2. Song, "As Pants the Hart".......Lily and Mamie Siebe and Lottie and Clara Glasshoff.
3. Recitation.......J. N. Junken.
4. Vocal Solo.......Mrs. C. Wilson.
5. Recitation, "The Little Maid in the Pale Blue Hood"... Sadie Glasshoff.
6. Vocal Solo.......J. H. Neitzel.
7. Song, "The Master Stood in His Garden".......Lottie and Clara Glasshoff and Lulu Herbison.
8. Recitation.......Miss Rose Harrison.
9. Vocal Solo, "Queen of the Night".......Miss Gussie Mason.
10. Recitation, "Early Settlers' Story" (Carlton).......B. J. Waugh.
11. Vocal Solo.......Miss Lottie Bauman
12. Recitation.......Miss Sallie Lewis.
13. Vocal Solo.......Mrs. Mastin.
14. Parasol Drill....... Lottie and Clara Glasshoff, Mamie and Lily Siebe, Lula Herbison, Neva Nichols, Katie Loeser, Sadie Glasshoff and Maud Mayhood.
15. Reading.......Miss Davis.
16. Duet.......Misses Dottie and Gussie Mason.
17. Recitation.......Miss Gracie Williams.
18. Song.......Lottie and Clara Glasshoff and Lulu Herbison.

Entertainment given for Home and Foreign Missions.

REFRESHMENTS SERVED AFTER PROGRAM.

ADMISSION, : 25 CENTS.

Exercises commence promptly at 8 o'clock.

"Grand literary and musical entertainment!" Local churches often hosted literary and musical evenings as fundraisers for special projects. This evening's entertainment hosted a veritable who's who of young local talent. (VHC.)

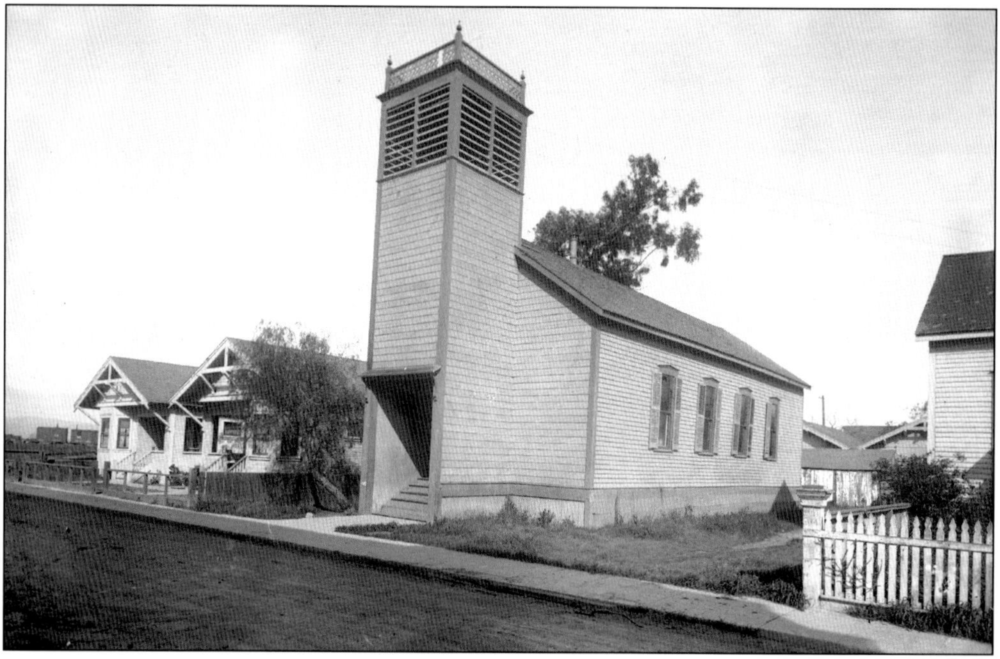

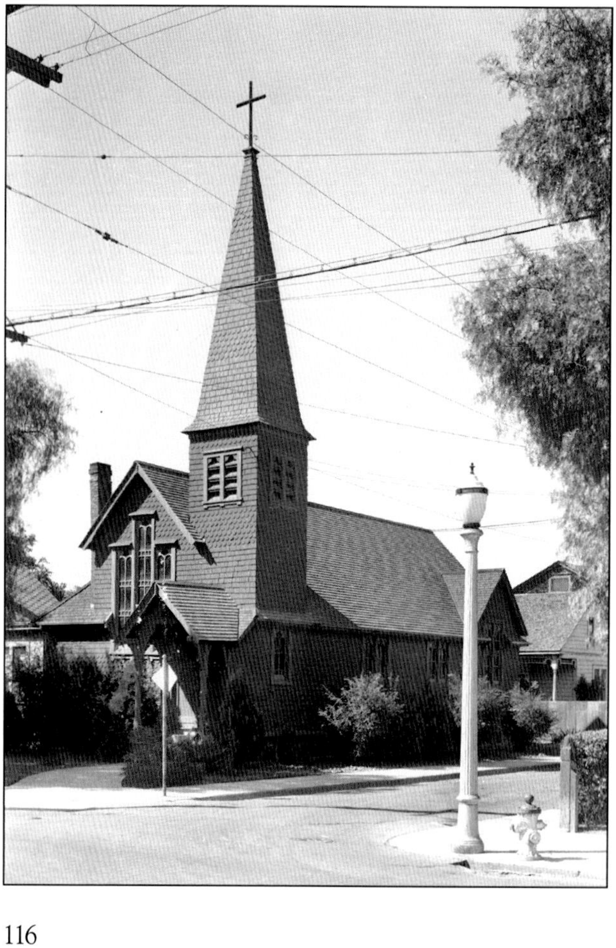

Pictured here is the very first church established in Suisun City, which was built in 1857 by "Old School Presbyterians." In 1861, the building was sold, and it became the Methodist house of worship. Soon thereafter, the Methodists shared their worship space with a small Episcopalian congregation. (VHC.)

The Episcopal congregation flourished, and by 1872, the newly incorporated Parish of Grace Episcopal Church purchased the building outright from the Methodists. Attendance continued to grow, and the need for larger accommodations became apparent. The Gothic Revival church seen here was built in 1888. Today, the building is home to First Church of Christ, Scientist. Grace Episcopal Church moved to Fairfield in 1954. (VHC.)

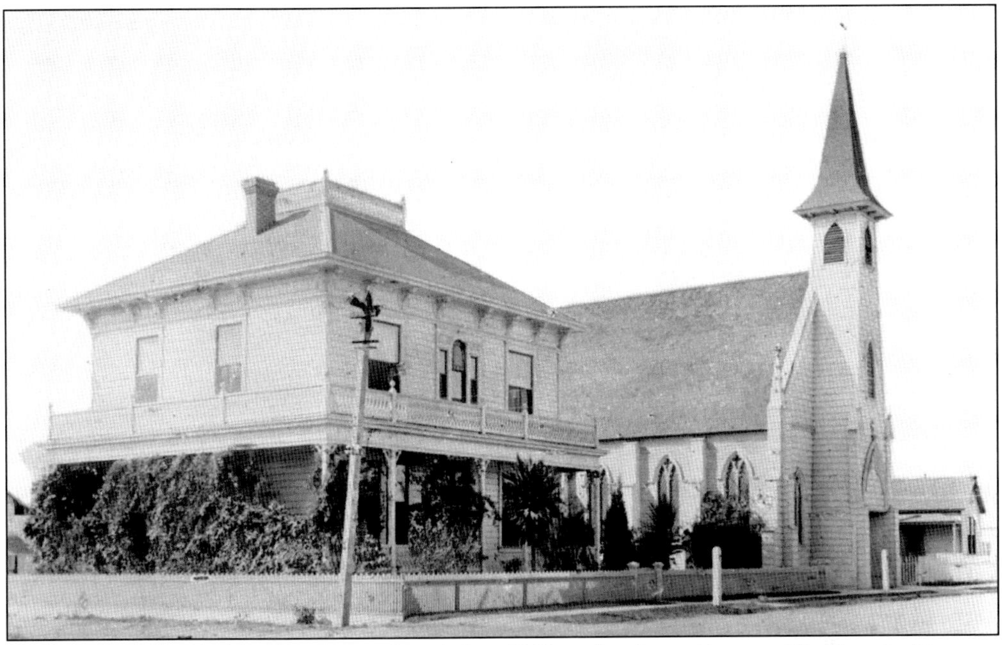

St. Alphonsus Catholic Church was founded in 1860 under the guidance of Fr. Peter L. Deyaert. Construction of the building seen here began in 1868 for the initial sum of $6,000. However, due to financial differences, builder J. Hamilton locked the congregation out of the building at one point. They in turn simply held services at Union Hall. Eventually, under Fr. Michael McNaboe, the mortgage for the church was paid in its entirety. In 1878, an addition was made to accommodate the growing congregation of nearly 300 members. (VHC.)

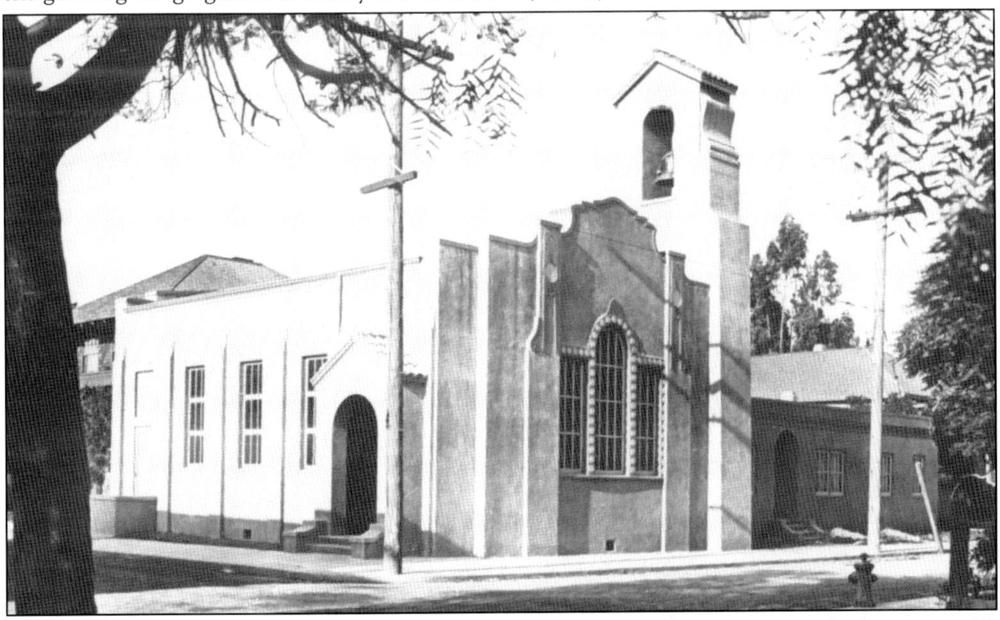

The Congregational Church at Suisun has been a continuously worshipping body since 1877, when it was first organized at the home of E.P. Hilborn Sr., husband of Josiah Wing's daughter Mary. Highly regarded educator C.W. Childs was the first Sunday school director. The building pictured here was dedicated February 23, 1919, after its predecessor burned down. (VHC.)

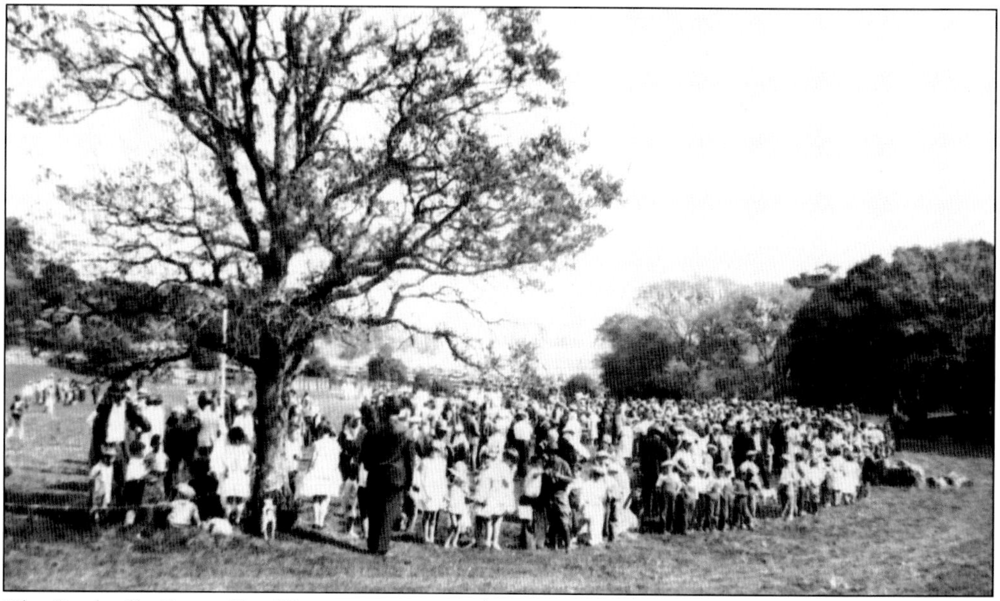

The Rockville Easter Egg Hunt was an annual community event held in the 1920s. On Easter morning each year, the local Boy Scouts would rope off an area out near Rockville Corners for the two-to-five-year-olds and another for the six-to-eight-year-olds. Everyone looked forward to the social event, which included games, races, and prizes. (VHC.)

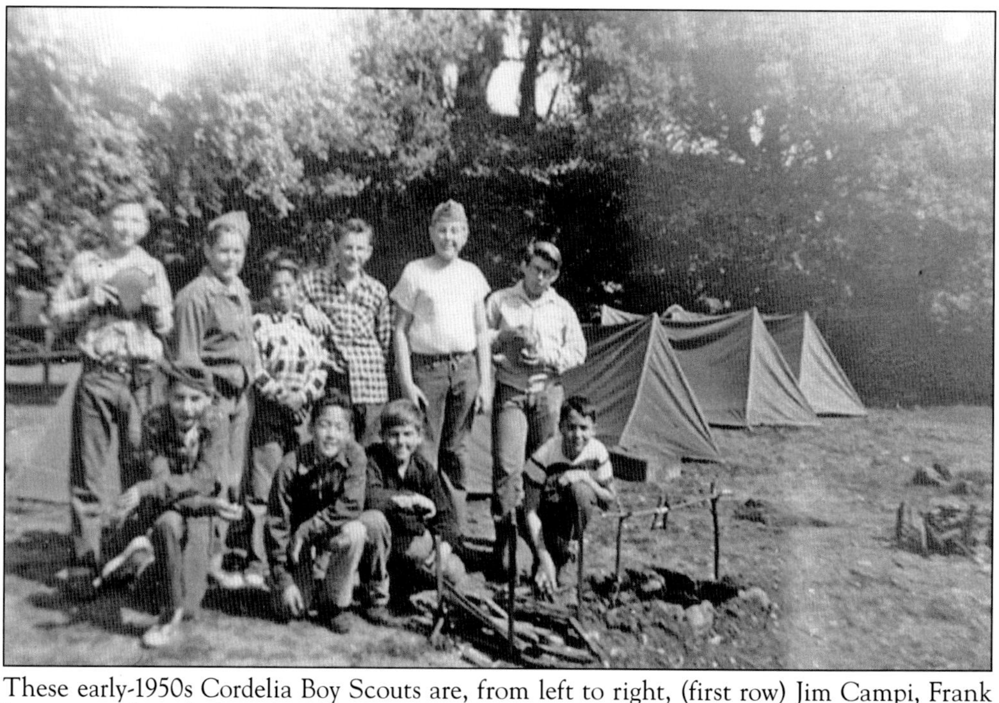

These early-1950s Cordelia Boy Scouts are, from left to right, (first row) Jim Campi, Frank Iwama, unidentified, and Bill Robbins; (second row) Harry Carender, Dell Reeves, Bobby Uchishiba, Bill Lockefeer, Frank Neitzel, and Earl Lawley. The leader of the troop was George Golinger. (VHC.)

Suisun Valley may not be tropical, but that did not stop Marlene Oberti from enjoying her ukulele and hula skirt, which were gifts from her uncle William C. Knecht upon his return from service at Pearl Harbor. William enlisted in 1941 at Suisun as a private with the National Guard. Prior to his service, he worked as a laborer at the Oberti Ranch. (MD.)

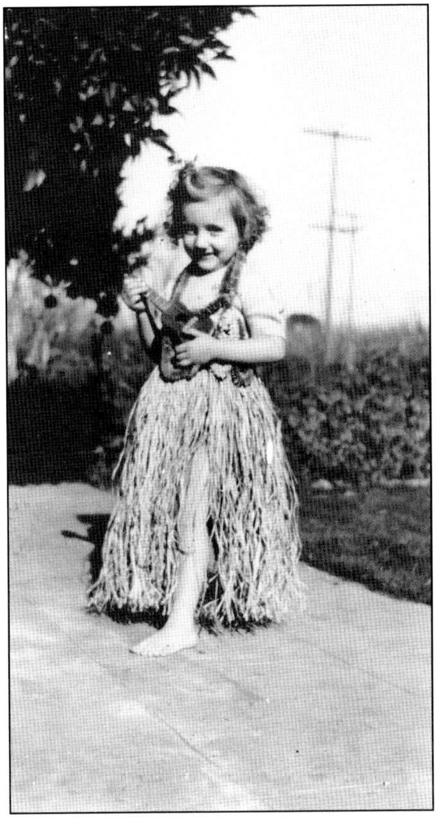

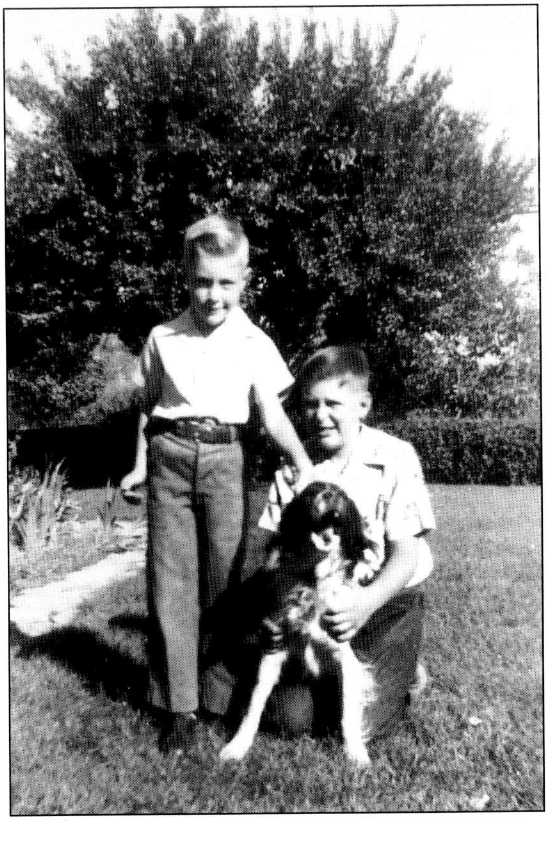

The Neitzel boys, Frank (left) and Joe, seen here with Wags, grew up on a 52-acre ranch in Suisun Valley. Frank was calm and studious. Joe enjoyed hanging out with his buddies and "dragging the main." Both grew up to become respected members of the community through their efforts on behalf of Native Sons of the Golden West and many other service organizations. (VHC.)

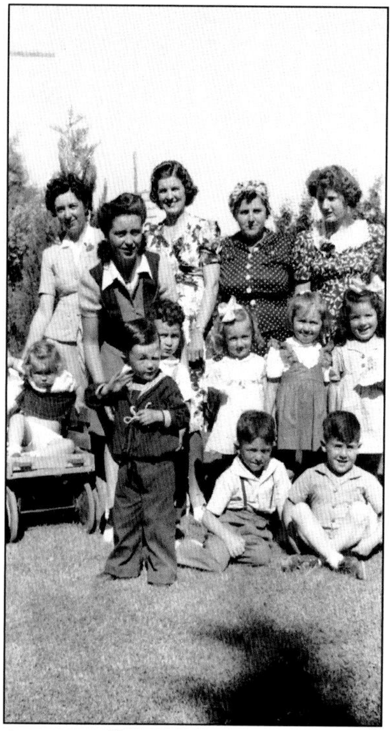

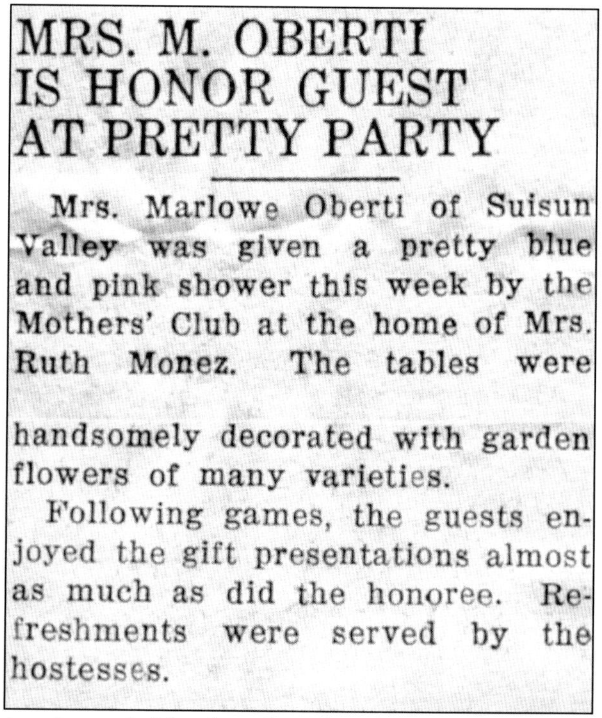

MRS. M. OBERTI IS HONOR GUEST AT PRETTY PARTY

Mrs. Marlowe Oberti of Suisun Valley was given a pretty blue and pink shower this week by the Mothers' Club at the home of Mrs. Ruth Monez. The tables were handsomely decorated with garden flowers of many varieties.

Following games, the guests enjoyed the gift presentations almost as much as did the honoree. Refreshments were served by the hostesses.

Suisun Valley was a close-knit community of extended family and good neighbors. Families came together at picnics, dances, and social clubs. The Mothers' Club, pictured here, was one such informal group of valley mothers who shared advice, support, and conversation while the little ones played. (Both, MD.)

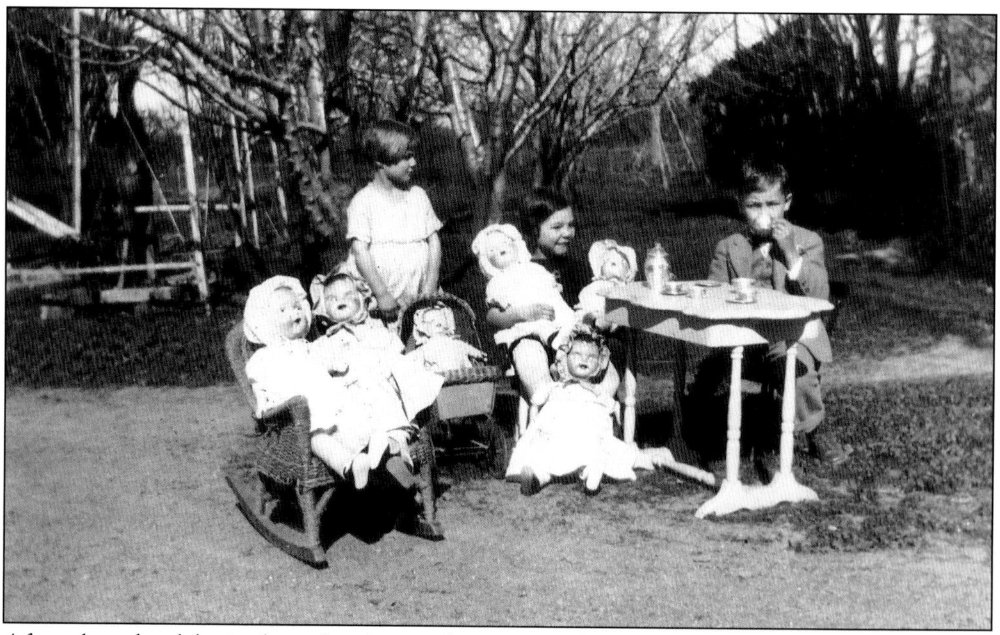

After a long, hard day in the orchards, it is always nice to have a tea party with friends and family, as seen in this photograph of, from left to right, siblings Dorene, Ruth, and Lester, children of Harry and Bessie Siebe. (DF.)

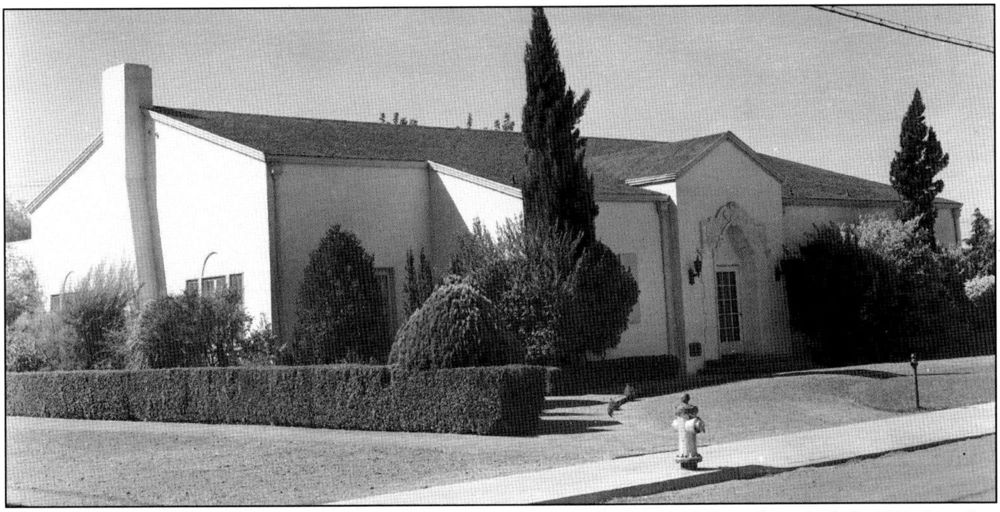

Sixteen local women with a common vision of improving the community founded the Wednesday Club on September 11, 1911. Initially, they met at Ellen Dinkelspiel's home, then at the Armijo Club, and then in a small wood-frame building purchased for $500. Finally, in 1925, architect W.H. Crim Jr. was engaged to design the building pictured above. Today, the Wednesday Club continues its tradition of promoting cultural, historic, and educational endeavors to improve the community. (VHC.)

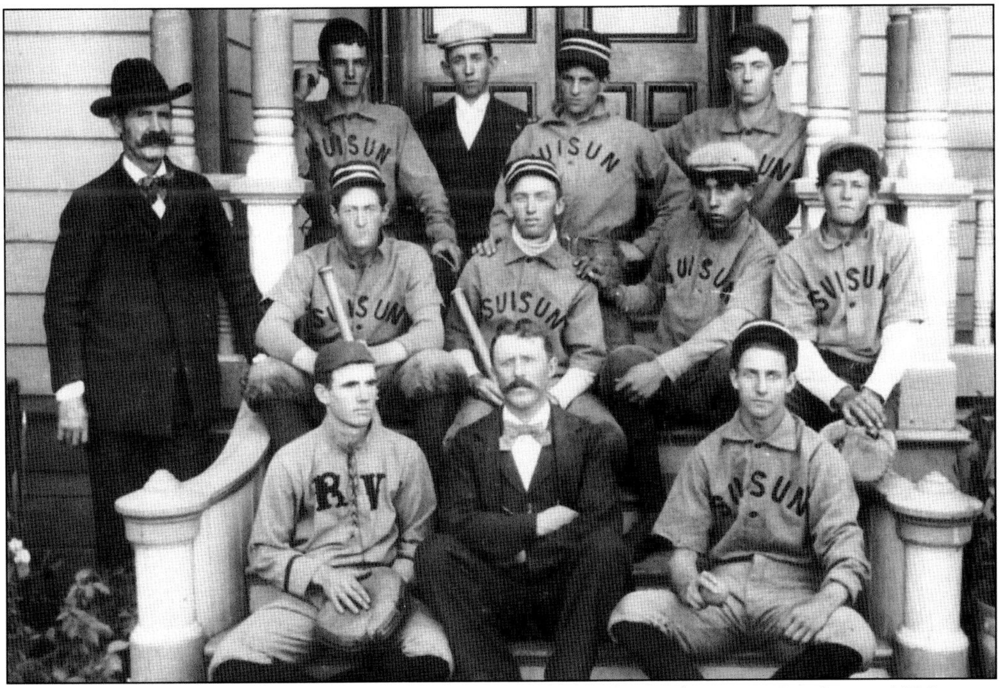

The Suisuns baseball team played competitively throughout the state. In this c. 1898 team photograph, pitcher Howard C. Bronson is seated on the right in the first row. Among his teammates are Barbour, Tillman, and Larkin. The *Sacramento Record-Union* newspaper noted the following about the team: "The Suisun club is composed of gentlemanly players, mostly residents of that Village. They are of the never-give-up class, and play as hard and earnestly when the score was 10 to 1 against them as at the beginning of the game." (VHC.)

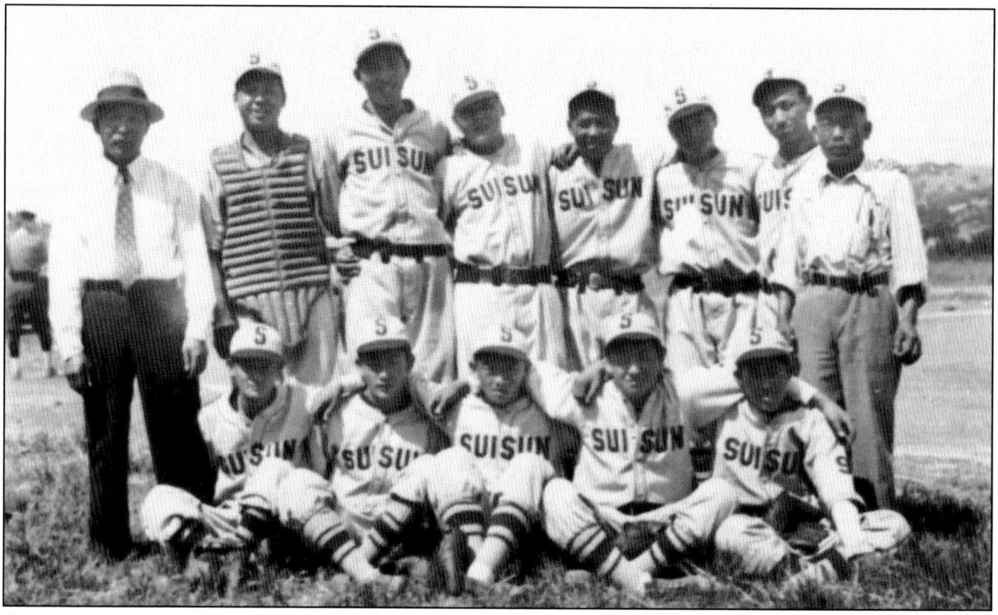

For over a century, Japanese Americans, such as these members of the Suisun Nisei team, have been playing baseball. Between 1903 and 1915, Nisei leagues were established throughout the West Coast, and as a result, great contributions were made to the development and international promotion of American baseball, at one point even inspiring baseball greats Babe Ruth, Lou Gehrig, and Moe Berg to embark on an all-American tour of Japan to play 18 exhibition games in 1934. (VHC.)

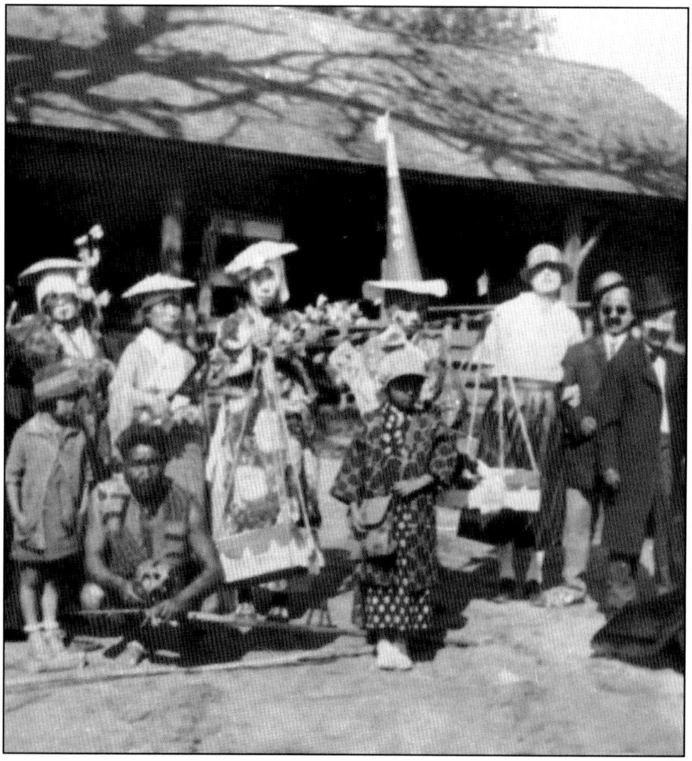

"*Oni wa soto! Fuku wa uchi!*" is what these Suisun children would say as they celebrated *Setsubun*, the Japanese festival marking the first day of spring. The phrase translates roughly to "Demons out! Luck in!" and is proclaimed during the *mamemaki* ritual, in which celebrants throw roasted beans at a "goblin" (seen kneeling) to symbolically drive away evil spirits for the new year. It is also customary to wear disguises in order to ward off wandering spirits. After the *mamemaki*, everyone eats one bean for every year of his or her age to ensure good health for the coming year. (VHC.)

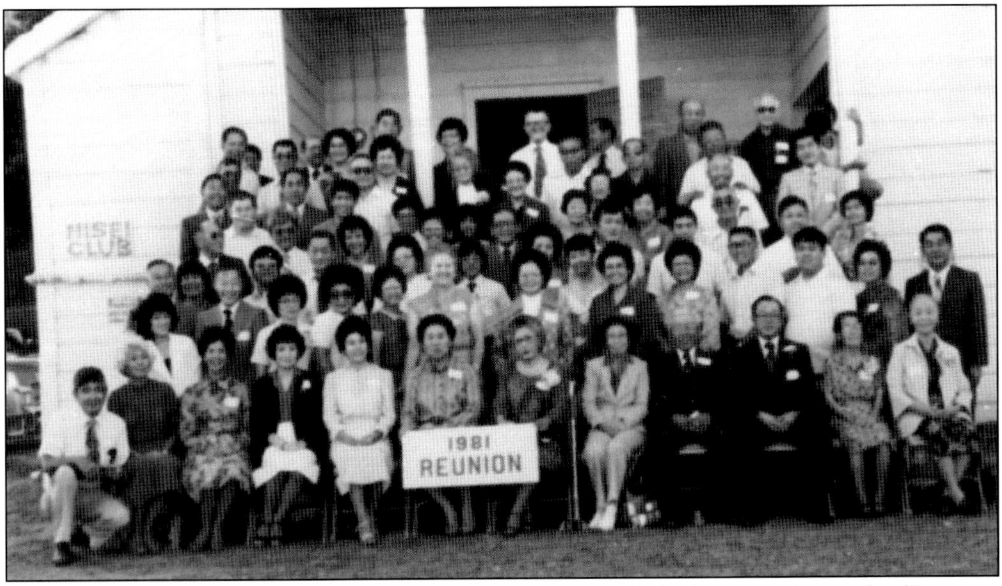

As early as 1877, Japanese community organizations were established to meet the needs of Japanese immigrants and their families. The clubs provided a means to continue Japanese cultural identity, while assimilating to the American way of life. Educational and recreational opportunities were provided for young and old alike. The Suisun Nisei Club was incorporated in 1932 and is housed in the former Rockville Schoolhouse, as seen in this photograph taken at the 1981 reunion of its founding members. (VHC.)

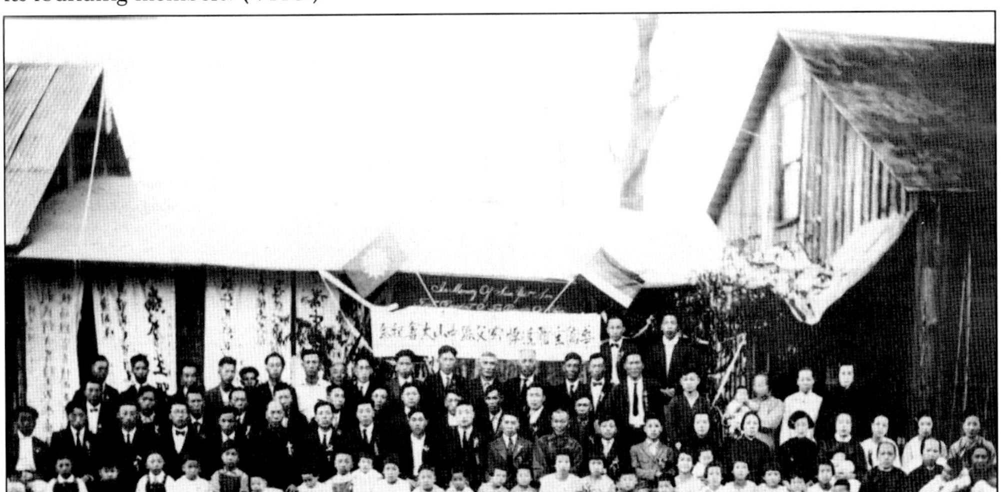

The contributions by Chinese immigrants to the success of Suisun Valley orchardists cannot be overstated. They provided much-needed labor and excelled at harvesting and packing crops. Big Camp, where the majority of local Chinese resided, was located along the bank of Suisun Creek on A.T. Hatch's ranch property and is the backdrop for this 1925 photograph of the memorial service for the Chinese revolutionary Sun Yat-sen. (SCHS.)

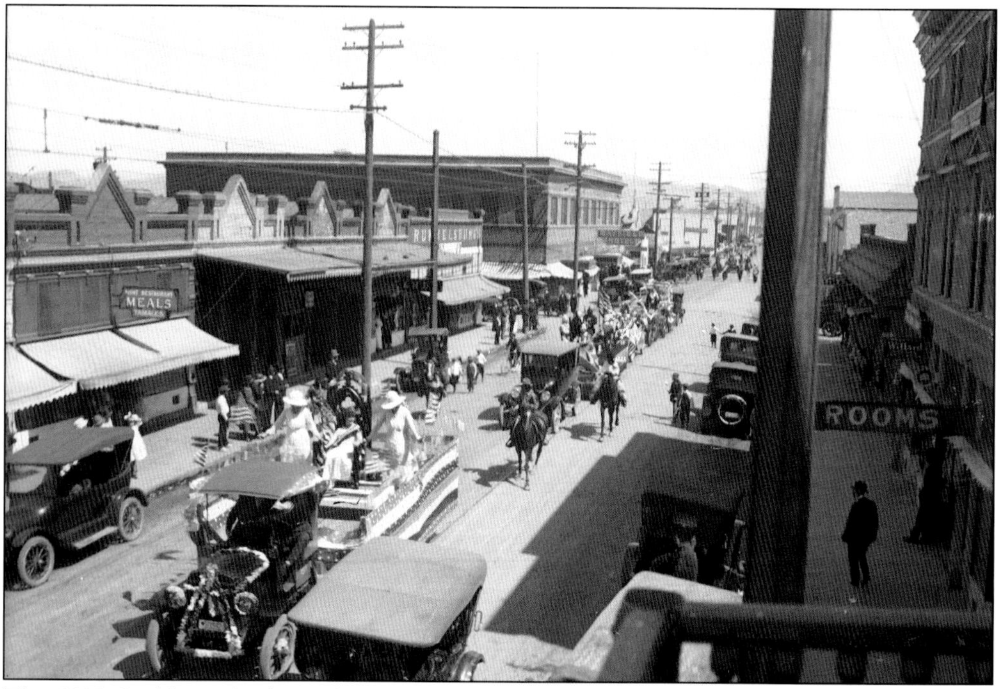

The 1919 Goddess of Liberty leads the Suisun City Fourth of July Parade south on Main Street. (VHC.)

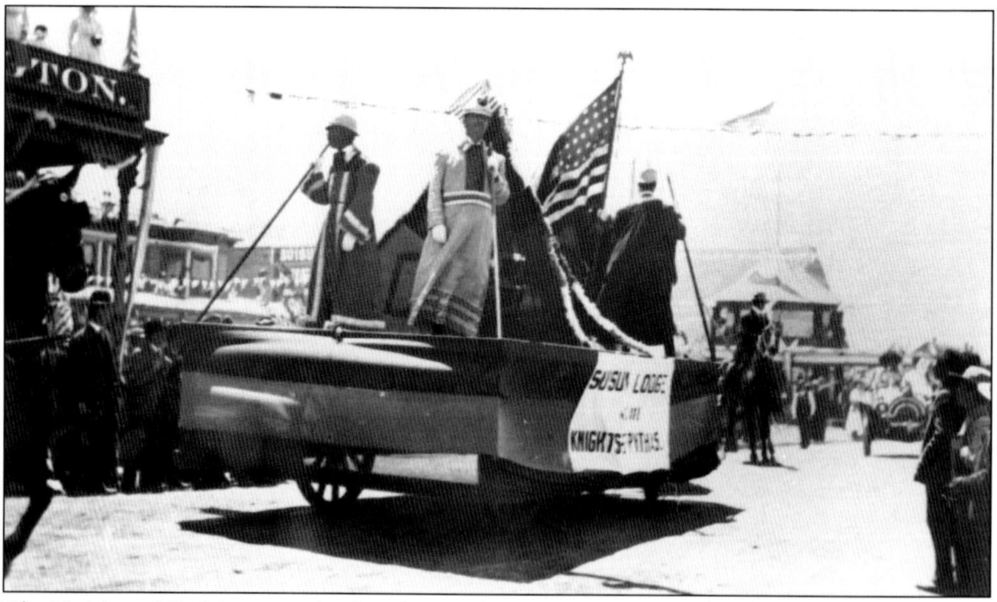

The Knights of Pythias were the first fraternal organization granted a charter by US Congress in 1864 and count loyalty, honor, and friendship as their ideals. Members of Suisun Lodge No. 111 progress past Suisun City Plaza during a Fourth of July parade in this photograph. Solano County superintendent of schools Dan H. White, at left on the float, was one of Suisun's many members. (VHC.)

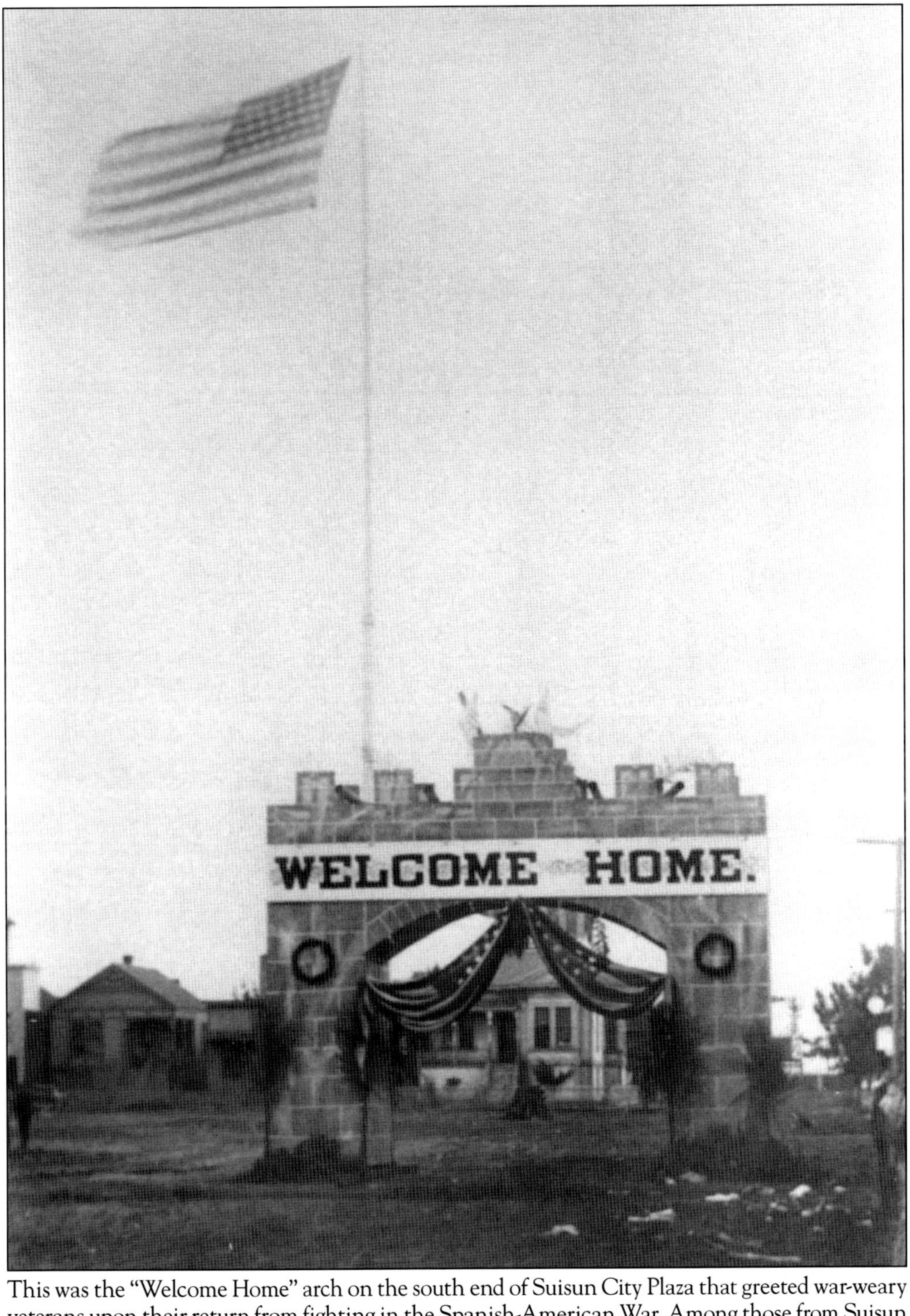

This was the "Welcome Home" arch on the south end of Suisun City Plaza that greeted war-weary veterans upon their return from fighting in the Spanish-American War. Among those from Suisun who served were Fred W. Rush, Jackson W. Oliver, George Cooper, Howard Bronson, and Seranus Hastings. While stationed in the Philippines, Rush, the son of Benjamin Rush, wrote letters to his family that offered glimpses of the harsh and monotonous realities of war. (VHC.)

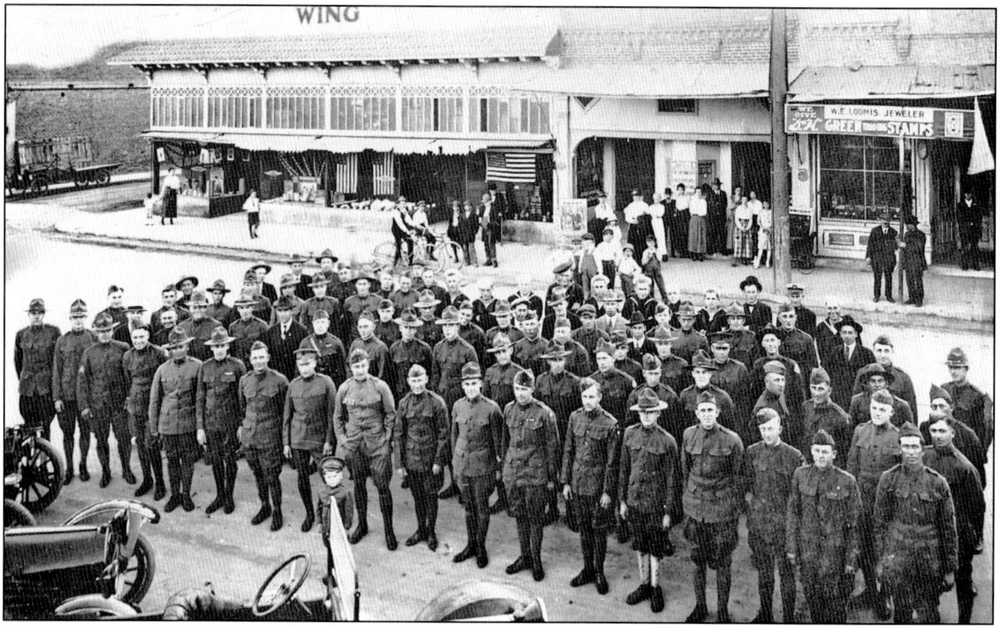

World War I soldiers are pictured on Suisun City Plaza. The B&L Wing store, Suisun Theater, and the jewelry shop of W.E. Loomis can be seen in the background. Veterans of the Spanish-American War and World War I would later found the Veterans of Foreign Wars Post No. 2333 and name it after World War I casualty Sgt. Melvin Simmons and World War II casualty Capt. Milton J. Sheldon. (VHC.)

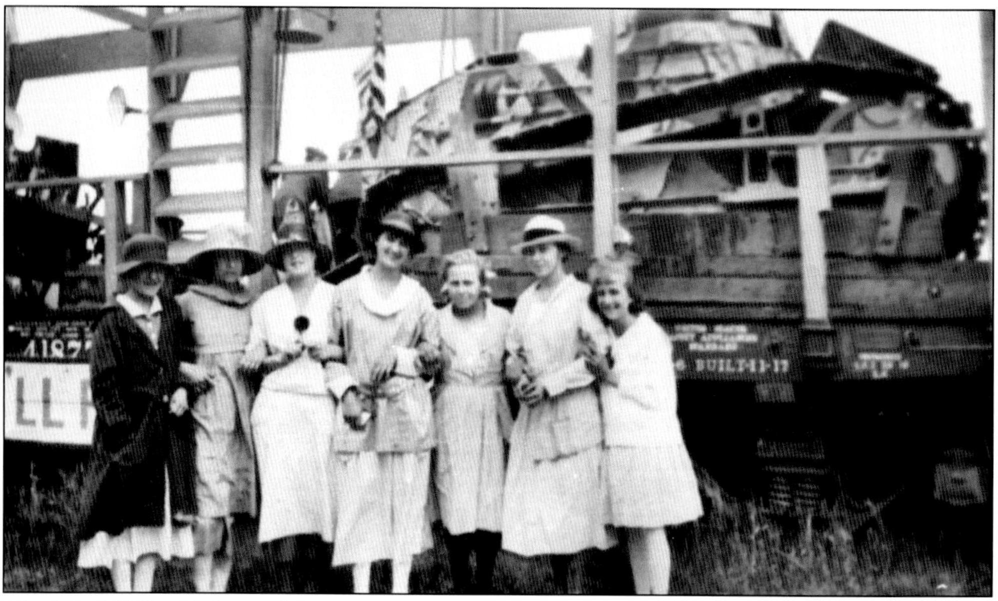

The World War I Victory Liberty Loan war train came to town in 1919 laden with German equipment captured by American troops. The festivities of rousing speeches and grand displays were intended to inspire residents to invest in Victory Liberty Loans to help fund the cost of the war. Among those who viewed the attractions were, from left to right below, Gladys Swanson Huck, Ruby Shively Grigsby, Leah Babe Shively Carpenter, Evelyn Crandall, Grace Burdick Mason, Hazel Burdick Sarasin, and Marjorie Crandall. (VHC.)

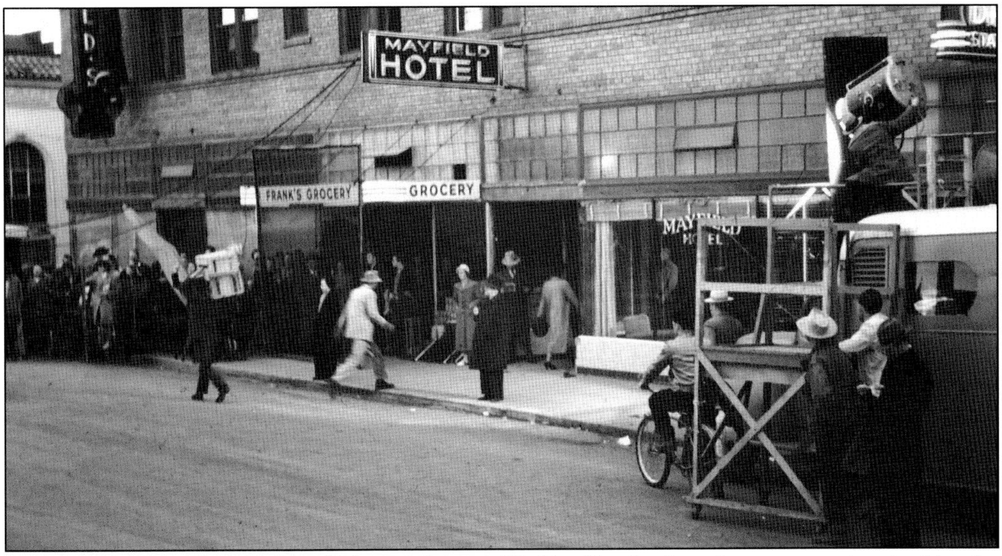

Filmed partly in Suisun City, *All the King's Men* (1949) tells of political corruption inspired by the story of Huey Long. The film utilized local residents in natural settings, such as this scene at the Mayfield Hotel, to create a backdrop of greater realism, setting a precedent for cinematography. A winner of three Academy Awards and deemed "culturally significant," it was selected for preservation in the National Film Registry in 2001 by the Library of Congress. Acclaimed character actor Will Wright, who had a role in the film, is buried at the Fairfield-Suisun Cemetery. (VHC.)

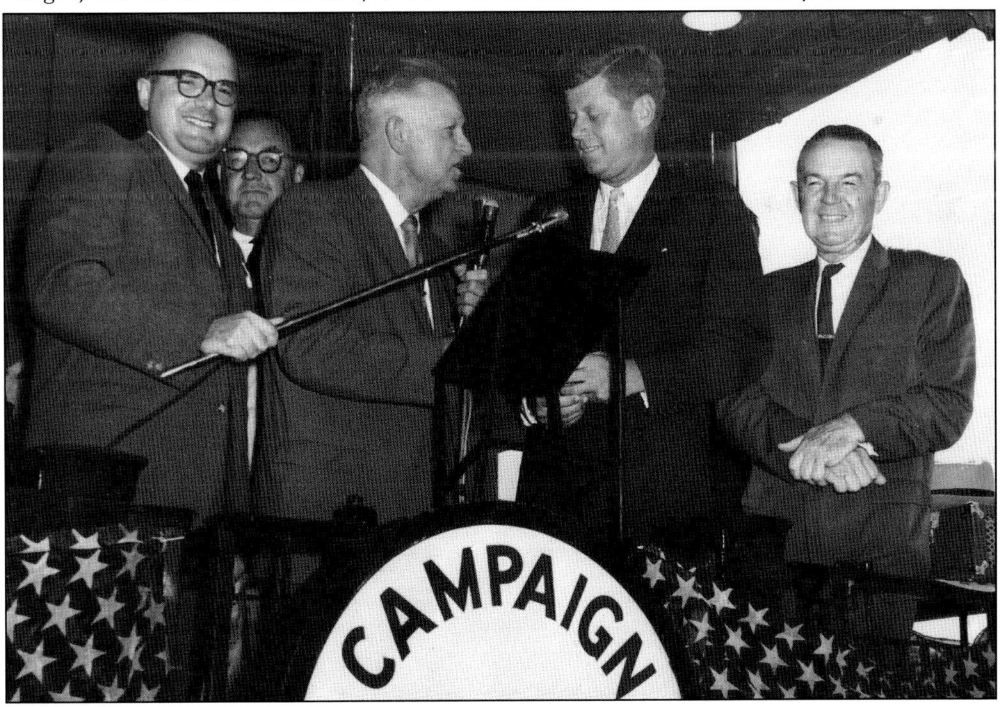

Mayor Julian "Tubby" Morrison greets Sen. John F. Kennedy on the deck of Kennedy's 1960 whistle-stop campaign tour railcar. Also pictured are, from left to right, Congressman Robert L. Leggett, Gov. Pat Brown (behind Morrison), and California State senator Luther E. Gibson, publisher of the *Vallejo Times-Herald* (to the right of Kennedy). (SHEC.)

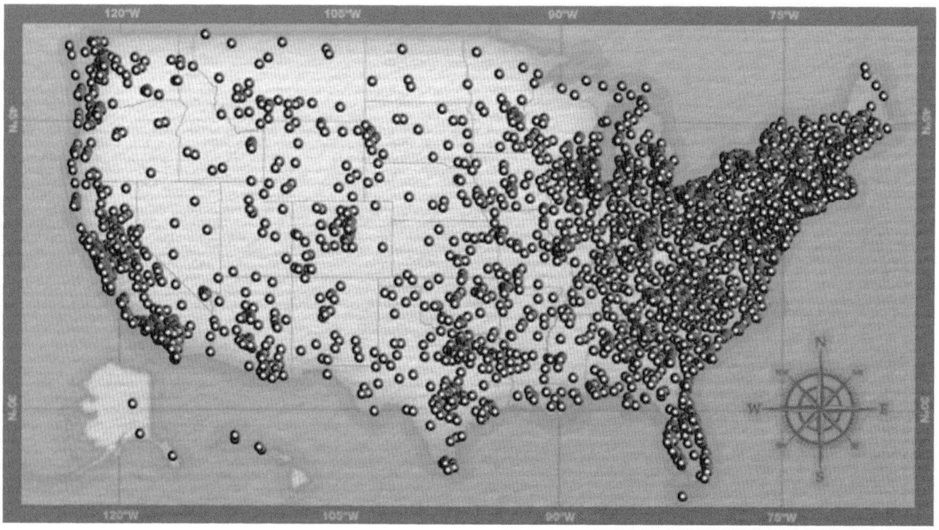